The State

The State

Anthony de Jasay

Basil Blackwell

© Anthony de Jasay 1985

First published 1985

Basil Blackwell Ltd
108 Cowley Road, Oxford OX4 1JF, UK

Basil Blackwell Inc.
432 Park Avenue South, Suite 1505,
New York, NY 10016, USA

British Library Cataloguing in Publication Data

De Jasay, Anthony
  The State.
  1. State, The
  320.1'01   JC11
  ISBN 0-631-14025-5

Library of Congress Cataloging in Publication Data

De Jasay, Anthony, 1925–
  The state.

  Includes index.
  1. State, The.   2. Welfare state.   I. Title.
  JC325.D38 1985   320.1   84–20512
  ISBN 0–631–14025–5

Typeset by Freeman Graphic, Tonbridge, Kent
Printed in Great Britain by Pitman Press Ltd, Bath

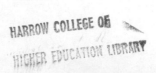

Contents

Preface

Though this book leans on political philosophy, economics and history, it leans on each lightly enough to remain accessible to the educated general reader, for whom it is mainly intended. Its central theme – how state and society interact to disappoint and render each other miserable – may concern a rather wide public among both governors and governed. Most of the arguments are straightforward enough not to require for their exposition the rigour and the technical apparatus which only academic audiences can be expected to endure, let alone to enjoy.

If nothing else, the vastness of the subject and my somewhat unusual approach to it will ensure that specialist readers find many parts of the reasoning in need of elaboration, refinement or refutation. This is all to the good for, even if I wanted to, I could not hide that my object has been neither to provide a definitive statement nor to solicit the widest possible agreement.

The reader and I both owe a debt to I. M. D. Little of All Souls College, Oxford for scrutinizing the major part of the draft for consistency and clarity. It is not his fault if I persevered in some of my errors. Without his encouragement, this book would not have been completed. Without his advice and criticism, it would be shallower than it is.

My thanks are also due to Mrs Jo Wimpory, who applied intelligence and care to transforming a labyrinthine manuscript into an impeccably typed printer's delight.

Paluel   A. J.
Seine Maritime
France

Introduction

What would you do if *you* were the state?

It is odd that political theory, at least since Machiavelli, has practically ceased asking this question. It has devoted much thought to what the individual subject, a class or the entire society can get out of the state, to the legitimacy of its commands and the rights the subject retains in the face of them. It has dealt with the obedience the hopeful users of the state's services owe it, the manner in which they participate in making it function and the redress the victims of its eventual malfunction can claim. These are vitally important matters; with the passage of time and the growth of the state relative to civil society, they are becoming steadily more important. Is it, however, sufficient to treat them only from the point of view of the *subject*, what he needs, wants, can and ought to do? Would not our understanding become more complete if we could also see them as they might look from the *state's* point of view?

The present book is an attempt to do this. Braving the risks of confusing institutions with persons and the difficulties of passing from the prince to his government, it chooses to treat the state as if it were a real entity, as if it had a will and were capable of reasoned decisions about means to its ends. Hence it tries to explain the state's conduct towards us in terms of *what it could be expected to do*, in successive historical situations, if it rationally pursued ends that it can plausibly be supposed to have.

The young Marx saw the state 'opposing' and 'overcoming' civil society. He spoke of the 'general secular contradiction between the political state and civil society' and contended that 'when the political state . . . comes violently into being out of civil society . . . [it] can

1

and must proceed to the abolition of religion, to the destruction of religion; but only in the same way as it proceeds to the abolition of private property (by imposing a maximum, by confiscation, by progressive taxation) and the abolition of life (by the guillotine).'[1] In other isolated passages (notably in 'The Holy Family' and the 'Eighteenth Brumaire') he continued to represent the state as an autonomous entity, going its own way without, however, offering a theory of why this should result in 'overcoming', 'confiscation', 'contradiction', why the autonomous state is an adversary of society.

As Marx moved toward system-building, he fell in with the main body of political theory whose unifying feature is to regard the state as essentially an instrument. Thus, for the mature Marx, and more explicitly still for Engels, Lenin and the socialist thought they continue to inspire, the state became a tool, subservient to the interests of the ruling class and assuring its dominance.

For non-socialist mainstream theory, too, the state is an instrument, designed to serve its user. It is seen as generally benign and helping to further the purposes of *others*. The shape of the instrument, the jobs it performs and the identity of the beneficiary may vary, but the instrumental character of the state is common to the major strains of modern political thought. For Hobbes, it keeps the peace, for Locke it upholds the natural right to liberty and property, for Rousseau it realizes the general will, for Bentham and Mill it is the vehicle of improving social arrangements. For today's liberals, it overcomes the incapacity of private interests spontaneously to co-operate. It *forces* them to produce collectively *preferred* volumes of the public goods of order, defence, clean air, paved streets and universal education. Under a stretched definition of public goods, its coercion also enables society to reach for distributive justice or just plain equality.

There are, to be sure, less starry-eyed variants of the instrumental view. For the 'non-market choice' or 'public choice' school, the interaction of private choices through the instrument of the state is liable to overproduce public goods and fail in other ways to attain preferred outcomes.[2] This school deals with the unwieldiness of the

---

1 K. Marx, 'The Jewish Question', *Early Writings*, 1975, pp. 220, 226, 222.
2   As one of the founders of this school puts it, welfare economics is about market failures, public choice theory is about government failures (James M. Buchanan, *The Limits of Liberty*, 1975, ch. 10). Note, however, the different tack adopted by certain public choice theorists, referred to in chapter 4, pp. 247–8, n. 39.

tool that is the state and its potential to hurt a society that tries to wield it. Nevertheless, the state is a tool, albeit a defective one.

What, however, are defect, faulty design, inherent malfunction? And what is internal consistency? On the way from democracy to despotism, does Plato's *Republic* degenerate? Or is it conforming to its own purposes?

A first step to an adequate understanding of the state is to think about an environment without one. Taking our cue from Rousseau, we tend gratuitously to associate the *state of nature* with savage and perhaps not very bright hunters at the dawn of history. It has become our conditioned reflex to think of it as some early, primitive stage of civilization, a more advanced stage both requiring, and being required for, the formation of a *state*. As a matter of empirical fact, this is as it may be. As a matter of logic, it does not follow from the sole necessary feature of the state of nature, which is that in it the participants do not surrender their sovereignty. No one has obtained a monopoly of the use of force; all keep their arms. But this condition need not be inconsistent with any given stage of civilization, backward or advanced.

Nation states are in a state of nature and show no inclination to pool sovereignty in a superstate. Yet contrary to what Hobbes is usually taken to have implied, most of them manage to avoid war a good deal of the time. They even cooperate in armed peace, most conspicuously and bravely in international trade, investment and lending, all in the face of sovereign risk. Social contract theory would predict that in these areas, there will be international thieving, default, confiscation and beggar-my-neighbour behaviour, and contracts will be worthless bits of paper. In effect, despite the lack of a superstate to enforce contracts across national jurisdictions, international cooperation is not breaking down. If anything, there is some movement the other way. International relations tend to cast doubt on the standard view of people in the state of nature as myopic simpletons clad in animal skins clubbing each other on the head. Instead, there is some reason to hold that the more civilization advances, the more viable becomes the state of nature. The fearfulness of advanced armaments may yet prove to be a more potent enforcer of abstinence from war, saving people from a 'nasty, brutish and short life', than were such historic super-states as Rome, the Carolingian or the British Empire, though it may be too soon to tell.

Among men and groups of men, it is harder to judge the viability of the state of nature than among nations. Civilized men have long been the subjects of states, so we have no opportunity to observe how well they would cooperate in the state of nature. Hence we cannot even pretend empirically to assess the difference it makes to have a state. Would people honour contracts in the absence of an enforcing agent possessing the monopoly of last-resort force? It used to be held that since it is every man's interest that all other men should keep their word and that he should be free to break his, social cooperation could not be maintained on a voluntary basis. In the technical language of decision theory, a properly constructed 'prisoners' dilemma' could not have a non-imposed cooperative solution. Recent contributions of mathematics and psychology to the social sciences teach us that if men confront such dilemmas repeatedly, this need not be so. Results teach them, and expected results induce them, to cooperate spontaneously. Any argument that, since the state must force them to cooperate, they would not have done so without being forced is, of course, a *non sequitur*.

On the other hand, the longer they have been *forced* to cooperate, the less likely they are to have preserved (if they ever had it) the faculty to cooperate *spontaneously*. 'Those who can, do', but the converse, 'those who do, can', is no less true, for we learn by doing. People who have been made to rely on the state never learn the art of self-reliance nor acquire the habits of civic action. One of Tocqueville's most celebrated insights (though he had more subtle ones) was in fact about English and American 'government' which left both room and need for grass-roots initiatives and, by benign neglect, induced people to run their own affairs, and French 'administration' which did neither. The habit-forming effects of the state, the dependence of people's values and tastes on the very political arrangements which they are supposed to bring about, is a basic *motif* which keeps surfacing throughout my argument.

Its other basic and recurrent element is the waywardness of cause and effect in social relations. State action may or may not achieve its intended effect, for its proximate incidence gives no sure clue to the ultimate one. Nearly always, however, it will also have other effects, possibly more important and longer-lasting ones. These *unintended effects* may, in addition, also be positively unwanted, unforeseen and, in the nature of the case, often unpredictable. This is what lends such a gooseflesh-raising quality to the bland view that politics is pluralistic vector-geometry, and that civil society governs itself and controls the state, which is just a machine to register and execute 'social choices'.

The argument of this book is arranged in five chapters, spanning the logical (though not the real-time) progression of the state from one limiting extreme, where *its ends do not compete with the ends of its subjects,* to the other where it has come *to own most of their property and liberty.*

Chapter 1, 'The Capitalist State', first deals with the roles of 'Violence, Obedience and Preference' at the birth of the state. It then sets out to deduce the characteristic outline of a state which, if it existed, would not be in conflict with civil society. I call it 'capitalist' to stress the decisive character of its treatment of property and contract. Its conception of good title to property is that finders are keepers. It does not interfere in people's contracts for *their* own good (which also excludes its compelling them to conclude a comprehensive, omnilateral social contract designed to overcome their free-rider temptations). It does not indulge such compassion and sympathy as it may harbour for its less fortunate subjects by forcing the more fortunate to assist them. By the same token, it is also a *policy-less,* minimal state ('The Contours of the Minimal State').

It seems anomalous if not self-contradictory for the state both to have a will and to want to *minimize* itself. For this to be rational, its ends must lie beyond politics, and be unattainable through governing. The purpose of governing, then, is merely to keep out any non-minimal rivals (preventing revolution). There has of course never been such a state in history, though the style and overtones of one or two in the eighteenth and nineteenth centuries do faintly suggest it.

The 'political hedonist' who regards the state as the source of a favourable balance in the calculus of help and hindrance, must logically aspire to a more than minimal state and would invent it if it did not exist.[3] Political hedonism on the part of the individual subject underlies the wish for a more comprehensive and less optional scheme of cooperation than the patchwork of contracts that arises from voluntary negotiation ('Inventing the State: the Social Contract'). On the part of a hypothetical ruling class, political hedonism is supposed to call for a machine assuring dominance ('Inventing the

---

3 The term 'political hedonist' was coined by the great Leo Strauss to denote Leviathan's willing subject.

State: the Instrument of Class Rule'). Both versions of political hedonism presuppose a certain gullibility as to the risks of disarming oneself to arm the state. They involve a belief in the instrumental character of the state, *made to serve the ends of others* and having none of its own. Yet in any non-unanimous society with a plurality of interests, the state, no matter how accommodating, cannot possibly pursue ends other than its own. Its manner of resolving conflicts, and the respective weights it attaches to the ends of others, *constitute* the satisfaction of its own ends ('Closing the Loop by False Consciousness').

The questions whether political hedonism is sensible, prudent, rational, whether having the state around us makes us better or worse off, whether the goods the state, acting in pursuit of its interest, chooses to produce are what we should have chosen, are addressed again in chapter 2 in relation to reform, improvement and utility, and in chapter 3 in such contexts as one-man–one-vote, egalitarianism (both as a means and as an end) and distributive justice.

While violence and preference may stand respectively at its historical and logical origins, political obedience continues to be elicited by the state through recourse to the old triad of 'Repression, Legitimacy and Consent', the subject of the first section of chapter 2. Legitimacy is obeyed regardless of hope of reward and fear of punishment. The state cannot, except in the very long run, breed more of it at its choice. In getting itself obeyed, its alternatives are reduced to various combinations of repression and consent (though of course it will count the blessings of such legitimacy as it may enjoy). The consent of a minute fraction of society, e.g. the camp guards in a camp state, may suffice to repress the rest. Rewards, such as they are, then accrue *thickly* to the consenting *minority*; repression is spread *thinly* over the vast *majority*. *A reversal of this pattern* corresponds to greater reliance on consent.

For reasons which look valid at the time, though in retrospect they may be regretted as weak or foolish, the repressive state usually finds it opportune over time to seduce some of those it used to repress and to lean more on consent ('Taking Sides'). This process combines steps towards wider political democracy and moves to do good, with an adversary, divisive role for the state, for it is now soliciting the support of broad sections of society by offering them significant rewards to be taken from other, perhaps narrower but still substantial sections. A by-product of this process of creating gainers and losers is that the apparatus of the state grows bigger and cleverer.

It seems to me almost incontrovertible that the prescriptive content of any dominant ideology coincides with the interest of the state rather than, as in Marxist theory, with that of the ruling class. In other words, the dominant ideology is one that, broadly speaking, tells the state what it wants to hear, but more importantly what it wants its subjects to overhear. Rather than the 'superstructure' of ideology being perched on the 'base' of interest (as it is usual to place them), the two hold each other upright. There may well be no ruling class in a society, yet state and dominant ideology will thrive and evolve together. This view is advanced to justify the attention devoted to utilitarianism ('Tinker's Licence' and 'The Revealed Preference of Governments'), an immensely powerful though now mostly subconscious influence on past and present political thought. The utilitarian operations of 'mending', judging changes in arrangements by their expected consequences, and comparing utilities interpersonally so that the state can, in evaluating a policy, deduct the harm it does to some from the greater good it does to others and *strike a balance* of greater happiness, lend a moral content to acts of government. The doctrine which recommends such operations represents the perfect ideology for the activist state. It provides the moral ground for policies adopted by the state when it has discretion in choosing whom to favour. However, when the question whom to favour is no longer discretionary, but is prejudged for the state by the rise of electoral competition, interpersonal comparisons are still implicit in its affirmations that what it is doing is good or just or both, rather than merely expedient for staying in power.

Social justice as the avowed objective, the ethical excuse for seductive policies, is seemingly a break with utilitarianism. A basic continuity between the two as criteria for justifying policies, however, results from the dependence of both on interpersonal comparisons. One compares *utilities,* the other *deserts.* Either comparison can provide a *warrant for overriding voluntary contracts.* In both, the role of the 'sympathetic observer', of the 'discerning eye' performing the informed and authoritative comparison, falls naturally to the state. Stepping into this role is as great a conquest for it as is the derivative chance to favour, among its subjects, one class, race, age-group, region, occupation or other interest over another.

However, the *discretion to choose whom to favour at whose expense,* which the state enjoys when it first sets out to assemble a base of support by reform and redistribution, is almost bound to be short-lived. The argument of chapter 4 offers reasons why it tends to vanish with political competition and with society's progressive addiction to a given redistributive pattern.

A fully fledged redistributive state, at whose behest 'the property-less come to legislate for the propertied',[4] and which in time transforms the character and structure of society in largely unintended ways, has its doctrinal counterpart, its ideological match. The development of neither can be very well conceived without the other. Chapter 3, 'Democratic Values', deals with the liberal ideology which is dominant when the state, depending increasingly on consent and exposed to competition for it, overwhelms people while serving their ideals.

In agreeing to and, indeed, aiding and abetting the advent of democracy as the vehicle for moving from rule by repression to rule by consent, the state commits itself to certain procedures (e.g. one-man–one-vote, majority rule) for the award of the tenure of power. The procedures are such that the state, in search of support, must proceed by a simple headcount. Its policies must, putting it crudely, simply create more gainers than losers instead of, for example, favouring the most deserving, those it likes best, those with more clout, or some more subtle objective. 'More gainers than losers' can always be more lucratively achieved by condemning to the role of losers a number of rich people than the same number of poor people. This rule is, however, merely expedient. It may not command the approval of bystanders who do not expect to gain from its application. Some of them (including many consequential utilitarians) might prefer the rule 'create more *gains* rather than more *gainers*' and forget about the headcount. Others might want to add 'subject to respect for natural rights' or, possibly, 'provided liberty is not infringed', either proviso being sufficiently constricting to bring most democratic policies to a dead stop.

Consequently, it helps a good deal if the liberal ideology establishes a case or, to be on the safe side, a number of parallel cases, for holding that democratic *policies* do create democratic *values,* i.e. that

4   Marx, 'The Jewish Question', p. 219.

political expediency is a reliable enough guide to the good life and to universally prized ultimate ends.

I look at four such cases. One, whose great advocates were Edgeworth (impeccably) and Pigou (more questionably), seeks to establish a strong presumption that equalizing income maximizes utility. My counter-argument ('Through Equality to Utility') is that if it makes sense at all to add different persons' utilities and maximize the sum, it is more reasonable to hold that it is *any* settled, time-honoured income distribution, whether equal or unequal, that will in fact maximize utility. (If there is a case for equalizing, it is probably confined to the new rich and the new poor.)

A more fashionable, if less influential, case constructed by John Rawls, recommends a modified, tempered egalitarianism as corresponding to the principles of justice. I take issue on several grounds with the principles he derives from the prudential interest of people negotiating about distribution in ignorance of their selves and hence of any differences between them. I dispute the purported dependence of social cooperation, not on the terms which willing participants settle bilaterally among themselves in making *actual* cooperation unfold, but on the readjustment of these terms to conform to principles negotiated separately, in an 'original position' of ignorance set up for the purpose. I also question the deduction of principles of justice *from* democracy rather than the other way round ('How Justice Overrides Contracts'). In the section 'Egalitarianism as Prudence' I challenge the alleged prudential character of a certain egalitarianism and the roles assigned to risk and probability in inducing self-interested people to opt for it. In passing, I reject Rawls's bland view of the redistributive process as painless and costless, and of the state as an automatic machine which dispenses 'social decisions' when we feed our wishes into it.

Instead of contending, in my view unsuccessfully, that certain economic and political equalities produce final, uncontested values like utility or justice, liberal ideology sometimes resorts to a bold short cut and simply elevates equality itself to the rank of a final value, *prized for its own sake* because it is inherent in man to like it.

My main counter-argument ('Love of Symmetry'), for which there is perhaps unexpected support in Marx's 'Critique of the Gotha Programme' and in a priceless outburst by Engels, is that when we think we are opting for equality, we are in fact upsetting one equality in making another prevail. Love of equality in general may or may not be inherent in human nature. Love of a particular equality in preference to another (given that both cannot prevail), however, is like any other taste and cannot serve as a universal moral argument.

Somewhat analogous reasons can be used against the case that democratic policies are good because, in levelling fortunes, they reduce the pain people suffer at the sight of their neighbour's better fortune ('Envy'). Very few of the countless inequalities people are liable to resent lend themselves to levelling, even when the attack on difference is as forthright as Mao's Cultural Revolution. It is no use making everyone eat, dress and work alike if one is still luckier in love than the other. The source of envy is the envious character, not some manageable handful out of a countless multitude of inequalities. Envy will not go away once chateaux have all been burned, merit has replaced privilege and all children have been sent to the same schools.

Incentives and resistances, the exigencies of staying in power in the face of competition for consent and the character of the society whose consent must be elicited, should duly lead the state to adopt the appropriate pattern of policies for taking property and liberty from some and giving them to others. However, would not this pattern, whatever it was, be bound to remain hypothetical, and property and liberty inviolate, if the constitution forbade the state to touch them, or at least laid down fixed limits to what it may touch? It is to come to terms with the constitutional constraint on democratic policies, that chapter 4, 'Redistribution', starts with some remarks on 'Fixed Constitutions'. It is suggested that the ostensible constraint of a constitution may be positively useful to the state as a confidence-building measure, but that it is unlikely to remain fixed if it does not coincide with the prevailing balance of interests in society. The prospective pay-off from amending it is available as an inducement for a coalition of the required size for passing the amendment (though this is not a sufficient condition for triggering off constitutional change).

The mechanics of obtaining majority support under democratic rules are first considered in a highly simplified abstract case in the section on 'Buying Consent'. If people differ from each other only in how much money they have, and if they vote for the redistributive programme under which they gain most (or lose least), the rival programmes offered by the state and the opposition will be closely similar (one being marginally less bad for the rich than the other). Under the spur of competition for power, everything that *can* safely be taken from the prospective losers *has to be* offered to the prospective gainers, leaving no 'discretionary income' for the state to dispose of. As a consequence, its power over its subjects' resources is all *used up* in its own reproduction, in merely staying in power.

A less abstract version ('Addictive Redistribution') where people, and hence their interests, differ in an indefinite variety of respects, and the society within which preponderant support must be obtained is not atomistic but can have intermediate group structures between man and state, yields results which are fuzzier but hardly less bleak for the state. Redistributive gains tend to be habit-forming both at the individual and the group level. Their reduction is apt to provoke withdrawal symptoms. While in the state of nature the integration of people into cohesive interest groups is held in check by (potential or actual) 'free riding', the emergence of the state as the source of redistributive gains both permits and incites unchecked group formation to exact such gains. This is so in as much as state-oriented interest groups can tolerate the free riding among their members that would destroy market-oriented groups.

Each interest group, in turn, has an incentive to act as a free rider in relation to the rest of society, the state being the vehicle permitting this to be done without meeting serious resistance. There is no reason to expect the corporatist ideal of constituting *very large* groups (all labour, all employers, all doctors, all shopkeepers) and having *them* bargain with the state and with each other, greatly to alter this outcome. Thus, in time, the redistributive pattern becomes a crazy quilt of loopholes and asymmetrical favours along industrial, occupational or regional dimensions or for no very apparent rhyme and reason, rather than along the classic rich-to-poor or rich-to-middle dimension. Above all, the evolution of the pattern increasingly escapes the state's overall control.

In the section 'Rising Prices' the group structure of society promoted by addictive redistribution is assumed to impart an ability to each group to resist or recover any loss of its distributive share. One symptom of the resulting *impasse* is endemic inflation. A related one is the complaint of the state about society becoming ungovernable, lacking any 'give' and rejecting any sacrifice that adjustment to hard times or just random shocks would require.

The social and political environment resulting in large part from the state's own actions eventually calls forth a widening divergence between gross and net redistribution ('Churning'). Instead of robbing Peter to pay Paul, *both* Peter *and* Paul come to be paid *and* robbed on a growing variety of counts (much *gross* redistribution for a small and uncertain *net* balance); this causes turbulence and is destined to generate disappointment and frustration.

The state has, at this stage, completed its metamorphosis from mid-nineteenth-century reformist seducer to late twentieth-century redistributive drudge, walking the treadmill, a prisoner of the unintended cumulative effects of its own seeking after consent ('Towards a Theory of the State'). If its ends are such that they can be attained by devoting its subjects' resources to its own purposes, its rational course is to maximize its discretionary power over these resources. In the ungrateful role of drudge, however, it uses all its power to stay in power, and has no discretionary power left over. It is rational for it to do this just as it is rational for the labourer to work for subsistence wages, or for the perfectly competitive firm to operate at breakeven. A higher kind of rationality, however, would lead it to seek to emancipate itself from the constraints of consent and electoral competition, somewhat like Marx's proletariat escaping from exploitation by revolution, or Schumpeter's entrepreneurs escaping from competition by innovation. My thesis is not that democratic states 'must' all end up doing this, but rather that a built-in totalitarian bias should be taken as a symptom of their rationality.

Autonomy of action in the passage from democracy to totalitarianism need not be regained in a single unbroken move, planned in advance. It is, at least initially, more like sleep-walking than conscious progress towards a clearly perceived goal. Chapter 5, 'State Capitalism', deals with the cumulative policies likely to carry the state step by step along the road to 'self-fulfilment'. Their effect is so to change the social system as to maximize the potential for discretionary power, and to enable the state fully to realize this potential.

The agenda for increasing discretionary power ('What is to be Done?') must first address the problem of decreasing civil society's autonomy and capacity for withholding consent. The policies the democratic state managing a 'mixed economy' tends to drift into will unwittingly erode a large part of the basis of this autonomy, the independence of people's livelihoods. What the Communist Manifesto calls 'the winning of the battle of democracy' in order 'to wrest, by degrees, all capital from the bourgeoisie, to centralize all instruments of production in the hands of the state' is the completion of this process. The socialist state thus puts an end to the historical and logical freak of economic power being *diffused throughout civil society* while political power is centralized. In centralizing and *unifying the two powers,* however, it creates a social system which is inconsistent with, and cannot properly function under, the classical democratic rules of awarding tenure of state power. Social democracy must evolve into people's democracy or the next best thing, the state now being powerful enough to enforce this development and ward off systemic breakdown.

'Systemic constants' *versus* the variables of the human element are considered in the context of private and state capitalism ('The State as Class') to assess the place of the managing bureaucracy. As the thesis that separation of ownership and control really means loss of control by the owner is untenable, it must be accepted that the bureaucracy has precarious tenure and its discretionary power is limited. The nice or nasty disposition of the bureaucrats manning the state, their 'socio-economic origin' and whose father went to which school, are variables, the configurations of power and dependence characterizing private and state capitalism respectively are constants; in such phrases as 'socialism with a human face', the weight of the constants of socialism relative to the variables of the human face is best seen as a matter of personal hopes and fears.

In state capitalism more inexorably than in looser social systems, one thing leads to another and, as one inconsistency is eliminated, others emerge, calling in turn for their elimination. The final and futuristic section of this book ('On The Plantation') deals with the logic of a state which owns all capital, needing to own its workers, too. Markets for jobs and goods, consumer sovereignty, money, employee-citizens voting with their feet are alien elements defeating some of the purposes of state capitalism. To the extent that they are dealt with, the social system comes to incorporate some features of the paternalistic Old South.

People have to become chattel slaves in relevant respects. They do not own but owe their labour. There is 'no unemployment'. Public goods are relatively plentiful, and 'merit goods' like wholesome food or Bach records, cheap, while wages are little more than pocket money by the standards of the outside world. People have their ration of housing and public transport, health care, education, culture and security *in kind,* rather than receiving vouchers (let alone money) and the corresponding onus of choosing. Their tastes and temperaments adjust accordingly (though not all will become addicts; some may turn allergic). The state will have maximized its discretionary power, before eventually discovering that it is facing some new predicament.

An agenda for a rational state gives rise, by implication, to an inverted agenda for rational subjects, at least in the sense of telling them what must be done to help or to hinder it. If they can purge any inconsistent preferences they may have for more liberty and more security, more state and less state at the same time – probably a more difficult undertaking than it sounds – they will know how far they want to assist or resist carrying out the state's agenda. On such knowledge must depend their own stand.

1

The Capitalist State

Violence, Obedience, Preference

*Preferences for political arrangements depend on people's
conception of their good as well as on the arrangements that are
supposed to be preferred.*

States generally start with somebody's defeat.

'The origin of the state is conquest' and 'the origin of the state is
the social contract' are not two rival explanations. One deals with
the origin of the state in real time, the other with logical deduction.
Both can be simultaneously valid. Historical investigation may establish that, to the extent that we can learn about such things, most
states trace their pedigree to the defeat of one people by another;
more rarely to the ascendancy of a victorious chief and his war gang
over his own people; and nearly always to migration. At the same
time, widely acceptable axioms will also help 'establish' (in a different sense of the word) that rational people, in pursuit of their good,
find it advantageous to subject themselves to a monarch, a state.
Since these two types of explanation of the state deal in unrelated
categories, it is no use trying to relate them or accord priority to one
over the other. Nor is it sensible to infer that because states have
come into being and flourished, it must have been rational for people
who pursued their good to subject themselves to them – otherwise
they would have put up more of a fight before doing so.

Consider in this light a well-regarded attempt at reconciling the
(historically) violent origin of the state with the rational volition of
the subject which underlies the analytical type of ontologies such as

15

the social contract.[1] In this essay, any person living in the state of nature forms an estimate of all future incomes he is likely to get in the state of nature and another estimate of all future incomes he would receive in civil society endowed with a state. The second estimate is taken to be larger than the first. The two estimates are discounted to present value. It takes time to get everybody else round to concluding the social contract that provides the passage from the state of nature to civil society. The high incomes resulting from the creation of the state are, therefore, some way off in the future and the present value of their excess over state-of-nature incomes is small. It may leave insufficient incentive for undertaking the task of getting everybody round to agree to the social contract. On the other hand, a state can be quickly created by violent means. The higher incomes engendered by the existence of the state thus begin to accrue quickly. They do not shrink so much when translated to present value. The comparison of the present value of incomes under a state formed slowly by peaceful negotiation of a social contract, with that of incomes under a state entering society by the short-cut of violence, must favour violence. If so, the income-maximizing rational person can presumably be expected either to welcome the violence done to him by whoever is bringing in the state, or himself resort to violence to organize it. The reader may either take it (though this cannot have been the author's intention) that this is the reason why most states were not created by peaceful negotiation but by violence or that, whatever was the historical cause in any particular case, this theory of rational motivation is at least not inconsistent with it.

Like the contractarian theories before it, this sort of theory invites the careless conclusion that because states have come into being by violence, and flourished, and because it can make sense for people serenely to submit to violence leading to the creation of the state which they desire but cannot manage to achieve, people did welcome state-creating violence *after the event*. The underlying assumption is that the state, regardless of its peaceful or violent origin, helps people in the pursuit of their good.

Astonishingly, this assumption is hardly ever cast in a more general form, for instance by allowing for algebraic sign. If it were, it should read 'the state helps/hinders', with the actual balance of the expression depending on the empirical content of the terms 'help' and

1   Robert L. Carneiro, 'A Theory of the Origin of the State', in J.D. Jennings and E.A. Hoebel (eds), *Readings in Anthropology*, 3rd edn, 1970.

'hindrance'. More informatively, the assumption could be cast in a form like 'the state helps/hinders some people, hinders/helps others and leaves the rest unaffected'. The affected are helped and hindered in different ways and to different extents. Unless by a fluke the hindered set is empty (i.e. everybody is either helped or left alone), the algebraic sum is a matter of comparisons between the helped and the hindered. Running up against interpersonal comparisons so early is a sign that our reflections are at least headed in the right direction, towards the central questions of political theory.

If ever there were people in the state of nature, and as a matter of repeated historical fact it took violence to impose a state upon them, it seems pertinent to ask, Why does standard political theory regard it as a basic verity that they preferred the state? The question really breaks down into two, one 'ex ante' and the other 'ex post': (i) Do people in the state of nature prefer *it* to the state? and (ii) Do people, *once in the state*, prefer the state of nature to *it*? These questions very sensibly allow for people's preferences to be related, in some way, to the political environment in which they actually happen to live.[2] However, once they are framed in this way, they are seen to have a peculiar character. When social scientists say that they know that Smith prefers tea to coffee because he just said so, or because he has revealed his preference by taking tea when he could have taken coffee, they deal in objects which are presumed to be both familiar and accessible to Smith. When Smith is talking about his preferences for things he can at best know from hearsay, difficulties begin to

---

2 A more succinct statement of the same point is found in Michael Taylor's excellent *Anarchy and Cooperation*, 1976, p. 130: 'if preferences change as a result of the state itself, then it is not even clear what is *meant* by the desirability of the state.' See also Brian Barry, *The Liberal Theory of Justice*, 1973, pp. 123–4, for the related argument that since socialization adapts people to their environment, a heterogenous or pluralistic society is unlikely to turn homogenous and *vice versa*, although 'only one generation has to suffer to create orthodoxy (as the absence of Albigensiens in France and Jews in Spain illustrates).'

However, Barry's use of the socialization argument seems to me somewhat lopsided. Must we exclude the possibility that the environment can generate not only *positive*, but also *negative* preferences for itself? Enough examples from second-generation socialist countries and even from third-generation Soviet Russia, attest to a virulent allergy to totalitarian ways and a yearning for diversity on the part of some unknown but perhaps not negligible part of the population. In the pluralistic West, there is a parallel yearning for more cohesion of purpose, for moral attitudes, an allergy to admass, to what Daniel Bell calls the 'porno-pop culture' and the 'psychedelic bazaar'.

This is perhaps saying no more than that all societies tend to secrete corrosive elements (though in only some societies do the rulers suppress them). Yet it is not trivial to generalize the 'endogenous preference' argument by admitting that social states may generate both likes and dislikes. Otherwise, the endogenous generation of preferences would ceaselessly *cement any status quo* and historical change would become even more mysterious, incomprehensible and random than it is anyway.

arise. They are compounded when he could not possibly translate his avowed preference into a practical act of choice, because some alternatives are simply not feasible. People who live in states have as a rule never experienced the state of nature and *vice versa*, and have no practical possibility of moving from the one to the other. It is often a historical anachronism and an anthropological absurdity to suppose such movement. On what grounds, then, do people form hypotheses about the relative merits of state and state of nature?[3]

It appears that among certain South American Indians (though conceivably elsewhere, too) an increase in the size of the demographic unit is recognized as favouring the likelihood of the creation of a state, possibly because of the changed scale and kind of wars that this entails. A war chief supported by his quasi-professional warrior followers can coerce the rest of the people into durable obedience. In a book by Pierre Clastres which should prominently figure in any bibliography of the social contract,[4] it is reported that the Tupi-Guarani people used to abort this process by swarms of them seceding, going off to distant and fearsome lands on prophet-led flights from the greater dread of subjection, of the state which they identify with evil. The American Indian people studied by Clastres typically live in the state of nature, a condition which has little to do with the level of technical civilization and everything to do with political power. Their chiefs can exhort but not command, and must rely on oratory, prestige and liberal hospitality to get their way. Their prestige depends in part on seldom risking interference in a matter where their exhortation is liable to go unheeded. There is no appar-

---

3   In the luxuriant literature that has sprouted around John Rawls's *Theory of Justice*, 1972, no objection appears to have been raised against the 'original position' on this ground. The participants in the original position are devoid of all knowledge of their particular persons. They do not know whether they are representative white Anglo-Saxon men or representative Red Indian women, tenured philosophers or welfare recipients. They do not even know the age they live in (though this seems hard to reconcile with their knowledge of 'political affairs and the principles of economics'). They are induced to seek a 'cooperative solution' to their existence (in game-theory terms), which can be summarily interpreted as agreement on a social contract for a just state.

Failing agreement, in leaving the original position they would exit into the state of nature. They seek to avoid this outcome, because they know enough about themselves and the state to prefer it to the state of nature. They know their 'life-plans' whose fulfilment depends on command over tangible and intangible 'primary goods'. They also know that the state, through the 'advantages of social cooperation', entails a greater availability of primary goods than the state of nature. In technical language, the participants thus know that they are playing a 'positive-sum game' in bargaining for a social contract (which is just in the sense, and only in the sense, that everybody is willing to stick to its terms). This means that if the cooperative solution is reached, more primary goods can be distributed than if it is not.

atus among them for enforcing obedience and the Indians would not dream of voluntarily contracting to obey, though they may choose to agree with the chief on a case-by-case basis.

Theirs are, according to Clastres, true affluent societies, easily capable of producing surpluses but choosing not to do so, a two-hour working day being sufficient amply to provide for what they consider adequate subsistence. Though there is little or no production for exchange, there is private property; there could be no private hospitality, no invitations to feasts without it. There is no obvious obstacle to the division of labour and hence to capitalism, but the goods that the division of labour may provide are not prized. Work is held in contempt. Hunting, fighting, story-telling and party-going are preferred to the sort of goods labour could produce. The question is staring us in the face, Is it because of their preferences that the Indians abhor the command–obedience relation inherent in the state, and choose to stay in the state of nature? Or is it living in the state of nature which predisposes them to like, above all else, the tangibles and intangibles that typically go with it?

Marx would no doubt frown at the role tastes and preferences are allowed to play in this way of posing the question, and would presumably decide that subsistence agriculture, gathering and hunting were phenomena of existence, of the 'base', while the institutions of the state were those of consciousness, of the 'superstructure'. It was thus the former which must have determined the latter. Clastres, for one, asserts the contrary.[5] Analytically (as distinct from historically), both views are true in the same sense as 'the chicken caused the egg' and 'the egg caused the chicken' are both true. My conten-

---

The comparison of two bundles of primary goods, however, requires indexing, and the weights adopted for the index (for instance, the relative valuation of time off against real income), cannot help but reflect a logically prior preference for a type of society. In other words, people in the original position cannot say that the bundle of primary goods available in the state of nature (containing, for instance, much leisure) is smaller than that available under the state (containing, for instance, many tangible consumption goods) unless they already know that they prefer to live in civil society. Comparison of the state-of-nature bundle and the state bundle presupposes the very preference which it is employed and required to explain.

The state-of-nature bundle of primary goods contains more of the things which people living in the state of nature are *used to* and have learnt to appreciate. It is, for them, the bigger bundle. The converse is true of the bundle available under conditions of social cooperation. It is the bigger bundle for people who have *learnt to like* what it contains and not to mind its constraints. But can people *in the original position* really tell which bundle is bigger?

4   Pierre Clastres, *La société contre l'état*, 1974; English translation, *Society against the State*, 1977.

5   Ibid., ch. 11.

tion here is that preferences for political arrangements of society are to a large extent produced by these very arrangements, so that political institutions are either *addictive* like some drugs, or *allergy-inducing* like some others, or both, for they may be one thing for some people and the other for others. If so, theories that people in general (Hobbes, Locke, Rousseau), or the ruling class (Marx, Engels), mount the political arrangements that suit them, need be approached with much mistrust. Conversely, the view (Max Weber's) that historical outcomes are largely unintended, deserves a *préjugé favorable* as the more promising approximation to many of the relations linking state and subject.

Title and Contract

The state is a capitalist state if it does not demand ownership to be justified, and does not interfere for his own good with a person's contracts.

The origin of capitalist ownership is that 'finders are keepers'.

This is the acknowledgement that permits the passage from possession to ownership, to good title to property, independently of *its* particularities, of *who* the title-holder may be and also of the *use* he may or may not make of the property. The state which recognized title to property on this ground (though it may do so on other grounds *as well*) fulfils one of the necessary conditions of being a 'capitalist state' in the sense I am using here (a sense which will become very clear as I proceed). The title is not invalidated by *scarcity*, is *contingent neither upon merit nor status*, and entails no obligation. The reference to scarcity may need some elucidation. What I mean is that if a man can own an acre, he can own a million acres. If his title is good, it is good regardless of whether, in Locke's famous words, 'enough and as good' is left for others. Ownership is not invalidted by the scarcity of the things owned nor by the non-owners' desire for it, so that in a capitalist state access to scarce goods is regulated by price and substitution and not by sovereign authority, however constituted.

Those brought up on the notions of primitive accumulation, division of labour and appropriation of surplus value as the source of continuing accumulation, might balk at this manner of approaching the origin of capital and the essence of the capitalist state. No doubt very little capital has ever been 'found' and a lot has been accumulated. Moreover, to both Marxists and perhaps most non-Marxists it might look like putting the cart before the horse to proceed from the 'relations of production' (which, as Plamenatz has demonstrated, mean relations of ownership 'if they are to have any identity at all')[6] to the 'means of production', the things owned. Yet it is not, or at least not generally, a change in the means of production or in the techniques applied to them, that transforms them into capitalist property. Land held by any major French or German noble family down to the Thirty Years' War was owned by it in the most tenuous sense only. It was a means of production but assuredly not capitalist property in the manner of English or Italian land. Land owned by the English nobility and gentry from the sixteenth century on, can rightly be regarded as capital and has in fact served as the main springboard of English capitalism. Shipping and other mercantile accumulation of capital got off to a flying start in late Tudor and Stuart times due, in great part, to the stakes put up by landowners. Non-capitalist (I am advisedly avoiding the term 'feudal') tenure of land usually originated in service and continued on the strength of a (more or less well-founded and realistic) expectation of future service. This was true of the landlord who was supposed to owe service, directly or indirectly, to the sovereign, and of his serfs who owed service to him.[7] It is characteristic of English social evolution that land tenure became so rapidly unconditional, and that such (light, and unwritten) conditions as remained, concerned local justice and charity where the landlord *supplanted* rather than *served* the state.

The peasant in the North and Central Russian 'repartitional' village held land because of who he was and because he had so many

6 John Plamenatz, *Man and Society*, 1963, vol. II, pp. 280–1. See also his *German Marxism and Russian Communism*, 1954, ch. 2.

7 Cf. C.B. Macpherson, *The Political Theory of Possessive Individualism*, 1962, p. 49, for the view that without unconditional ownership, there can be no market for *land*. The same argument must hold for any other 'means of production', including labour. (For Macpherson, no less than for Marx, the rot set in when the individual was acknowledged to own his labour and came to sell *it* rather than its products.) In Russia, service tenure of land meant that serfs ('souls') could not, prior to 1747, be sold off the land because they were needed to maintain the landlord's capacity to serve the state. The transferability of 'souls' (hitherto regarded as managed by the landlord on behalf of the ultimate owner, the state) was a symptom of social progress, a sign that private property was taking root in Russia. The reader must bear in mind that the Russian nobility had no title to its lands prior to 1785 and that its service tenure was quite precarious. In view of the recent nature of private property as a social institution, the progress of capitalism in Russia in the short run-up to 1917, was most remarkable.

adults in his family. His title, such as it was, could be argued to have depended on status, need for and capacity to use, the land. Every so many years, when the cumulative change in the needs of his and *other* families in the village demanded it, the caucus of influential peasants who ran the *obshchinnoe* might take away his strips of land and deal him out other, inferior strips. Nobody, however, could sell out or buy into the village; if they could have done, the land would have become capital. The land the American farmer 'found' on the frontier, or 'proved up' under the 1862 Homestead Act, or got from somebody else who did, was capital. The premises, tools and stock of materials of a master of a craft guild, were not capital. The physically very similar premises, tools and materials of his successor, the small entrepreneur-artisan under *Gewerbefreiheit* were the very essence of capital.[8] Unlike his guild predecessor, he could be anybody and could run his shop the way he saw fit. It is not the scale of the undertakings nor the fact of employing the labour of others which makes the first pre-capitalist and the second capitalist. Both generated 'surplus value' and enabled their owner to appropriate it. However (except perhaps in Italy north of the Papal States), the guild master's title to his business was contingent not only upon constraints on output, price and quality, but also upon who he was and how he lived.

Ownership which does not have to be born into, lived up to, served and atoned for, but just *is,* is of course no less an ideological phenomenon for that. Its recognition is a distinctive mark of the ideology defining the capitalist state, just as ownership which is contingent upon its conformity to some *principle of social utility, justice, equality or efficiency* and which is forfeit or at least *forcibly adjusted if it does not so conform,* satisfies an ideology which is variously called democratic, liberal, socialist or combinations of these words.

Unsurprisingly, the relation connecting the finders-are-keepers principle of ownership to the capitalist state runs both ways. Like other implicit functions which mostly make up the base of the social sciences, it does not feature an independent and a dependent vari-

---

8   *Gewerbefreiheit*, the freedom to engage in a particular craft or commerce, was introduced in Austria-Hungary in 1859 and in the various German states in the early 1860s. Prior to it, a cobbler needed a state licence to cobble and even a mercer needed one to sell thread. The licence was granted, or not, at the state's discretion, ostensibly on grounds of proficiency and good standing, in fact as a means to regulate competition. At all events, because of the licence, the goodwill of the business could not be easily negotiated.

able, an unmistakeable cause and an effect. The relation really asserts that it takes the capitalist state to accept and uphold such a quintessentially positivist, non-normative principle of ownership, and that it takes such a severe, contingent-upon-nothing kind of ownership to make the state a capitalist state.

There is a second necessary condition of capitalism, which is inevitably bound up with the first without being part of the same thing. It is the freedom of contract. When, as in most of medieval Europe, the tenure of property involved onerous obligations and was open to persons of a defined status or other defined characteristics, alienation by free contract could not have been countenanced by the sovereign. Even the marriage contract was subject to state approval and for really prominent families remained so into the eighteenth century. Property came gradually to be governed by contract rather than status, partly because servitudes in kind were commuted into money and partly because, from being the obligations of the owner, they became those of the property – of the *marquisat* rather than of the *marquis* – so that the state interest was not harmed by letting it pass into the hands of any upstart tax farmer or venal magistrate. Much the same mutation led from a man's debts, which he had to discharge or go to prison, to the no-recourse mortgage on property and to the liabilities of an undertaking which permitted its changing hands, even before formal limited liability became widespread.

Freedom of contract, as a necessary condition for the state to be a capitalist one, can be construed as the freedom of the finder not just to keep what he found, but to transfer all his rights in it to another on whatever terms he chooses, and by extension the freedom of the latter to transfer it to yet another. The capitalist state must let freedom of contract prevail over both ideas of *status* and propriety, and ideas of *just* contracts (*fair* wage, *just* price).

If all the world's goods were divided up into random bundles belonging to nobody, and if everybody were blindfolded and could pick one bundle, and when the blindfolds were taken off all could see their own and anyone else's bundle, we would have a properly translucent setting for the interaction of free contracts, status and just contracts. If some of the bundles contained beaver hats, and some people liked beaver hats more than other things while for other people it was the other way round, after some scurrying about they could all end up holding what they liked best, subject of course to the constraints of feasibility fixed by the initial bundles. If (as used to be the case before the late seventeenth-century flooding of the European market with Canadian pelts), people below a certain status were then forbidden to wear beaver hats, their price in terms of other things would decline and even so a number of swaps of hats for other things would be prevented from taking place, for some people of the requisite high status but not so keen on beaver, would half-heartedly hang on to the hats they found in their bundles. If, in addition, there was an authority entitled to outlaw unjust contracts and it felt that the just price of beaver was what it has always been, the number of mutually agreeable exchanges would be further restricted, only people of the requisite status and very keen on beaver being prepared to pay the just price. A number of hats would go begging, their holders being unable either to wear or to swap them.

Analogous, though less outlandish, problems arise when we imagine bundles made up of all sorts of talents, skills, knowledge and muscle-power, and various job opportunities, outlets for this talent, needs for that skill or muscle. As we can expect from a random distribution, there would be a hopeless mismatch *within* each bundle between talents and opportunities, skills and the occasions for using them. Status rules and the banning of unjust bargains, e.g. the setting of minimum wages or of a 'rate for the job', would prevent at least a part of the possible matching *between* bundles from taking place. In this context, the capitalist state is naturally one that will not enforce status-related and justice-related rules and constraints on the freedom of contract,[9] passively allowing the ideas which gave rise to them to be eroded by the tide (when such a tide is running) of the capitalist ideology and the exigencies of capitalist business practice. The state which will actually outlaw and suppress such rules, however, may learn to like outlawing and suppressing in a general way, and may not remain a capitalist state for very long.

Pareto has laid down the precise sense in which the voluntary reshuffling by their owners of the contents of random bundles, results in the 'best' distribution of the world's goods. If two consenting adults close a contract, and there is no independent evidence of duress (i.e. evidence *other than the contract looking unfavourable to*

---

9 One must not confuse injustice and cheating. An unjust man will, if he can, hire you for wages you cannot be expected to work for. (What this may precisely mean is a large question. As I am not concerned with substantive questions of justice, happily I can pass it by.) A cheat will not pay you the wages he said he would. The capitalist state must, of course, go after the cheat.

one party), we accept a *prima facie* case that they like the terms of this contract better than not entering into a contract with each other. (The precise condition, in fact, is that one of them prefers and the other either prefers, or is indifferent to, contracting.) There is also an (albeit weaker) case for holding that there is no other contract which these two people, given their respective situations, could have concluded instead such that it would be preferred by one of them to the contract they did conclude, while leaving the other party at worst indifferent. If, then, it cannot be shown that their contract violates the rights of a third party (it may violate his interests), no one – neither the third party, nor anyone purporting to defend his interests – has the right to hinder them in executing their contract as agreed. Overriding the contract, or forcibly amending its terms *ex post*, let alone insisting that, as amended, it is still binding on the parties, are the ways of 'hindering' typically reserved for the state (cf. pp. 103– 104).

The condition 'it cannot be shown that their contract violates the rights of a third party' is, however, obviously neither straightforward nor easy, though it is putting the onus of proof where it belongs. Sometimes the onus is allowed to shift the other way, the contracting parties having to prove that they are not violating third-party rights. This is not an unfair characterization, for instance, of the practice of some American regulatory agencies. Norms for judging the rights of someone in relation to a contract to which he is not a party cannot be laid down independently of culture and ideology and may, even so, remain contentious. For instance, to stay safely in a realm of capitalist culture and ideology, does it violate the rights of the lowest bidder if he is not awarded the contract, assuming that the tender specified no explicit rule about accepting the lowest bid? Must the best qualified candidate for a job get it? Can land use be changed if it spoils the view for the neighbours? Different capitalist answers appear to be possible. Different capitalist jurisprudence might interpret the 'third party' condition in a more or less austere manner, and careful thought may be needed before one can say that a particular state is not respecting the freedom of contract and is, on this ground, an adversary of capitalism.

What, on the other hand, *is* an unambiguous denial of the freedom of contract is the interdiction or forcible amendment of a contract (in order, for example, to tilt its terms in favour of one of the parties) on grounds not involving the rights of third parties. Admission of such grounds appear to presuppose that a person, in entering into a contract, is capable of *violating his own rights* and it is incumbent upon the state, whose proper function is the defence of recognized rights, to prevent him from doing so. This is the key to a whole boxful of cases where it can be claimed that a person needs to be protected against himself. One oft-cited case (which involves other problems, too) is the puzzle about a man's freedom (in the sense of right) to sell himself into slavery.[10] A fundamentally different case for denying the freedom of contract arises out of the claim that, in agreeing to a certain set of terms, a person would be *mistaking his own preference or interest*. The ground for stopping him is no longer one of his right, and *a fortiori* not one of a conflict between two of his rights, but of *his utility* as seen from the outside by the sympathetic observer. On this ground, prohibition stops a man from buying whisky because his *real* (or 'rational', 'true', 'long-term' or 'unconfused' as it is sometimes called to distinguish it from plain) preference is for sobriety. The weakness-of-will argument may have to be invoked to justify the distinction between plain revealed preference for whisky and unconfused long-term preference for a sober life. However, much the same distinction must be agreed to support other applications of the principle of paternalism: the payment of wages in kind, the provision by the state of welfare services (e.g. health) in kind, compulsory insurance, education, etc., each of these in contradistinction to giving the recipient cash *in lieu,* to be spent as *he* saw fit.

Another's conception of a person's good or utility, another's diagnosis of his real preference or long-term interest, is adequate ground for interfering with his freedom to enter into contracts a consenting adult partner is prepared to agree to if, and only if, it is

---

10   The answer consistent with the capitalist ideology whose contours I am trying to sketch, might run like this: 'Yes, a man should be left free to sell himself into slavery; there is no more competent judge than he of his reason for doing so.' The state has nonetheless the duty to withhold legal protection from the institution of slavery, contributing to its removal as an option available under contractual freedom. Contracts under which slave-traders sell captured Africans to slave-owners obviously violate the Africans' rights. If plantation-bred third-generation slaves, for reasons which will always remain debatable but which are *their* reasons, do not seek freedom, we have to think again. Note that the British government first prohibited the slave trade without prohibiting slavery. The state must simply ensure that if he wants to walk off the plantation, he should not be prevented from doing so, i.e. it should not help enforce a contract under which the planter owns the slave. This is patently not an abolitionist position. It is doubtful whether it would have been an acceptable compromise to Calhoun and Daniel Webster.

accepted that it is a proper function of the state to use its monopoly power of coercion to enforce A's conception of B's good. Now A may be anybody, or the sympathetic observer, or the majority of voters, or the foremost socio-psycho-economic research institute, or the state itself. Different kinds of states could be distinguished according to which of these potential sources they would *profess* to follow. The test of the capitalist state is that it follows neither source, for it gives priority to the freedom of contract, including under it the extremely important freedom *not to contract at all*. Anticipating chapter 2, I might say broadly that other states profess to follow one or more of the possible sources. The choice of 'sources', whose conception of the good is to be listened to, is inevitably determined by the *state's own conception* of the good; it will choose to be guided by congenial spirits, kindred intellects. Selection of the adviser, no less than selection of what advice to accept, is tantamount to doing what one wanted to do all along. In choosing to promote B's good, the state is in effect pursuing its own ends. This, to be sure, is a quasi-tautology; it calls for more attention to the nature of the state's ends.

The Contours of the Minimal State

Indifference to the satisfactions of governing gives rise to self-imposed limits on the scope of the state.

It is strange but not patently irrational for the state to minimize itself.

A theory, or at least an approximative definition, of the capitalist state, which requires it to respect the freedom of two parties to enter into contracts that do not violate the rights of a third, looks incomplete, as is – by customary standards – the state in question. For what are the third-party *rights* which the state ought to protect and what are mere *pretensions* which it ought to ignore? There is a virtually limitless list of potential claims which third parties could make against the terms of a given contract. Laws must be made and administered both to define the category of claims that shall be treated as justified and to reduce the area of doubt (and hence of arbitrariness) between those that shall and those that shall not be so treated. Once there is a state, it is incumbent upon it to deal with these tasks.

There is some presumption that in the state of nature a spontaneous cooperative arrangement would arise and fulfil this function,

for the same general reasons which let us suppose that other functions habitually regarded as proper to the state would also be looked
after, though there is neither a certitude that they would be nor a
definition of the particular shape they would take. Once a state is
formed, however, at least some of these non-coercive arrangements
are liable to become unworkable and may, indeed, be impossible to
bring about in the first place. In the state of nature, anyone disliking
the way a voluntary arrangement is working, has only two choices:
to accept the way it works, or to bargain for its amendment, a
breakdown in bargaining carrying the danger of the whole arrangement breaking down and its benefits being lost.[11] The risk of such an
outcome provides some incentive for everyone to keep things going
by reciprocal accommodation.

In the presence of a state, however, the dissident member of a
voluntary arrangement has an added reason to be intransigent (and
the other members an added reason to call his bluff), i.e. the faculty
of recourse to the state. If he cannot get his way, he can still appeal to
the state to uphold the justice of his case, and so can the other
cooperators. Whoever wins, the voluntary arrangement is transformed into a coerced one. Turned upside down, this is the same
logic as the one in Kant's argument about the subject's right to
disagree with the sovereign. If there were such a right (which Kant
denies), there would have to be an arbiter to whom the disagreement
could be referred. The sovereign would then cease to be the sovereign, and the arbiter would take his place. Conversely, if there *is* a
sovereign he *will* get disagreements referred to him, for there is less
reason to yield in private compromise if an instance of appeal exists.
What the state must do, to make its life and that of its less litigious
subjects tolerable, is to lay down as clearly as possible the laws
predicting how it *would* rule if cases of a given description were
appealed to it (thus warding off many appeals), as well as a general
description of the cases in which it would not hear an appeal at all.[12]

---

11   This assumes that the arrangement requires unanimity. If it does not, and the arrangement
continues to produce its benefits after the withdrawal of the person who failed to get his way in
bargaining, the well-known free-rider problem arises and might destabilize the arrangement. If
the non-cooperator benefits as well as the cooperators, an incentive is created for the latter to
defect. As each successive cooperator becomes a free rider, ever fewer cooperators carry ever-
more free riders and the incentive to defect keeps increasing. Various devices, some practicable
in some situations and others in others, can be conceived to hinder this outcome and give the
arrangement some stability. (Cf. pp. 217–18.)
12   The reader will have spotted that while one type of state would have an interest in
proceeding as above, other types of state might want to do the precise opposite, to make their

Admitting, then, that if the state exists at all, it will somehow or other assume the task of sorting out disputes arising out of third-party claims, what are the guidelines the capitalist state would adopt for doing so while still remaining capitalist, an upholder of the freedom of contract? There is no question of drawing up a design, a sort of *code capitaliste* for the laws of such a state, the less so as it is reasonable to believe that more than one such *code,* containing significant variations on the same themes, could each be consistent with the basic capitalist conditions relating to unconditional property and free contract. Perhaps the most economical way of grasping the spirit common to all such possible *codes,* is to consider that if there is a state (which is not the same as claiming that there could really be one) which is prepared to agree to these basic conditions, it must be one which finds its satisfactions *elsewhere than in governing.*

Such a statement may look obscure and require a little elaboration. When we reflect about choice, we incline at least tacitly to suppose that 'behind' the choice there is a purpose, an end. It used even to be said, for instance that consumers seek satisfaction and producers seek profit, and their choices can be thought of as rational (or not) in terms of a corresponding maximization assumption. But what end or ends does the state pursue, the maximization of what can qualify its conduct as rational? Various answers of varying degrees of sincerity and seriousness could be proposed: the sum of the satisfactions of its citizens, the well-being of a particular class, the gross national product, the might and glory of the nation, the state budget, taxes, order and symmetry, the security of its own tenure of power, etc. (I address the question more seriously on pp. 244–7.) The likely *maximands* all seem on closer scrutiny to require that the state possess some specialized capacity, equipment to attain them. In addition, greater rather than lesser capacity looks desirable for guiding the course of events, dominating the environment, and actively working upon the maximand (increasing the pay-off, e.g. enlarging the dominion rather than merely the power over a given dominion). Even if there are *maximands* which do not require a vast capacity to act for their attainment – unwordly objectives like, say, the peaceful observation of rare butterflies – would it not be pointless

---

subjects appeal to them as frequently as possible; this may well coincide with the interest and the perhaps-unconscious wish of the legal profession. Laws breed lawyers who, in turn, breed laws.

for the state pursuing them, voluntarily to bind its hands and renounce in advance the use of a fully-fledged apparatus for exercising power, of the richest possible set of 'policy tools'? Might they not come in handy one day?

My definition of the capitalist state, however, requires it to opt for a sort of unilateral disarmament, for a self-denying ordinance concerning the property of its subjects and their freedom to negotiate contracts with each other. A state whose objectives needed, for their realization, a strong capacity to govern, would not willingly adopt such a self-denying ordinance. This is the sense in which we say that the ends of the capitalist state, whatever they are (we need not even seek to find their particular content) lie *outside government*.

What, then, is the *point* for the state in being a state? If it finds its satisfaction in what we could term 'metagovernmental' *maximands*, rare butterflies or plain peace and quiet, why not resign and *stop governing*? The only plausible answer that suggests itself is to keep *them* out, to stop *them* from getting hold of the levers of the state and spoiling it, the butterflies, the peace and all. The very special rationale of being a minimal state is to leave few levers for the zealots to get hold of and upset things with if, by the perversity of fate or of the electorate, *they* manage to become the state.

Inheriting a strong, centralized state apparatus is part of the secret of the successes both of the Jacobin terror and of Bonaparte. In what are, perhaps, the climactic passages of *L'ancien régime et la révolution* (Book III, ch. VIII), Tocqueville blames the pre-revolutionary French state for having set over everyone the government as 'preceptor, guardian and, if need be, oppressor', and for having created 'prodigious facilities', a set of egalitarian institutions lending themselves to despotic use, which the new absolutism found, all ready and serviceable, among the debris of the old.

Marx, too, is perfectly clear about the value to the revolution of the 'enormous bureaucratic and military organization, with its ingenious state machinery' put in place by the regime it had overthrown. 'This appalling parasitic body, which enmeshes the body of French society like a net and chokes all its pores, sprang up in the days of the absolute monarchy. . . . The seignorial privileges of the landowners and towns became transformed into so many attributes of the state power. . . . The first French Revolution . . . was bound to develop what the absolute monarchy had begun: centralization, but at the same time the extent, the attributes and the agents of governmental power. Napoleon perfected this state machinery.'[13] Thus, it is not the state that mistrusts *itself* and would rather not have levers or powerful tools lest it should misuse them. It knows that *it* could not possibly be tempted to misuse power. It is its rivals for state power who would, by the nature of their ambition, misuse it. (The minimal state may even be aware that if it was succeeded by a rival with contestable ends in mind, the latter would need but a little time to put in place the rudiments of an apparatus of non-minimal government. However, even gaining a little time, and hence hope, would be better than handing it a ready-made system of pulleys and levers.) Seeking, as it does, aims which positive government is incapable of promoting, and fearing its capacity for wrong-doing in profane hands, the capitalist state is rational in adopting the contours of the minimal state.

Recalling the regimes of Walpole, Metternich, Melbourne or Louis Philippe (only more so), with a blend of indifference, benign neglect and a liking for amenities and comforts, the capitalist state must have sufficient *hauteur* not to want to be bothered by petty disputes among its subjects. The more quietly they get on with their business, the better, and it may occasionally, and a little reluctantly, use a heavy hand to make them do so. Its distance from the mundane concerns of its subjects does not, on the other hand, imply the sort of heroic *hauteur* which a Nietzsche or a Treitschke wished to find in the state, which reaches out for some high purpose, risking in avoidable war the life and property of the subject; nor the *hauteur* of utilitarian ethics, which sees the subject and his property as legitimate means to a greater common good. In a seeming paradox, the capitalist state is aristocratic because remote, yet with enough bourgeois overtones to recall the governments of the July Monarchy of 1830–48 in France. At any event, it is a state which is very unlikely to be a republic. As a digression, it is worth remembering, though it may not prove much, that Alexander Hamilton was a convinced royalist. His is a good example of how little the essence of capitalism is understood by the public. If people were asked who was the most capitalist American statesman, some may be tempted to say 'Grant' and think of railroad land grants, 'Garfield' and think of the Gilded Age, perhaps 'McKinley' and think of Mark Hanna and tariffs, 'Harding' and the Teapot Dome scandal and the Ohio Gang. Such

13 K. Marx, 'The Eighteenth Brumaire of Louis Bonaparte', in K. Marx and F. Engels, *Selected Works in One Volume*, 1968, p. 169.

answers miss the point. These Presidents caused or condoned corruption and scandal by favouring some interests over others, which means using state power for *their* ends. If any American statesman was good for capitalism, which is not evident, it was Alexander Hamilton.

Such a state, then, will make few and simple laws and not enforce many of the laws it may have inherited. It will make it clear that it dislikes adjudicating claims against established situations resulting from people's freely negotiated contracts, will do so gingerly if it must but only as a last resort.

It will be reluctant to promote the good of society, let alone to order the more fortunate of its subjects to share their good fortune with the less fortunate, not because it lacks compassion, but because it does not consider that having creditable and honourable feelings entitles the state to coerce its subjects into indulging them. We must leave it at that, and not try to find out (nor could we if we tried) whether it is 'belief in *laissez faire*' or some other, more subtle conviction about the proper role of the state which is holding it back, or simply *indifference to the satisfactions that may be found beyond the limits of the minimal state.*

If States did not Exist, should they be Invented?

People come to believe that because they have states, they need them.

Neither individual nor class interest can justify a state on *prudential* grounds.

We have derived some of the characteristic features of a state which would be 'best' (alternatively, 'least harmful') for capitalism, proceeding from the ideal conditions of capitalist ownership and exchange to how the state fulfilling these conditions might behave, and what reason it could possibly have for doing so. The image which is beginning to emerge is that of an unusual creature, bearing a relatively remote likeness to any real state that ever existed. The few real states I have alluded to in order to illustrate a point were chosen more for their style, flavour, and lack of governing zeal, than for being really close incarnations of the ideal being. The reverse procedure could, perhaps, be used to show that a less bizarre, more likely sort of state would really be more harmful to capital and capitalism, even if it was an unprincipled tool of the Two Hundred Families and sent gendarmes or the National Guard to help grind the face of the poor.

The real-life states people are stuck with, more often than not because their distant ancestors were beaten into obedience by an invader, and sometimes due to Hobson's choice, to having to take one king so as to escape the threat of getting another, are not primarily 'good for this' or 'least harmful for that'. They are not shaped to meet the functional needs of a system of beliefs, preferences, life-styles or 'mode of production'. This affirmation of the autonomy of the state and the separateness of its ends does not exclude all scope, over time, for some mutual adaptation whereby the state comes to conform to people's customs and preferences, just as they learn to accept and, from time to time, to enthuse about some of the state's demands upon them.

Any real state, given its *de facto* origin, is primarily an historical accident *to which* society must adapt. This is unsatisfactory to those who, by both training and inclination, see political obligation as resting either on moral duty or on prudential purpose. Instead of a trivial theory showing obedience to result from the threat of coercion, more interest will be shown in theories which derive the state from the subject's own volition, if only because it is intellectually comforting to find coherent reasons for believing that we actually need what we have.

There are, in particular, two rival theories with the identical basic thesis that if the state did not exist, we should invent it. Both, I shall argue, rest on self-delusion. One holds that it is people in general who need the state which alone can fulfil the function of turning general conflict into general harmony. People not only need this, but are aware of their need, and by the social contract create the state and give it authority over themselves. The other theory proposes that it is the possessing class which needs the state as the indispensable instrument of class rule. The source of the state's political power is, in some fashion, the economic power which ownership confers upon the possessing class. The two powers, economic and political, complement each other in oppressing the proletariat. The purest, least ambiguous theorist of the social contract is Hobbes, and Engels is that of the instrument-of-class-oppression theory.

Both theories have an irreducible common core: both require

people ('the people' in the one case, 'the capitalist class' in the other), to abdicate a *de facto* faculty, the recourse to force. One and the other, each in the manner proper to it, confers a monopoly of the possession (and hence obviously of the use) of force upon Leviathan, the monarch or the class state. One's motive is fear, the other's greed; not moral but prudential reasons.

Neither provides any good ground for supposing that the state, once it has the monopoly of force will not, at times or forever, use it *against* those *from* whom it received it. Neither is a theory of the state in the proper sense, i.e. neither really explains why the state will do one thing rather than another. Why, in fact, should it stop people from killing and robbing each other rather than indulging in some robbery and, if need be, killing, on its own account? Why should it help the capitalists oppress the workers, rather than engage in the probably more rewarding pursuit of oppressing the capitalists? What *maximand* does the state maximize, what is its pay-off, and how does it go about getting it? The conduct of the state is assumed (it keeps the peace, it oppresses the workers) rather than derived from *its* rational volition.

The state, under either the contractarian or the Marxist hypothesis, has got all the guns. Those who armed it by disarming themselves, are at its mercy. The state's sovereignty *means* that there is no appeal against its will, no higher instance which could possibly *make* it do one thing rather than another.[14] Everything really depends on Leviathan giving no cause to people to rebel (Hobbes is *assuming* that it would not), or on the state oppressing only the right people, i.e. the workers.

14   Locke, seeking to oppose Hobbes and to present a more palatable doctrine, saw that if people's natural right was to remain inviolate (i.e. if the state was not to trespass upon property which, in turn, was coextensive with liberty), sovereignty could not be absolute. It had to be limited to the upholding of natural right (*Second Treatise*, 1689, section 135). Subjection of the executive to a strong legislature was to safeguard this limit.

Two objections arise. First, the sovereignty of the legislature being absolute, we are back in the Hobbesian situation: the legislature is the monarch; why should it not violate natural rights? *Quis custodiat ipsos custodes?* Second, why should the executive choose to stay subjected to the legislature?

Locke was really arguing from the circumstances of a historical fluke: property-owners have managed to dethrone James II and put William III in his place, therefore the legislature has the upper hand over the executive. He was manifestly unaware that by giving the majority the right of rebellion, he did not provide them with the *means for rebelling successfully* in less exceptionally propitious historical circumstances than those of the Glorious Revolution (1688). It is fairly probable that had he been writing in the age of armoured vehicles, automatic weapons and proper telecommunications, he would have avoided the concept of a *right* to rebel altogether. Even within the technical civilization of his own day, he failed to allow for a state which is neither inept at keeping power nor insensible to its subjects' property.

There are certainly good reasons, both *a priori* and empirical, why such assumptions should, at least some of the time, be wrong. One cannot seriously expect people in general, or the capitalist class, to take such a gamble with an essentially *unpredicted* state for prudential reasons, though they might do so as an act of faith. The one plausible condition under which self-interest could induce rational people to take this risk is when the likely consequences of *not* disarming themselves in favour of the state look more dangerous still.

Inventing the State: the Social Contract

Political hedonism requires a benign state or a conformist subject. Failing both, it is a foolhardy attitude.

Hobbes, who could be mischievous, saw that every man has reason to fear his fellow man if they are alike.

All men, needing self-approval, seek eminence over others. If I let my fellow man seek eminence, he will invade my property, therefore I must attack his first. Self-preservation must drive both of us to fight each other, and there will be 'savage war for glory'. Both our lives will become 'nasty, brutish and short'.

While self-preservation is said to be the spring of all Hobbesian conduct, it is clear that I would not have to worry about preserving myself if my neighbour, whether to become eminent or to forestall me, did not invade my property. Is there a way of persuading the neighbour to desist? Perhaps by letting him know that I am not seeking eminence over him and he has nothing to fear? If self-preservation no longer obliged him to keep up his guard, and he lowered it, I could pounce and gain eminence over him; and so could he if I agreed to let him be and lowered my guard. As he is like me, I have to fear him, and cannot prudently make the first step which *would* break the vicious circle if he were unlike me.

In modern decision theory, such situations are called 'prisoners' dilemmas'.[15] As set up, they have no spontaneous cooperative solution. Left to themselves, both 'prisoners' must, if they are rational, seek to get the better of each other by 'confessing' first, and both end up with a longer sentence than if they had both played 'thief's

---

15 I submit that 'prisoners'' is preferable to the more usual 'prisoner's', for the dilemma is always that of two or more persons and its essence is the fatality of *mutual* betrayal. It cannot ever be a game of *solitaire*.

honour' and refused to confess. In Hobbes, they both end up with a shorter and nastier life. Their sole escape is to abandon the state of nature and conclude a 'covenant of mutual trust' whereby a designated sovereign is invested with whatever power it takes to enforce peace (or natural right). Thus nobody need fear that, by behaving trustingly, he will be taken advantage of by the others; therefore all can behave trustingly. The sovereign will, for some reason, use his absolute power only for obtaining this result. His subjects have no right to rebel but nor do they have any reason for doing so. It is not clear whether, if they did have cause, they would have a right to rebel.

The prisoners' dilemma implicit in Hobbes requires, for its proper study, the state of nature where no sovereign authority stops the participants from making themselves miserable if they are so inclined.[16] States are in a state of nature in that they retain the faculty of recourse to force against each other and do not transfer their arms and their sovereignty to a super-state.[17]

I will consider, in this context, two Hobbesian dilemmas, those of *war* and *trade*. While I am at it, I will go on briefly to look at Rousseau's problem of general *social cooperation* also, though the latter is quite different in nature (it is not a 'prisoners' dilemma' and requires a special psychological assumption in order *not* to result in voluntary cooperation).

Let there be two sovereign countries (to borrow the language of army manoeuvres, 'Blue' and 'Red'). Both want 'eminence' in Hobbes's sense. The order of their preferences is: (1) victory in war, (2) disarmament, (3) armed peace and (4) defeat in war. They must choose between two 'strategies' – arming and disarming – without

16 Hobbes's dilemma is more natural and less rigorous than the one set up under the conventions of formal game theory and it should, much of the time, have a cooperative solution. In a formal game, the player must make his move all the way, he is not allowed pauses, feints or tentative half-moves whose second half depends on the equally tentative reactions, *tâtonnements* of the other player. In the state of nature a player, before even making a half-move, may make speeches, brandish his weapon, cajole, etc. Depending on the other player's reaction or rather on his reading of it, he may walk away (if the other stands his ground), or strike a blow (either because the other looks about the strike first, or because he is looking the other way), or perhaps hear and consider an offer of Danegeld.

17 In his remarkable *Anarchy and Cooperation*, Taylor rightly raises an eyebrow at Hobbes not applying to a state of nature composed of *states*, the analysis he applies to a state of nature composed of *persons*. This reproach looks particularly grave from an empiricist's point of view: for a state of nature composed of states is available in the real world, while a state of nature composed of persons is a theoretical construct, or at least it was that for Hobbes and his readers who had no inkling of what modern anthropologists were going to find in remote corners of the world.

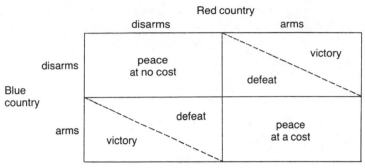

Figure 1

knowing what the other country chooses. The 'pay-off matrix' resulting from this situation will then be as in figure 1.

Though Blue does not know whether Red will arm or disarm, he will choose to arm because by doing so he avoids defeat, gets peace at a cost as the worst-case pay-off and may get victory if Red is a sucker. Red is like Blue, and reasons similarly. He, too, chooses to arm. They end up in the southeast corner of the figure, in armed peace which is the 'maximin' (the best worst-case) solution proper to hostile players. The northwest corner of costless peace is denied them, though they would both prefer it, because of their even greater preference for victory over each other. Once in the northwest corner, Blue would try to go into the southwest and Red into the northeast quadrant, i.e. the 'cooperative solution' of costless peace would be unstable in the absence of a super-state *enforcing disarmament*.

This is, broadly, the result we actually find in the real world. States are most of the time in the southeast quadrant of the figure, i.e. they live in costly armed peace. From time to time they slip into the southwest or northeast quadrant and make war. Whether this is by virtue of unequal arms, a freak cause, or for another of the innumerable historical causes of war, is beyond our present concern. Despite their preference for northwest over southeast, however, they do not surrender sovereignty. We must carefully note this fact and consider it presently.

The dilemma of trade is formally identical to the dilemma of war. Let there be the same two countries, Red and Blue. Each wants the other's goods. Both have the same order of preferences: (1) get foreign goods for free, (2) trade home goods for foreign goods, (3) retain the home goods (no trade), and (4) forgo the home goods and get no foreign goods (total loss, confiscation, expropriation, write-

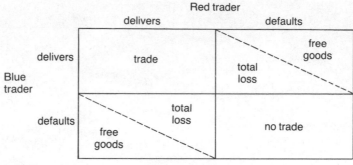

Figure 2

off). The two countries contract to deliver goods to each other (or to lend for later repayment, or invest for a return). As there is no enforcing super-state, they can either perform the contract or default, as in figure 2.

Game theory would once again predict that neither trader will give the other the chance to play him for a sucker, so that 'maximin' is the dominant strategy for both and they end up not trading. The structure of their preferences and the structure of the pay-offs jointly deny them the benefit of trading in the absence of a contract-enforcer. This prediction, of course, is belied by the widespread fact of trade, investment and lending across national jurisdictions, which those who engage in them find on the whole worthwhile in the face of a certain frequency of bad debts and defaults of one kind or another. States are in certain circumstances even prepared to give redress to foreign nationals and enforce performance by their own defaulting nationals; an altogether quixotic act by the standard conceptions of basic social contract theory. Equally quixotic is the voluntary sub-mission, by medieval traders and bankers, of cases of default or disputed contract performance to the judgments of their peers ap-pointed for the purpose but possessing no arms and commanding no police, especially when you consider the danger that the decision might have gone against them!

If history demonstrates that two ostensibly identical dilemmas regularly give rise to contrasting outcomes, the war dilemma result-ing in armed peace (with occasional war) and the trade dilemma resulting in trade, the ostensible identity must hide some significant difference. Intuitively, war is more easily seen as a single isolated act than is trade. A war can even be fought 'to end all wars', to have hegemony in peace forever after. Trade is typically an indefinite series of recurrent acts, which the participants fully intend to prolong. Everything that mathematics and psychology finds conducive to cooperative solutions in 'iterated' prisoners' dilemmas applies to trade, much less of it to war. Neither dilemma and its real-world resolution, however, lends convincing support to the Hobbesian reason for inventing a state and escaping from the brutish misery of the state of nature, into its encircling arms.

Is there more force in Rousseau's thesis, that people in the state of nature are unable to organize the social cooperation necessary for the realization of their common good (the general will)? His basic statement of the problem is in the Second Discourse, and is known as the parable of the Hunting Party.[18] If (two) hunters stalk a deer, they are sure to catch it if only each one will stand faithfully at his post. They can in this way unconsciously acquire the idea of mutual obligation (which, for Rousseau, forms the passage from the state of nature to civil society), but only if their present and palpable interest demands it. However, they lack foresight and 'hardly think of the morrow'. Therefore, if one sees a hare passing, he will quit the deer stalk and run off to catch it, depriving the other hunter of the deer and, indeed, of bagging anything at all. The pay-off matrix of their interaction will have the form of figure 3.[19]

As both hunters prefer the deer, or even half of one, to a hare, neither has an incentive to 'sucker' the other, leaving him standing

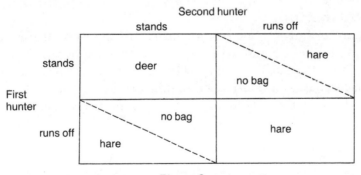

Figure 3

18   J-J. Rousseau, *Discours sur l'origine de l'inégalité parmi les hommes*, 1755.
19   I am borrowing this formulation from Raymond Boudon and François Bourricaud, *Dictionnaire critique de la sociologie*, 1982, p. 477. In attributing the crucial role in the creation of the problem to myopia, I have been preceded by Kenneth M. Waltz, *Man, the State and War*, 1965, esp. p. 168. Myopia can make the deer worth less than the hare because it is further away; the second hunter's awareness of the first hunter's myopia can induce the *former* to run off after a hare even though it is the *latter* who is too shortsighted to see the deer!

while he runs off after the hare. Neither would, therefore, rationally opt for a 'maximin' strategy (go for the hare in the southeast corner). The deer hunt, then, is critically different from the genuine, Hobbesian prisoners' dilemma. Social cooperation is *not a dilemma* and *does not for that reason* require *coercion*. A problem (but not a dilemma) is only created for the hunting party by the myopia of one of the hunters who cannot see that a sure deer at the end of the hunt is better than a sure hare. (If *both* hunters suffered from such complete lack of forethought, they might 'objectively' have a pris-oners' dilemma without feeling it. Neither would worry about the end-result of the party; they would not perceive the missed deer, let alone invent an arrangement, such as the social contract creating a state, enabling them to catch the deer *rather than* the hare, which is the only reason they would have for *not* letting the hunt take its course, with both hunters running off after the game, if any, they happen to *see*.)

Supposing, then, that at least the second hunter is alive to the advantage of getting the first hunter to keep his place, what solutions are available for overcoming the latter's myopia or fecklessness? The contractarian solution is to get him to become a party to the social contract, voluntarily submitting to coercion when needed. But it is difficult to see why he would see the advantage of the social contract if he does not see that of standing fast.[20] He is either shortsighted and sees neither, or he is not and the hunters don't *need* the social contract.

A more promising line of thought is to suppose that the hunters have hunted before and, as by happy chance no hare crossed their paths, they did catch the deer. The second hunter (the far-sighted one) has saved up a quarter. Next time out he dangled it before the myopic eyes of the first hunter, keeping him at his task and letting

---

20   To be led, by a scrutiny of the core structure of mutually advantageous cooperation, to the conclusion that Rousseau's social contract has an insufficient basis in rational self-interest, is certainly unexpected. The theory of the social contract has always served as *the* rational foundation for the state, making mystical-historical foundations both of the pre-Reformation and the romantic-Hegelian type redundant. Part II of Ernst Cassirer's *The Myth of the State* (1946) is entitled 'The Struggle against Myth in the History of Political Theory', and deals with the Stoic heritage in political philosophy, culminating in contractarian theory. In it, he writes: 'if we reduce the legal and social order to free individual acts, to a voluntary contractual submission of the governed, all mystery is gone. There is nothing less mysterious than a contract.'

However, a contract which it is impossible to derive from the perceived interest of the contracting parties is mysterious, and presumably mystical in its genesis.

him have it at the end of the day while he kept the whole new deer they successfully caught together. (He has, of course, not forgotten once more to set aside a quarter, to maintain the 'wage fund'.) This, in a slightly abridged version, is the story of abstinence, capital accumulation, natural selection, the differential contributions and rewards of entrepreneurial initiative and wage labour, and in fact the organization of social cooperation and the determination of the *terms* on which the participants are willing to carry it on. (In 'How Justice Overrides Contracts' [pp. 150–3], we will meet the claim that willing social cooperation is not a matter of the terms the participants *agree*, but of the terms being *reasonable*. If the terms that have proved capable of bringing about social cooperation need not, for that reason alone, be considered reasonable, difficulties arise about the very meaning of social cooperation. What, then, is cooperation on unreasonable terms?)

The story, however, does not naturally lend itself to the sort of happy ending which we have learnt to associate with the exit from the state of nature. It does not explain why rational persons, living in a state of nature, *should* have a preference for the state and seek to invent one (and it is silent on the civic preferences of persons who have been educated in and by the state and have never had occasion to try the state of nature).

Persons *are* in states, have been there for many generations, and would have no practical means of getting out if they wanted to. States are in the state of nature; many of them have known something approaching the security offered by the super-state when they were part of the Roman Empire, or a British colony; and if they wanted to surrender their sovereignty to a super-state, there are at least some practical steps they could take to try and organize one. They do nothing of the sort. They are quite content to listen to their own voice at the United Nations, leaving it the fatuous irrelevance that it is. Is it, then, beyond reasonable doubt that persons *would* rush and negotiate a social contract if, like states, they had the option *not* to do so?

States have known both peace and war throughout history. Some states have died as such because of war, though more states have been born. Most, however, have survived more than one war and continue to muddle through, without finding existence so 'nasty and brutish' as to make life within a world state look enticing. Even the very particular prisoners' dilemma in which two nuclear superpowers are exposed to the threat of destruction and to the expense of maintaining a counter-threat, has not so far induced them to seek shelter and assured self-preservation in a Soviet–American contract.

On a less apocalyptic level, 'beggar-thy-neighbour' policies in international trade seem to be a perfectly good practical illustration of the prisoners' dilemma as applied to states. Generally speaking, all states could be better off if, by cooperative conduct, they allowed the potential gains from trade to be fully realized, just as all prisoners would be better off if none betrayed the other by confessing. The 'dominant strategy' of each state (as the 'optimum tariff' argument demonstrates), however, is to engage in discriminatory trade practices, high tariffs, competitive devaluations and so forth. This strategy is 'dominant' on the argument that if other states behave nicely and adopt free-trader conduct, the first state will reap advantages from its misbehaviour, while if other states misbehave, it would suffer by not also misbehaving. The supposed outcome of every state adopting its dominant strategy is an escalating trade war with everybody rapidly getting poorer and being unable to do anything about it in the absence of a super-state with powers of coercion. In actual fact, many states much of the time behave reasonably well in international trade. They either do not have a dominant strategy or, if they do, it is not to misbehave. Most states most of the time adhere to GATT rules (which stand for the 'cooperative solution' in game-theory parlance). Trade wars are generally minor skirmishes, limited to a few products of a few states and instead of escalating as they should, they usually subside. Such 'partial free trade' is achieved, just like 'partial peace', without benefit of a state above states and the transfer of power to it. Complete free trade, like total peace, may from most points of view be more satisfactory, but the cost of the added satisfaction must appear prohibitive to the participants; states do not willingly submit to domination even if the dominant entity is to be called the Democratic Federation of Independent Peoples.

People, in the sense of natural persons, however, are supposed by contractarian theory to submit willingly. Unlike states in international relations, people as persons have no opportunity to contradict this supposition. For centuries, since Hobbes if not before, political theory has been assuming that people did not, in fact, very much mind the potential threat of being coerced, being too frightened of the hurt they might suffer in un-coerced 'chaos' (this is the Hobbesian version of the social contract), or too interested in the beneficial results of coercion (which is the broader basis of the social contract, laid by Rousseau).[21] I believe this is how one should read the cryptic and profound observation of Leo Strauss (few others have thought more powerfully and deeply about these matters), that Hobbes 'created' *political hedonism,* which transformed life 'on a scale never yet approached by any other teaching'.[22] It is a not very important detail that instead of pleasure (as hedonists are supposed to seek), Hobbes spoke of self-preservation as the end which explains action.[23] Since Hobbes, it is tacitly treated as a self-evident truth that people need, or want to have, the state because their hedonistic pain-and-pleasure calculus is *ipso facto* favourable to it.

Recent research into the prisoners' dilemma, both deductive into its logical structure and experimental into actual behaviour in such situations, has established that acceptance of coercion by the participants is not a necessary condition for their finding a 'cooperative solution'.[24] Some of the crucial steps toward getting this result are: (a) to admit that the dilemma can be confronted more than once (it can be an iterative or sequential 'game'), so that reliance on single-stage rationality may not correctly predict the moves of rational players; (b) to make a player's move depend in part on the other player's move in a previous stage of the sequential game, or in some other game altogether (i.e. to make it depend on experience), either player taking account of the reputation established by the other for

21   'If, in a group of people, some people act so as to harm my interest, I may readily submit to coercion if this is the pre-condition of subjecting *them* to coercion' (W.J. Baumol, *Welfare Economics and the Theory of the State,* 2nd edn, 1965, p. 182). This statement is presented as enabling the state's generally recognized functions to be logically derived from what its subjects want. It is not explained why the fact that some people act to harm my interest is sufficient to persuade me to submit to coercion (in order to submit *them* to it, too), *regardless* of the sort of harm they are doing to my interest, its gravity, eventual possibilities of a non-coercive defence, and *regardless* also of the gravity of the coercion I am submitting to, and all its consequences. Yet it is not hard to interpret history in a way which should make me prefer the harm *people* do to my interest, to the harm *people organized into a state* and capable of coercing me, can do to my interest.
22   Leo Strauss, *Natural Right and History,* 1953, p. 169.
23   Ibid., p. 169, note 5.
24   Taylor, *Anarchy and Cooperation* ch. 3; David M. Kreps, Paul Milgrom, John Roberts and Robert Wilson, 'Rational Cooperation in the Finitely Repeated Prisoners' Dilemma', *Journal of Economic Theory,* 27, 1982; J. Smale, 'The Prisoner's Dilemma and Dynamical Systems Associated to Non-Cooperative Games', *Econometrica,* 48, 1980. For a broader review of the problem, cf. Anatol Rapoport, 'Prisoners' Dilemma — Recollections and Observations', in Anatol Rapoport (ed.), *Game Theory as a Theory of Conflict Resolution,* 1974, pp. 17–34. The important point seems to be that the players must not be stupid and totally without foresight. Fairly alert, wordly-wise players will generally cooperate in iterated prisoners' dilemmas. Cf. also Russell Hardin, *Collective Action,* 1982, p. 146.

toughness or softness; (c) to make him play as he ought to if the other player were playing tit-for-tat; (d) to introduce some regard for the relative value of present and future; and (e) to let the increased pay-off of a cooperatively solved game teach people to go for the cooperative solution in subsequent games. It is intuitively plausible that in a state of nature where people do not instantly club each other to death in a single-stage non-cooperative performance of the di-lemma game, but where they survive for some time and have both occasion and incentive to assess and heed each other's capacity for retaliation, vengefulness, mutual protection, gratitude, fair play, etc. the prisoners' dilemma becomes both very much more complicated and loses much of its inexorability.

Nor need one limit the application of this result to the sole *bellum omnium contra omnes*. Hobbes makes people choose Leviathan to produce order out of purported chaos. But people need not have chosen Leviathan, since some kind of cooperative solution, some kind of order emerges in the state of nature, too, though it may not be the same kind of order as that produced by the state. Both qualitative and quantitative differences are possible, indeed ex-tremely likely, though it is very hard to form sensible hypotheses about what the voluntary solution would exactly be like. Whether the voluntary product, in turn, is inferior or superior to the state product, will have to remain a matter of taste. The important thing is not to confuse the question of how we like either *product,* with the far more vital question of *how we like the entire society in which order is state-produced,* compared to the entire society (the state of nature) in which it is a voluntary arrangement.

What goes for order goes, by simple extension of the argument, for other public goods as well, whose production was supposed to have been altogether prevented by a rigidly interpreted prisoners' dilemma and the related, rather looser free-rider problem.[25] Once a public

___

25 Prisoners' dilemma and free riding are *not* just different words describing the same structure of interaction. The former imposes on each rational prisoner one dominant strategy, i.e. to confess before the other can betray him. This alone secures the least bad of two alternative worst-case outcomes (maximin). The free-rider problem *imposes no dominant strategy,* maximin or other. It is not inherently inconsistent with a cooperative solution. Where would the free rider ride free if there were no cooperative transport service?

To make it into a prisoners' dilemma, its structure must be tightened up. Let there be two passengers and a bus service where your fare buys you a lifetime pass. If one passenger rides free, the other is the sucker and *must pay double fare.* Each likes free riding best, riding the bus at single fare second best, walking third best and riding the bus at the double fare least. If both try to ride free, the bus service ceases. As they choose one course of action for a lifetime, good, say clean air, paved streets or national defence, gets produced, people cannot be excluded from enjoying it regardless of whether they have paid their share of the cost of producing it. (We shall have occasion in chapter 4, pp. 214–15, to question what 'their share', in the sense of the part of the cost that a particular person *ought* to bear, can possibly mean.) Therefore, many will choose not to bear 'their share' and the public good will not get produced or maintained, unless the state steps in to coerce all would-be free riders to pay, at the one hit both overcoming 'isolation' by making each individual act as he would if all had one common will, and providing 'assurance' to each individual who pays that he is not a lone sucker, for all others pay too.[26] If the general dilemma is conceived of as a sequential game, a *society's perpetual learning process*, it seems obvious that it can have a solution for each intermediate stage, and arbitrary to rule out the likelihood of at least some of the solutions being cooperative, so that as a general proposition, at least some quantities of some public goods will get produced on a voluntary basis.

'Some quantities' of 'some public goods' as a result of non-coercive spontaneous solutions, sounds insufficiently affirmative. The reflex reaction of capitalism's adversary may well be that, because of external economies and diseconomies, only an *all-embracing* compulsory arrangement, i.e. a state, can ensure that the right amount of public goods gets made. In this view, the prisoners' dilemma would represent one limiting case, that of total failure to 'internalize', and the state would be the other limiting case in which the entire benefit of an external economy gets internalized from the state's aggregative point of view. The in-between case of the voluntary association, the spontaneously formed interest group, would stop short of complete internalization and as a consequence would typically tend to fall between the two stools of the unresolved prisoners' dilemma and

---

and independently of one another, they will both choose to walk, i.e. with this structure, the free-rider problem will work as a (non-iterated) prisoners' dilemma and will be inherently inconsistent with the mutually preferred cooperative solution, i.e. a bus that runs.

The special 'tight' feature, it will be remarked, is that free riding by one makes the fare unacceptably high for the other, leading to cessation of the service. In the 'loose', general form of the free-rider problem, there are many passengers and another free rider may not greatly increase the fare payable by the others, so that it may be rational for them to carry on paying. There is no *perceptible penalty* attaching to the role of the sucker.

26   The allusions are to A.K. Sen's 'Isolation, Assurance and the Social Rate of Discount', *Quarterly Journal of Economics*, 81, 1967.

state provision of the *right* amount of the good. Nor is it, of course, always true of any and all levels of output that if the state has in fact chosen that level, it considered it (given all constraints, scarcities and competing claims) the 'right' one. If the claim that the output of a public good chosen by the state is the right output, is to be more than a tautological statement of the state's 'revealed preference', it must somehow be related to some independently derived standard of the optimum.

In the case of individually consumed goods, this standard is, by and large, the Pareto-optimum reached by equating the marginal rates of substitution and transformation between any two goods. But as it is nonsense to speak of a marginal rate of substitution between a public and a private good (a person cannot decide to give up a dollar's worth of chocolate to get a dollar's worth of clean air, law and order or paved street), this standard does not work. When the post-1981 Polish state imports one more water-cannon and reduces chocolate imports by the corresponding sum, the decision can hardly be related to the marginal Polish chocolate-eater's relative liking for law and order and chocolate. If it expresses anything, the decision must express the state's balancing of the *real* interests of society that *it* considers important, in proportion to the importance *it* attaches to each. The individual chocolate-eater is obviously unable to attach the proper weights to the interest of the vanguard of the working class, of the Organs, of proletarian internationalism, etc. How much tax to surrender to the state so it may buy law and order or clean air for the use of the individual taxpayer in question is not a matter of any taxpayer's choice. The state cannot buy a collective good *for him*.

A standard which will do for 'collective choice' (if we *must* resort, for the sake of argument, to this question-begging concept) what Pareto-efficiency does for individual ones, can always be contrived by supposing either (a) that society has but one will (e.g. a will manifested by unanimity, or possibly the general will), or (b) that the several more-or-less divergent wills (including, arguably, the will of the state itself) which are present in society can, by a system of weights attached to each, be expressed as one will (what Robert Paul Wolff disdainfully calls 'vector–sum democracy').[27]

Whoever fixes the relative weights to be attached (i.e. makes the interpersonal comparisons, or reads the general will, or whichever

27 Robert Paul Wolff, Barrington Moore Jr and Herbert Marcuse, *A Critique of Pure Tolerance*, 1965.

way the reader prefers to phrase it), fixes the 'right' output of public goods with respect to the standard he has thus set up for himself. Whatever he decides, he will, therefore, always be in the proud position of having fixed the right output; for *there can never be independent proof to the contrary*. It is a redundant apology for the state to say 'by reading the general will', 'by balancing the merits of conflicting claims', 'by duly considering public need against the background of its disinflationary policy', etc. it has determined the right output of public goods. For, whatever the output it chose on whichever considerations, it would not have been, according to its own lights, the *wrong* one, and no one can ever say that somebody else's lights would have led it to a more nearly 'correct' determination.

It remains to add that the political hedonist who is content to sign the social contract must somehow or other have convinced himself that he is getting a good deal. The incremental *pleasure* he expects to derive from having the state arrange the production of the correct amount of order and other public goods, instead of relying on a possibly quite inadequate patchwork of spontaneous arrangements, must outweigh the *pain* of coercion he thinks he will suffer at the state's hands.

The obvious case where this must hold true is when he does not expect to suffer at all. He will, as a matter of fact, never be coerced if he wills what the state wills, or *vice versa*, if he can rely on the state to will only what he wills. He must either be the perfect conformist, or he must believe in a benign state which has the power of coercion but lets itself be controlled by those who have none.

Inventing the State: the Instrument of Class Rule

The state is autonomous and subjects the ruling class to its own conception of its interest; it 'serves the bourgeoisie despite the bourgeoisie'.

'Autonomy' and 'instrument', rule and subjection are terms that yield their real meaning only to the dialectic method.

Attempting to interpret the Marxist theory of the state carries more risk than reward. The young Marx, superbly talented political journalist that he was, said incisive and original things about the state, but he did so more under the impulsion of events than in search of a general doctrine. In his later system-building periods, on the other hand, he was not very interested in the state (Engels was a little more so), presumably deflected from the subject by the very force of his theory of class domination, which may be thought implicitly to provide an understanding of the state. In any case he made little effort to make it explicit. This was consistent with his confining the determinants of social change in the 'base' and allowing the state, a phenomenon of the 'superstructure', either no autonomy or only an ambiguous one. This implicitness is the reason why, despite the much greater respect later Marxists (notably Gramsci and his intellectual descendants) paid the superstructure, one is reduced to speculation about what Marxist theory 'must mean', what view it may hold of the forces acting upon and exerted by the state, in order to preserve logical consistency with the whole of its construction.

Such speculation is rendered doubly hazardous by the combination, in much Marxist writing, of the dialectic method with verbose discourse aimed at the *ad hoc* needs of the day. Owing to the latter, one can nearly always find, in some hallowed text, passages to support almost any stand and its contrary, so that for every 'on the one hand' the adept can cite an 'on the other' and a 'yet we must not overlook that …'. The dialectic method, in turn, enables its practitioner to nominate any one out of a pair of contradictory propositions for the role of survivor, of the third member of the triad of thesis–antithesis–synthesis. He can for instance decide, according to the requirements of his argument, that where an object is black but also white, it is in reality white (though black in appearance), or possibly *vice versa*. It is in this way that the relation of state and subject in Hegel,[28] and that of the state and the capitalist class in Marx, turn out to be perfectly pliable according to the needs of the moment and of the context. (This is also, in a general way, the reason why the average dialectician can virtually always devastate the average non-dialectical argument.)

Having said this, let us nevertheless venture to put forward the bare outline of an interpretation where we will remain committed, as far as possible, to a non-dialectical (hence easy to refute) meaning. It is quite legitimate to take Marxism to hold that the victory of the

---

28   For Hegel, man is free; he is subjected to the state; he is *really* free *when* he is subjected to the state. The alternative way of completing the triad, of course, is that when he is subjected to the state, he is unfree; but few Hegelians would content themselves with such a simplistic version.

working class and the extinction of class antagonism *means*, by definition, that the state withers away. Lenin, understandably, has a strong interest in adopting the contrary interpretation. He goes to immense trouble to argue that the cessation of class conflict does not *entail* the withering away of the state. There are no classes but there is a (coercive) state under socialism. Only in the abundance corresponding to full communism can the state wither away. Its doing so it not a logical *implication*, but a *process* in real historical time, about whose required length it would be naive to speculate in advance.

Though there will still be an apparatus for the 'administration of things', there will be none for the 'government of men'. Close reflection is needed to grasp, if grasp one can, how it is possible to 'administer things' without telling people to do this or that about them; and how telling people differs from 'governing people'. A tentative answer, for what it is worth, would seem to be that this becomes possible when men will do what is required of them in order for things to get administered, without being made or commanded to do so.

The classless society, then, can tentatively be defined as a state of affairs where this holds true, i.e. where men spontaneously administer things without being administered themselves. However, if men freely do what they have to do, what is the residual need for the administration of things and what is the residual non-coercive quasi-state which is said to subsist after the state proper has withered away? A necessary condition for the non-withering-away of the coercive state is the existence of more than one class. The interests of 'historic', principal classes are necessarily antagonistic. The ruling class needs the state to deter the exploited class from attacking its property and breaking the contracts which provide the legal framework of exploitation. As history proceeds on its preordained course towards the victory of the proletariat and the one-class society, functionally obsolete classes fall by the wayside. The last-but-one surviving class is the bourgeoisie, which possesses all capital and appropriates the surplus value produced by labour. The state is the protector of property. If it is the bourgeoisie that possesses property, the state *cannot but serve the bourgeoisie* and any state would do so. This is why such autonomy as Marxism (sometimes, not always) allows the state, is so ambiguous. The absolute monarchy, the bourgeois republic, the Bonapartist, the 'English', the Bismarckian and the Czarist states which Marx and Engels admitted differed from each other, were all said to be states obliged to further the interests of the possessing class, just as the compass needle is obliged to point northwards, no matter in what exotic corner we set it down.

The reduction of the state to the role of blind instrument of class oppression is obviously unsatisfactory. Engels and Lenin make intellectually more exacting Marxists wince when they resort to it. Yet the concept of an autonomous state, a state with a will of its own which keeps surfacing in Marx's early political writings, is even less acceptable; to elevate the state to the rank of a *subject* is revisionism, Hegelian idealism, fetishism if not worse, inconsistent with the mature Marxism of the *Grundrisse* and of *Capital*. It leads to deep political pitfalls. Among them, mainstream socialism is menaced with lukewarm reformist notions of the state reconciling society's inherent contradictions. promoting worker welfare 'despite the bourgeoisie', taming 'crises of overproduction', etc. The proponents of planned 'state monopoly capitalism' as the means to mitigate capitalist chaos, and Juergen Habermas and his Frankfurt friends with their doctrines of legitimation and conciliation, are all considered as carriers of this menace.

A synthetic solution of some elegance, elaborated mainly by modern West Berlin Marxist scholars, consists in grafting social contract theory on to the trunk of Marxism. Capital in the 'fragmented' (i.e. decentralized) capitalist mode of production consists of 'individual capitals' (i.e. separate owners have separate bits of it). These 'capitals' require that workers be docile, trained and healthy, that natural resources be renewed, legal relations enforced and streets paved. No individual capital, however, can profitably produce these goods for itself. A problem of 'externality' and a problem of 'free riding' stand in the way of capitalist reproduction and accumulation. Non-imposed cooperative solutions, sparing capital the risks involved in surrendering itself to a state, are not envisaged. There is, thus, an objective necessity for a coercive state 'beside and outside society' to protect workers' health, provide infrastructures, etc. From this necessity, its form and function can be logically derived (*Ableitung*).[29] It leads to the state's monopoly of force, just as various other forms of political hedonism lead to it in the systems of Hobbes

---

29 A relatively readable exponent of this *Ableitung* is Elmar Altvater. Several other contributors to the Berlin journal *Probleme des Klassenkampfes* employ a rather steamy prose through which, however, much the same contractarian *motif* of capital's general interest (general will?) can be discerned. They are criticized (cf. Joachim Hirsch, *Staatsapparat und*

and Rousseau. Yet the 'doubling' (i.e. splitting) of the economic and the political sphere and the *Besonderung* (separateness) of the state are subject to the 'dialectic of appearance and essence'. The state appears neutral and above classes because it must stand *above* 'individual capitals' in order to *serve* general capital; it must subjugate the individual bourgeois in order to secure the interests of the bourgeoisie. Any state having the power of coercion, whether absolute monarchy, republic, democracy or despotism, seems able to fulfil this function.

However, the bourgeoisie must for some reason be requiring more than this, for otherwise it would not rise up in revolution, as it is supposed to do, to smash the pre-capitalist state. It is desperately important to Marxism to maintain, despite all contrary evidence, that revolutions reflect the economic requirements of the class which is called upon by the developing 'forces of production' to rise to dominance, and that the contradiction between capitalist techniques and pre-capitalist relations of production must be resolved by revolution.

This belief is a source of difficulties and for none more so than for historians who hold it. An historian who does not, and who did more than most to dispel many of the myths that used to be spread about the French Revolution, reminds us: 'neither capitalism nor the bourgeoisie needed revolutions to appear and become dominant in the main European countries of the nineteenth century,' remarking drily that 'nothing was more like French society under Louis XVI than French society under Louis Philippe.'[30] Starting off in 1789 firmly committed to the sacredness of property, in a little over four years this revolution reached the point where property rights were to become contingent upon active support for the state of the Terror (Laws of Ventôse). Ironically it was Thermidor – the counterrevolution – which called the state to order, rescued the inviolability of property and secured the bourgeois interests which were supposedly the *raison d'être* of the revolution. Once it ejected the Girondins, the revolution made the purposes of the state override the security of tenure of property and, contrary to the usual excuse made for it, it continued

---

Reproduktion des Kapitals, 1974) for failing to show why and how capital's 'general will' comes in fact to be realized in the historical process. This failure, if it is one, assimilates them even more closely to Rousseau. The criticism basically reflects the mystical character of contractarianism.

30   François Furet, *Penser la révolution français,* 1978. Both quotations are from p. 41.

to escalate its radicalism long after the tide of war had turned in its favour. Marx, who (notably in 'The Holy Family', 1845) recognized perfectly well that the Jacobin state 'became its own end', that it served only *itself* and *not* the bourgeoisie, considered this a perversion, an aberration, a departure from the norm. He diagnosed the trouble as the alienation, the detachment of the Jacobin state from its bourgeois class basis,[31] and in no wise suggested that it is *far from being an aberration for the state to detach itself* from its 'class base', if indeed it was ever attached to it.

Nor is Marxist theory better served by the historical facts of other revolutions. Engels is reduced at one point to grumble that the French have had a political and the English an economic revolution – a curious finding for a Marxist – and at another juncture that the English have, in addition to their bourgeoisie, a bourgeois aristocracy and a bourgeois working class. It has been pointed out that while the view that the 'big', 'real' revolutions were brought about by the interest of a class, fits badly 1776 (USA), 1789 (France), 1830 (the Low Countries) and 1917 (Russia), it fits worst of all the two English revolutions of 1640–9 and 1688 – the Puritan and the Glorious.[32] Nor did capitalism need a revolution to rise to dominance of a sort in the Italian city states. Moreover, Russian peasant and mercantile capitalism between the seventeenth and nineteenth century throve to such good effect that it colonized the Black Soil region and Siberia, without noticeable hindrance from Moscow, which was the seat of a decidedly pre-capitalist state.[33] (It may be, though, that such 'frontier' phenomena should be regarded as exceptions, i.e. that capitalism can colonize and settle a frontier, without being helped or feeling hindered by the state.)

Whether with or (in deference to historical evidence) without the benefit of revolution, the capitalist class nevertheless ends up with the state serving *its interest*. Sometimes, in aberrant, 'untypical' situations, however, the bourgeoisie does not *dominate* the state. The

31   This is a comfortable diagnosis which foreshadows, in its *Deus ex machina* character, the more recent one ascribing the doings of the Soviet state for a quarter-century to the Cult of the Personality.
32   J.H. Hexter, *On Historians*, 1979, pp. 218–26.
33   Apart from agricultural colonization in the south, Russian peasants also played a pioneer role, as principals, in industrial capitalism. Interestingly, many bonded serfs became successful entrepreneurs from the last third of the eighteenth century onwards, while remaining serfs. Cf. Richard Pipes, *Russia under the Old Regime*, 1974, pp. 213–15. If there is a pre-capitalist hindrance to playing the role of capitalist entrepreneur, being a serf must surely be it.

distinction is important as it admits an at least quasi-autonomy of the state in particular historical settings. Engels formulates this as follows: (The state) 'in all *typical periods* is exclusively the state of the ruling class, and *in all cases* remains essentially a machine for keeping down the . . . exploited class.'[34] We must, I think, take this to mean that there are periods (which we can thus recognize as typical) when the state is an instrument of class oppression acting at the behest of the ruling class, while at other times it escapes the control of the ruling class yet continues to act on its behalf, for its good, in its interest. The ruling class, of course, is the class which owns the means of production, whether or not it 'rules' in the sense of governing.

Just as the weather is not unseasonable in Russia except in spring, summer, autumn and winter, so there have not been untypical periods in the history of capitalism except in the golden ages of the English, French and German bourgeoisie. In England, the bourgeoisie has purportedly never sought political power (the Anti-Corn Law League and later the Liberal Party for some reason do not count), and was content to leave the state in the hands of the landowners, who could attract atavistic popular loyalties and whose *apparent* even-handedness and social concern helped retard the development of proletarian class-consciousness. It is not clear whether the English state is to be regarded as autonomous – Engels speaks of the aristocracy being properly *remunerated* by the capitalists for governing – but no doubt is left that it represents the capitalist interest more effectively and cleverly than the politically inept bourgeoisie could have done.

In France, at the fall of the July Monarchy the bourgeoisie momentarily found itself with political power on its hands. It was unfit to wield it, parliamentary democracy (viz. the election of March 1850) unleashing popular forces which endangered the bourgeoisie more than any other group or class.[35] (Contrast Marx's diagnosis with the astonishing position taken by Lenin in 'The State and Revolution'

34 F. Engels, 'The Origin of the Family, Private Property and the State', in Marx and Engels, *Selected Works*, my italics.
35 In 'The Class Struggles in France', *Political Writings*, 1973, p. 71, Marx points unerringly at the risk the bourgeoisie runs under elective democracy with a broad franchise. The latter 'gives political power to the classes whose social slavery it is intended to perpetuate . . . [and] *it deprives the bourgeoisie . . . of the political guarantees of* [its social] power.' (my italics) Once more, the young Marx recognizes reality, only to leave his brilliant insight unexploited in favour of his later, unsubtle identification of ruling class and state.

that parliamentary democracy is the ideally suited system for the requirements of capitalist exploitation.)[36] In 'The Eighteenth Brumaire of Louis Bonaparte', Marx talks of the bourgeoisie abdicating power, condemning itself to political nullity; he compares the dictatorship of Napoleon III to a Damocles sword hanging over the head of the bourgeoisie. It is not clear whether Marx thought that in abdicating, it was aware of the dangerous aspects of Bonapartism, lower-middle class populism, state parasitism, etc. He felt sure, though, that in doing so the bourgeoisie bought itself the secure enjoyment of property and order, which would suggest that the Damocles sword was not really poised over *its* head. Engels, as usual plainer in meaning, states that Bonapartism upholds the wider interests of the bourgeoisie *even against the bourgeoisie*. Like the rod for the good of the child, the autonomous state of the Second Empire was really for the good of the capitalist class even at times when the latter felt restive under it.

Germany, while being (as ever) a case apart, with its bourgeois revolution of 1848–9 coming much too late and miscarrying into the bargain, has nevertheless this in common with England and France; the Prussian state and, after 1871 the Reich, did what it had to do to further capitalist exploitation without being in any way under capitalist direction or control. When Engels says that Bismarck cheated both capital and labour to favour the 'cabbage Junkers' (who, despite the favours, the grain tariff and the Osthilfe, stayed stubbornly poor), he is admitting the autonomy of the state (for subservience to the landed interest did not make the state class-controlled, as landowners no longer constituted a functionally real, live class – only the capitalists and the workers did that), without suggesting that this cheating gave the capitalists cause for complaint, any more than did the treacherous alliance of Bismarck with the despised Lassalle, and Bismarck's whole reformist, 'social', welfare-statist drift. Solid bourgeois interests were being consistently served throughout, despite the bourgeoisie.

The Marxist prototype of the state, in short, allows it a good deal of autonomy outside 'typical periods', i.e. virtually all the time, yet obliges it always to use this autonomy in the sole interest of the capitalist class. Nothing much is made by Marx, nor by his successors down to the present, of his original insights into the phenom-

36   V.I. Lenin, 'The State and Revolution', *Selected Works*, 1968, p. 271.

enon of the state *lacking a particular class base* and serving its own ends, nor into bureaucracy, parasitism, Bonapartism and so forth.

In the end, Marx could not admit that it really mattered whether the state was or was not controlled by the ruling class. It had to act in its interest regardless. It made little odds whether the state was directed by true representatives of their class like Casimir Perier and Guizot, Peel and Cobden, or by a classless adventurer like Louis Bonaparte, not to speak of men like Castlereagh or Melbourne in England, Roon or Bismarck in Prussia or Schwarzenberg in Austria-Hungary, who had little time for bourgeois concerns. Any state, it would seem, would do. Any state could be relied on to do what was good for capitalism.

Pursuing this logic further, we find moreover that the converse is also asserted: not only will any state do, but whatever it does turns out, on examination, to be good for capitalism. When in December 1831 Marshal Soult leads 20,000 troops against 40,000 striking silk workers in Lyons, when in June 1832 General Lobau reaps 800 dead or wounded rioters in putting down the Montmartre disorders, when in April 1834 there are 300 casualties in Lyons again while in Paris Bugeaud's troops fire into women and children, the state is helping the exploiters. When the English Combination Acts of 1799 and 1800 make it (broadly speaking) a criminal conspiracy for employees to organize, the state is an ally of capital.

When the 1802 and especially the 1832 English Factory Acts make it illegal to work children under eighteen the same hours in industry as on the land, the state is somehow *still* helping the manufacturers. When trade union organization is (to put it simply) made lawful in England in 1824, in Prussia in 1839, in France and most German states in the early 1860s, when a ten-hour day is laid down by law in much of the USA in the 1850s, the state is still acting in the capitalist interest, properly understood. (The Marxist hypothesis of the state always acting in the interest of the ruling class is as irrefutable as the vulgar Freudian one of a person's actions always being the result of his sexual drive, both when he yields to it and when he resists it. Damned if he does and damned if he doesn't.)

The sole difference between the manifestly pro-capitalist and the ostensibly anti-capitalist acts of the state is that we need the dialectic method correctly to place them in a triad of thesis–antithesis–synthesis in order to see that the latter are the same as the former. Virtual, formal, superficial, ephemeral anti-capitalist appearance will thus dissolve into basic, genuine, long-term, true pro-capitalist reality.

In fact it is hardly feasible to reconstitute what might be the Marxist theory of the state, without recourse to dialectics. The state engages in acts that harm capital and capitalists, like progressive taxation, the grant of legal immunities for trade unions, anti-trust legislation, etc. These acts are pro-capitalist. The state serves the ruling class,[37] and as these *are* acts of the state, they *are* necessarily in the ('real') interest of the ruling class. Individual members of the capitalist class may be too short-sighted to recognize their real interest, and may be restive about the state's actions, joining the John Birch Society in opposition to bourgeois democracy, but the class as such will see the identity of its interest with that of the state, for this is how Marxism *defines* the concepts of ruling class, class consciousness and state.

The same iron-clad reasoning goes today for the socialist state, the working class and proletarian class consciousness. Many (or for that matter all) workers may be individually opposed to the actions of the socialist state. These actions are, nevertheless, in the interest of the working class, for the necessary terms are so defined as to make this true. Antagonism between the socialist state and the working class is a nonsense term; empirical evidence of conflict is admitted only on condition of redefining one of the terms, for instance in the 1953 East Berlin or in the 1956 Hungarian uprising the security police becomes the working class, Russian tank crews are friendly workers, while those rising against the state are either not workers or are 'manipulated'. (It is hard to find a more impressive example of the two-fold function of words, the *semantic* and the *magical*.) Although all this is no doubt tediously familiar to the contemporary reader, it has the merit of being a replica of, and an aid better to appreciate, the Marxist argument about the absurdity of the capitalist state (i.e. the

37 In modern Marxist literature this has at least two alternative meanings. One corresponds to the 'structuralist' view (notably represented by N. Poulantzas). Vulgarized, this view would hold that the state can no more fail to serve the ruling class than rails can refuse to carry the train. The state is embedded in the 'mode of production' and cannot help but play its structurally assigned role. The other view would have the state *choose* to serve the ruling class for some prudential reason, e.g. because it is good for the state that capitalism should be prosperous.

Presumably the state could, *if its interest demanded it*, also choose not to serve the ruling class; this case, however, is not, or not expicitly, envisaged. Such neo-Marxist writers as Colletti, Laclau or Miliband, who have got past the mechanistic identification of state and ruling class (rejoining in this Marx, the young journalist), do not for all that allow for antagonism between the two, despite the rich array of possible reasons why the state, in pursuit of its interest should choose to turn against the ruling class (which, in Marxist theory, only 'rules' because it 'possesses' *property*, whereas the possession of *arms* is reserved for the state).

state which Marxists conceive of as 'capitalist') turning against the capitalist class.

Turn where he may, the bourgeois as political hedonist is thus stuck in a dead end. At first blush, Marxism seems to be telling him that if the state did not exist, he ought to invent it the better to pursue his pleasure – the exploitation of the proletariat – for which the state is the appropriate instrument. On a closer look, however, the state is a peculiar instrument, for it subjects him to *its* conception of *his* best interest and it serves its conception even *despite* the bourgeois. This is obviously unsatisfactory to each capitalist, taken individually. It may be satisfactory to the capitalist class if, but only if, we admit the existence of a class consciousness which is unrelated to the consciousness of the actual members of the class. Though Marxists have no difficulty admitting this, it is hardly likely to find favour with a member of the class concerned, nor is it designed to do so.

What, then is the capitalist to do? The state is either indispensable or just helpful to him. If it is indispensable, a necessary condition, if capitalism cannot function without it, the capitalist must invent the state, or embrace it if it has already been invented. If the state is merely a helpful instrument, the capitalist might very well prefer, if he has the choice, to pursue his interest without its help, i.e. perhaps *less effectively* but also *unburdened* by the servitudes and constraints which the autonomous state's conception of the capitalist interest imposes on him.

On this choice, Marxism gives no clear guidance. The thesis that the state, if it exists at all, must necessarily further class oppression, does not entail that the state must exist if there is to be class oppression. Why not have private, small-scale, home-made, diversified oppression? Though Engels, at any rate, appears to have held that a state must arise if there is division of labour and consequently society becomes complex, he did not really imply that capitalism presupposes a state and that the exploitation of labour by capital could not take place in the state of nature. To assert that he did imply this is to ascribe to him a rigid economic determinism or 'reductionism', and though it is fashionable for modern Marxists to patronize Engels, they would still be reluctant to do that. The bourgeois, wondering whether he must unquestioningly opt for the state or whether he can try and weigh up the pros and cons (always assuming that by some miracle he is given the choice), is really left to make up his own mind.

The historical evidence points, as is its well-known habit, every which way, leaving it very much up to the capitalist to decide whether the state, with the risk its sovereignty involves for the possessing class, is really a desirable aid for the operation of capitalism. It is revealing of such perplexities to read of how inadequate the state can be as an instrument of class oppression, and of the remedies that were sought at one time. It appears that prior to the repeal of the Combination Acts in 1825, illegal unionism was rampant in Oldham, Northampton and South Shields (and no doubt elsewhere, too, but the account in question is a local one), the Acts being poorly enforced. Through three decades to 1840, unions grow muscle, 'frame rules . . . and inflict punishments': the state was useless, and an 1839 Royal Commission report on the county constabulary found that 'the owners of manufacturing property had introduced arms for self-defence, and were considering the formation of *armed associations for self-protection*,'[38] in some ways a more appealing idea than paying taxes and not getting the state's help they thought they were buying.

When hiring Pinkertons to break strikes and 'to protect manufacturing (and mining) property', the Pennsylvania steel industry or the Montana copper mines not only made up for the shortcomings of state and Federal 'instruments of class oppression', but have done so by taking up a private instrument which *they* could control and which in any case did not have the attributions and the scale to control *them*. No doubt armed voluntary associations or Pinkertons were only resorted to (in fact surprisingly rarely), when the state utterly failed to come to capitalism's aid as it was supposed to do. That sometimes it did fail is yet another support for the view that the political hedonist is really quite gullible in thinking that he has made a clever bargain, for there is precious little he can do to *make* the state keep its side of it.

Although there may be talk of 'armed associations for self-protection' and Pinkertons may be called in to give an expert hand, these devices are essentially aimed at supplementing the services of the state which are inadequate or afflicted by momentary political cowardice and weakness of will. There is no question, except briefly in the American West, of taking the law permanently into one's hands and getting by without the state, both because the national brand of

38   J. Foster, *Class Struggle and the Industrial Revolution*, 1974, pp. 47–8.

law and order is felt to be superior or safer, and because making it at home or in the village, without also producing strife and resentment, is a lost skill. This is basically the same misconception as the one identifying the state of nature with *bellum omnium contra omnes* and which overlooks some potent forces making for reasonably stable, peaceful cooperative solutions if, by a fluke, a learning process gets a chance to start operating. It is at any rate significant that, despite wishful gropings in this direction, there was until quite recently no good intellectual case for holding that one could give up the state without also wholly giving up certain services it renders, without which capitalism would find it awkward to function. There have since been good arguments making it plausible that the interaction of free contracts could spontaneously generate a supply of such services as contract enforcement and the protection of life and property, i.e. most of what the capitalist really wants from the state.[39] The point is not whether such voluntary arrangements are conceivable once a state is in place. Most likely they are not, if the very existence of the state breeds a civil society with a diminishing capacity for generating spontaneous civic cooperation. (It is not easy to think of any other good reason for the absence, in contemporary America, of *vigilante* action by desperate parents against drug-pushers in high schools.) It is, rather, that if they are conceivable and feasible *ab initio*, there is no compelling need for *willingly* subjecting oneself to the state. The capitalist who accepts coercion as being, *by common knowledge*, a cheap price to pay for the benefits he reaps, is suffering from 'false consciousness'.

Closing the Loop by False Consciousness

False consciousness helps people adjust their preferences to what their peace of mind requires, and prepares them for supporting an adversary state.

The most unselfish state could not pursue other ends than its own.

The political hedonist looks to the state for 'pleasure', for utility, for the furtherance of his interest. Were he to recognize that the state cannot administer things without also governing men including him,

---

39 Cf. Murray N. Rothbard, *Power and Market*, 1970 and David Friedman, *The Machinery of Freedom*, 1973.

so that he is liable to be coerced and constrained, he would still expect to enjoy a positive balance between the pleasure he derives from the state's help and the pain he may suffer from being hindered by it.[40] In fact, his general idea of the state is that it is none other than the professional producer of such a positive balance. If he had a different conception, he could still be a supporter of the state but not a political hedonist.

The state is equipped with powers to pursue its own pleasure, its 'maximand'. Were it to be a near-minimal state, it would still have at least the latent capacity to equip itself with powers to do so. Its maximand may be a sole and supreme end or a 'pluralistic' bundle of several ones, weighted more or less heavily. If the latter, it will juggle them as the feasibility of attaining each changes with circumstances, giving up some of one to get more of another, in order to reach the highest attainable index of the composite maximand. Some of these ends may, in turn, perfectly well consist of the individual maximands, pleasure–pain balances or utilities of its several subjects. In good faith, one should imagine an *unselfish* state which has *no other ends* in the bundle it seeks to maximize than several individual maximands of its subjects or of an entire class of them (e.g. the capitalists or the workers). In better faith still, one could seek to define the state which is *both unselfish and impartial* as one whose composite maximand consists solely of the individual maximands of *all of its subjects,* great and small, rich and poor, capitalist and worker alike in a spirit of true unity and consensus. Comic as the idea may look when set out like this, it should not be laughed out of court too fast, for (set out in softer lines) it represents most people's notion of the democratic state, and as such it is a very influential one.

By virtue of having to weigh them – for there is no other way of fusing them into a single magnitude, an index to be maximized – the state must, its unselfishness and impartiality notwithstanding, transform its subjects' ends, assimilating them into one of its own, for the choice of weights to be applied to each subject's end is nobody's but the state's. There is a quite unwarranted belief that in democracy, the state does not choose the weights, because they are given, incorpor-

---

40   The political hedonist could be defined as a person who signs the social contract because he holds this particular expectation. It is not unreasonable to argue that in *no* version of contractarian theory is the social contract signed by anybody for any other reason than the expectation of a favourable pleasure–pain balance, properly interpreted. If so, the fact of agreeing to the social contract is alone sufficient to define the political hedonist.

ated in some rule which the state cannot but follow as long as it stays democratic.

A typical rule of this sort would be one-man–one-vote, which assigns a weight of one to every elector whether the state likes him or not. The fallacy of this belief consists in the passage from votes to ends, maximands. The tacit assumption that a vote for a political programme or for a team in preference to another is approximately the same thing as an expression of the voter's ends, is gratuitous. The existence of a social mechanism, such as elections, for choosing one out of a severely limited set of alternatives, such as a government, must not be construed as proof that there exists, operationally speaking, a 'social choice' whereby society maximizes its composite ends. This does not invalidate the simple and totally different point that being able to express a preference for a political programme and for a person or team to wield power in the state, is a valuable end in itself.

If the state, in pursuit of impartiality, were to borrow somebody else's system of weights (to be applied to the several ends desired by its subjects), for instance, that of the sympathetic observer, the same problem would reappear, albeit at one remove. Instead of choosing its own weights, the state would choose the observer whose weights it was going to borrow.

None of this is new. It is merely a particular way of reiterating the well-known impossibility of aggregating individual utility functions into a 'social welfare function' without somebody's will deciding how it should be done.[41] The particular approach we have chosen to get to this conclusion has the merit, however, of showing up fairly well the short-circuit going straight from the state's power to the satisfaction of its ends. If the state were its subjects' father and its sole end were their happiness, it would have to try and reach it by passing alone a 'loop' consisting, in some manner, of the several happinesses of the subjects. But this is made inherently impossible by the 'layout' (plurality and conflict among the subjects, combined with the state's power to decide conflicts). The layout inevitably contains a short-circuit. Thus the state's end-fulfilment is quite direct, bypassing the loop going the long way round, *via* the social contract or *via* class rule and the satisfaction of the subject's ends.

---

41   This is known in the trade as Arrow's Impossibility Theorem, after its first rigorous statement by K.J. Arrow in *Social Choice and Individual Values*, 1951.

The capitalist state, as I have argued (pp. 29–30) is one to which it is logically possible (but only just) to attribute some imprecisely defined maximand ('butterflies'), lying outside the realm of goals which can be attained by making its subjects do things. For the essentially negative reason that it is best not to erect an apparatus for exerting power lest it should fall into the wrong hands, such a state would govern as little as possible. Since it would take an austere view of demands for public goods and of claims by third parties for amending, supplementing or otherwise overruling the outcomes of private contracts, there would be little common ground between it and the political hedonist who wants to get his good out of the state.

If a subject is to be contented, in harmony with a capitalist state, it would help him to be imbued with a certain ideology whose basic tenets are: (1) that property '*is*', and is not a matter of '*ought*' (or that 'finders are keepers'); (2) that the good of the contracting parties is not an admissible ground for interfering with their contracts and the good of third parties only exceptionally so; and (3) that requiring the state to do agreeable things for the subject greatly augments the probability that the state will require the subject to do disagreeable things.

The first tenet is quintessentially capitalist in that it dispenses with a justification for property. Some say that Locke has provided an ideology for capitalism. This seems to me off the mark. Locke taught that the finder is keeper on condition that there is 'enough and as good' left for others, a condition calling out for egalitarian and 'need-regarding' principles of tenure as soon as we leave the frontier and enter the world of scarcity. He also taught that the first occupier's right to his property springs from his labour which he 'mixed' with it, a principle on a par with the several others which make the owner-ship of capital contingent upon deserts: 'he worked for it', 'he saved it', '*il en a bavé*', 'he provides work for many poor people'. (If he did not do any of these meritorious things, what title has he got to his capital? Already the case of 'his grandfather worked hard for it' becomes tenuous because it is twice removed from such deserts.) To the extent that the rise of capitalism was accompanied by no political theory which sought to separate the right to property from notions of moral worth or social utility, let alone succeeded in doing so, it is true that capitalism never had a viable ideology. This lack, in turn, goes some way towards explaining why, in the face of an essentially adversary state and its accompanying ideology, capitalism has shown so little intellectual vigour in its own defence, and why such defences as it has managed to muster have been poor advocacy, lame compromises and sometimes offers of honourable surrender.

The second basic tenet of a proper capitalist ideology should affirm the freedom of contract. It must affirm it in particular against the idea that the state is entitled to coerce people for their own good. On the other hand, it would leave it ragged at the edge where it could cut into the interests of people not party to the contract whose freedom is being considered. The raggedness is due to a recognition of the indefinite variety of possible conflicts of interest in a complex society. It would leave the contract unprotected against a certain indefiniteness of right, of either too much or too little regard for the interests of those outside, yet affected by, a given contract.

This danger, however, is to some extent taken care of by the constraint arising out of the third tenet. The demand of *A* to have the state protect his interest which is affected by a contract between *B* and *C*, should be tempered by his apprehension of the consequential risk of finding himself under increased subjection as and when the claims of *others* are being attended to, for that is liable to mean that *his* contracts will be interfered with. These offsetting motivations can be more formally expressed as two imaginary schedules present in people's heads. For every person *A*, there should be a schedule of benefits (in the widest sense) that he would expect to derive from the state's progressively increasing degrees of concern for what could be called third-party interests in the deliberately neutral vocabulary I am attempting to use in discussing contracts. Another schedule should list the negative benefits (costs) which he would fear to suffer as a result of the state's escalating solicitude for the well-being of others. It is, of course, vain to pretend to empirical knowledge about such schedules even if it is admitted that they express something which is liable to exist in the heads of rationally calculating people. However, it could be suggested that poor people (and not only poor ones), people who feel helpless, who think they usually get the worst of any bargain, would have a schedule of expected benefits from state intervention which was, at any practicable level of the latter, always higher than the corresponding schedule of expected costs. In other words, they could never get too much help from the state, and never mind the restrictions, servitude and pain that this may entail. Conversely, rich people (but not only the rich), resourceful, self-confident people who think they can shift for themselves, could be regarded as carrying in their head a sharply rising schedule of negative benefits which soon mounts above the schedule of positive benefits at any but the most minimal scale of government activity.

I advance no hypothesis about the scale and shape of the cost–benefit schedules which describe real people's attitudes to these questions, nor about the ones they 'ought to' have if they all had the very highest order of political wisdom, insight and understanding. The implication of this duality is that the consequences of calling in the state to further one's interest are complex; they are partly unintended, and also largely unforeseen. People endowed with the political talents that take them as close as possible to perfect foresight would, therefore, presumably have different attitudes from those who assess proximate consequences only.

This concept of individual costs and benefits as a function of the state's concern for third-party rights will serve for the purpose of defining adherents to the capitalist ideology as people who consider (a) that as government intervention increases, the total disadvantages they will suffer increase faster than the total advantages; and (b) that the former exceed the latter at a level of state activity which is somewhere short of the actual level, so that when living in an actual state, such people expect that they would feel better off if there were less government interference with free contracts.

This does not, of course, mean that people adhering to the capitalist ideology must seek to go all the way and attain the state of nature. It means, however, that *at the margin* of actual experience they would seek to restrain and 'roll back' the state. It means that in terms of the direction of change, they would find congenial the capitalist state which (as we have seen) has intelligible reasons of its own to put restraints upon itself.

Such a state, it cannot be said too often, is an abstraction, an expository device. So is the person adhering to the capitalist ideology. He is not necessarily the abstract capitalist. He may be the abstract wage-earner. His identification with an ideology which (we contend) is the one *par excellence* conducive to the proper functioning of capitalism is not, as the Marxist theory of consciousness would have it, a necessary consequence of his role in the prevailing 'mode of production'. He need not 'exploit'; he may be 'exploited'. His consciousness with regard to the state can (if it really must!) be tautologically derived from his interest; if his personal pain-and-pleasure, cost–benefit, help-or-hindrance calculus tells him that he is better off under less government, he will be for less government. No *a priori* reason stops a wage-earner from reaching this conclusion, any more than it stops a real-life capitalist from wanting more government. Marxism, at least 'vulgar Marxism', would condemn both for false consciousness, for failing to recognize their 'real' interest which (again tautologically), is completely derived from their class situation. However, enough has been said by now to make clear that we find no convincing reason to suppose that a person is somehow making a mistake if his ideology is not the one purportedly 'corresponding' to his class situation. A capitalist and a worker may both be allergic to the state they know; they often are; their reasons may well be largely the same.

All theories of the benign state, from divine right to social contract, carry the tacit assumption that the satisfaction or happiness of the state is for some reason and in some manner attained through the happiness of its subjects. No good reason is offered for this, nor a plausible manner in which it *could* take place. Therefore, there is no warrant for this rather demanding assumption, least of all when it is made tacitly. Rational action by the state links its power to its ends in a natural short-circuit, without passing along the long and winding loop which is, so to speak, the *locus* of the subjects' own conception of their good. With the best will in the world, no state, not even the most direct democracy or the most enlightened absolutism, can make its power run round such a loop. If it has heterogeneous subjects, it can at the very best, in the limiting case, further its own composite conception of their several goods.

False consciousness can, with luck, close the loop; for subjects need only believe that their ends are no different from the ends the state is in fact furthering. This, it must be supposed, is the meaning of 'socialization'. Such a result is promoted by the state's ability (and in particular by the role it assumes in public education) to render society relatively homogeneous. It is closely allied to the process alluded to at the beginning of this chapter whereby people's political preferences adjust to the political arrangements under which they live.[42] Instead of people choosing a political system, the political

42   Jon Elster, 'Sour Grapes', in Amartya Sen and Bernard Williams (eds), *Utilitarianism and Beyond*, 1982, has a penetrating discussion of what he calls adaptive and counter-adaptive preferences, and which bear some relation to what I call, in the present work, 'addiction' and 'allergy'. He insists on adaptation and learning being distinct, notably in that the former is *reversible* (p. 226).
   It seems to me difficult to affirm that the formation of political preferences is reversible. It

...ystem can to a certain extent choose them. They need not with Orwell's Winston Smith, actually come to love Big Brother. If substantial numbers or perhaps a whole class of them develop sufficient false consciousness to identify their good with what the state is actually providing, and accept the collateral subjection *without doubting the attractiveness of the bargain,* the basis is laid for consent and harmony between the state and civil society, though the state is, inevitably, a presumptive adversary of its subjects.

---

may or may not be, and the historical evidence can be read either way. My intuitive inclination would be to regard it as irreversible, both in its adaptive and counter-adaptive manifestations. The question is of obvious importance if one form of government can, so to speak, 'spoil the people forever' for another form of government.

2

The Adversary State

Repression, Legitimacy and Consent

Reliance on consent, as a substitute for repression or legitimacy,
makes the state into a democratic and divisive force.

To tell one sort of state from another, one should first look at how
they go about getting obeyed.

In organizations that survive, a few command and the rest obey. In
all, the few dispose of some means of sanctioning disobedience. The
sanction may be the withdrawal of a good, like partial or total
deprivation of the benefits of belonging to the organization, or it may
be an outright bad like punishment. By suitably bending such terms
as command, obedience, punishment, etc. this can be recognized as
true for such institutions as the family, school, office, army, union,
church and so forth. The sanction, to be efficient, must be suited to
the nature of the offence and the institution. For the prosperity of an
organization it is probably equally bad to over- and to under-punish.
Usually, however, the graver the appropriate sanction, the less is the
discretion of those in command to apply it.

Max Weber, in an extension of this thought, defined the state as
the organization which 'successfully claims the monopoly of the
legitimate use of physical force'.[1] The vulnerable aspect of this
famous definition is the circularity of its idea of legitimacy. The use
of physical force by the state is legitimate for no more fundamental
and logically prior reason than that it *has* successfully claimed a

1   Max Weber, *Essays in Sociology*, 1946, p. 78.

monopoly of it and has thus become a proper state.[2] The use of force
by others is illegitimate by definition (except of course under delegation by the state). Thus doubt is cast on the existence of the state in
a society where masters could in their discretion flog their servants or
union militants can dissuade fellow workers from crossing picket
lines by unspoken threats of unspecified revenge. A definition which
might resist counter-examples rather better would lay down that the
state is the organization in society which can *inflict sanctions without
risk of disavowal* and can disavow sanctions by others. There are
sanctions which, due to their inappropriateness or gravity, risk
provoking appeal or need backing up by a more powerful organization. Only the state's sanctions, for lack of a more powerful
dispenser of sanctions, are certain not to be appealed.

This statement has the merit of expressing the state's sovereignty.
If there is nothing 'above' it, the state's decisions must be understood
as final. However, for some purposes, it is sometimes convenient to
treat the state, not as a homogeneous body with a single will, but as a
heterogeneous composite made up of higher- and lower- and side-
ways-differentiated 'instances'. In such a view, though appeal is
impossible *against* the state to something *beyond* it, it is possible
within it, against the bad local potentate to the good central bureaucracy, against the bad minister to the good king, against the axe-
grinding executive to the impartial judiciary. In fact, it was the
unease the very idea of sovereignty, of *no further recourse,* aroused in
sober minds which used to set them off on the grand quest for the
Holy Grail of political lore, the separation of powers, the supremacy
of the legislature and the independence of the judiciary.

A less hopeful view of the morphology of the state sees a rub in
this. Appeal from one instance of the state to another in general, and
the independence of the judiciary in particular, *presuppose the very
conditions they are designed to ensure,* like the raincoat which only
keeps you dry in dry weather. Appeal within the state is fine if there
are good ministers serving a good king and government is by and
large benign. The judiciary is definitely a safeguard against the
executive as long as the executive lets it be, but it has no powers to

2   An application of this particular principle to the special case of the legitimacy of the use of
force *between* states is Machiavelli's doctrine that war is legitimate when it is necessary, the
state itself being the only possible judge of necessity. For illuminating remarks on the
enforcement by states of the monopoly of war-making in the fifteenth and sixteenth centuries,
cf. Michael Howard, *War in European History,* 1976, pp. 23–4.

enforce its own independence. Like the Pope, it has no divisions, and like him, it cannot behave in temporal matters as if it had many. Its capacity to defy an executive unwilling to take defiance, is in the last analysis nothing but a dim reflection of the chances of successful popular revolt on its behalf – chances which are themselves usually the fainter the more the independence of the judiciary is waning. The 1770–1 clash between the French magistrature and the monarchy is a telling example of the point I am making. The *parlements,* in defying the king, had expected a broad popular clientele to stand behind them, but few would stick their necks out on their side. The magistrates, of course, actually owned their offices. They were nationalized and reimbursed. The new magistrates, chosen from among the old, became salaried officers of the king. They were assured security of tenure, presumably to ensure their independence!

The state may, of course, consider it positively useful to give its judiciary a measure of independence for ulterior reasons (cf. pp. 191, 193). On the other hand, it may also do so because, its ends being quite restricted and 'meta-political', it sees no particular point in having a subservient judiciary. Seeing no such point may perhaps be a serviceable preliminary criterion of the benignity of the state. Reflection will show, however, that ultimately such a criterion is not serviceable, for while guaranteeing the rule of law, it may just guarantee the rule of bad law (and a state which is bound by its own bad laws, though better than the state that readily subordinates or adjusts law to reason-of-state, is not benign). However, at least it clarifies the relation between the independence of the judiciary and the state's purposes. *The former cannot purify the latter.* The judiciary cannot render the state benign to ensure and perpetuate its own independence, any more than the proverbial man can lift himself by his own bootstraps.[3]

The separation-of-powers argument, once invoked, all too easily leads straight to the muddle of supposing the state to be benign *because* powers within it *are* separate, though causation runs the other way and only the other way; powers are genuinely separate

---

3 It may be reasonable to suppose that there is some probabilistic feedback from an independent judiciary *yesterday* to good government and hence the toleration of an independent judiciary *today*, a virtuous cycle running counter to the vicious circle, if there is one, of state power changing society and the changed society providing the state with yet more power over itself. Clearly, however, the virtuous cycle has little stability; if it is interrupted by bad government for whatever reason, the independence of the judiciary is soon taken care of.

only if the state is benign. We can, of course, tediously keep reminding ourselves that some powers are more real than others and that the test of reality is the ability of one to coerce the other, even if push never comes to shove because the latent chance of the use of force may always keep paper power in its place. Viewing the state as a plurality of instances including the caucus of the ruling party, the kitchen cabinet and the political police as well as the Weights and Measures Department, may save us from the sinful use of holistic, 'systematically misleading expressions',[4] but for our present purpose the assumption of a homogeneous body and a single directing will, *to* which one appeals and *against* which one does not, is going to obviate much wearisome repetition.

Any state obtains obedience in one of three ways. The most straightforward and historically often the first way is the threat of outright punishment which is implicit in the state's superior command over means of *repression*. The least straightforward and transparent way is the establishment of its *legitimacy*. For the present purpose, legitimacy will be taken to mean the propensity of its subjects to obey its commands in the absence of either punishments or rewards for doing so.

A little elaboration may be called for. It will be remarked that such a definition makes legitimacy, not an attribute of the state, but a state of mind of its subjects. Depending on history, race, culture or economic organization, one people may accept a given state as legitimate while another would, if it could, reject it as a hateful tyranny. Foreign conquerors bringing progressive government to a benighted race exploited by its own ruling class, seldom have the tact and patience needed to become legitimate. There may also be some truth in the belief that some people are more governable than others, so that White Russians, with their reputation for meekness, may have recognized as legitimate, and fairly willingly obeyed, each of the successive and quite different states represented by Lithuanian, Polish and Great Russian rule. On the other hand, people on the Celtic fringes seldom feel that the state deserves their obedience no matter what it does either *for* them or *to* them. In France, where rule by divine right had a long gestation and after a period of conceptual muddle came to dominate political consciousness roughly from

---

4   Gilbert Ryle's famous term for referring to the whole when we mean the part, as in 'The Russian occupation forces raped your sister.'

Henri II to Louis XIV, it was yet contested throughout by both Huguenot and Ultramontan ideologists and was twice near-fatally defied, by the League under Henri III and by the Fronde under Mazarin. If this proves anything, it is that concessions to the most potent counterforces in society, and the groping for consensus, are no recipe for breeding legitimacy.

Hume, who was firmly unimpressed by contractarian political theory, held that even if the fathers obeyed the state because they had become parties to a social contract, they have not bound their sons; the latter obey out of habit. Habit is probably nine parts of any good explanation of political obedience, but it does not explain much of legitimacy. Habitual obedience may itself rest on latent threats of coercion, on a dim sense of repression lurking in the background, or on the political hedonism the sons inherited in the form of 'common knowledge', from their contractarian fathers and which the state continued to nurture by an economical dripfeed of rewards.

Just as we want repression to be a logical limiting case of the spectrum of possible obedience-eliciting relations between state and subject, the case where unwilling people are all the time coerced by the threat of force to do the things the state wishes them to do and which they would not otherwise do, so we want legitimacy to be the limiting case at the opposite end, where the state can make people do things without possessing much in the way of the means of physical coercion or having many rewards to dispense. Thus when, in the Peasant Revolt of 1381, the young Richard II called out to the rebels: 'Sirs, will you shoot your King? I am your captain, follow me,'[5] it was the force of legitimacy which turned around the bereaved and furious bands of Wat Tyler. The King had, for the short run that alone mattered in that fateful moment, neither armed force to set against them, nor bribes for soothing their grievances, and he threw them no scapegoat. He needed neither.

Nothing, obviously, could suit a rational state better than to become legitimate in this sense. The only exception would be the state for which coercion, rather than being a more or less costly means to get people to obey it, would actually be an end, a satisfaction. It is no doubt tempting to view the state of a stylized Caligula, a simplified Ivan the Terrible, an unsympathetic Committee

5 *The Oxford History of England*, vol. V, Mary McKisack, *The Fourteenth Century*, 1959, p. 413.

of Public Safety or a schematic Stalin in this light. In reality, even where cruelty seems gratuitous and terror both redundant and of debatable efficacy, so that the observer would ascribe it to the perverse whim of a tyrant, in the mind of the perpetrators it may well have been the indispensable laying of a groundwork for future legitimacy. A case study of how Aztec Mexico, Inca Peru and nineteenth-century Buganda attempted to legitimize their respective states in the face of a hostile and heterogeneous mass of subjects, concludes that 'socialization involving benevolence and terror' were the principal ingredients of policy employed.[6] Others included the establishment of 'patterns of deference-demeanour', the claiming of infallibility, the shaking up and mixing of ethnic groups and education for citizenship rather than for knowledge, so as to inculcate a liking for the state's own values.

Though many of the ingredients must crop up again and again, it seems doubtful whether there is really a recipe in statecraft for getting from repression to legitimacy. Certainly no obvious one seems to have a decent success ratio, for legitimacy has been rare and elusive throughout history, needing ingredients simply not available at the snap of the state's finger. It took successful wars, prosperous peace, charismatic rulers, a great shared experience and perhaps, above all, continuity. The great value to the state of some undisputed rule of who gets the tenancy of power, like the Salic Law of dynastic succession, agreed and adhered to for some time and seen, like all good laws, to be impersonal and heedless of the merits of rival contestants, is precisely to retrieve continuity (albeit only a dynastic one) from death. It is partly for this reason that while, in general, it is no easier for a state to attain complete legitimacy than for the camel to pass through the eye of the needle, it is yet a little harder for republics than for monarchies. (Few political arrangements seem less apt to foster legitimacy than frequent elections, especially presidential ones focusing on a passing person. Every so many years, controversy is stoked up, to the effect that *A* would be a good and *B* a bad President and *vice versa*. After it has reached great heat, the controversy is supposed to be settled, by a possibly infinitesimal margin of votes, in favour of the good *or* of the bad candidate!)

No state relies on repression alone and none enjoys perfect legiti-

---

6   Donald V. Kurtz, 'The Legitimation of Early Inchoate States', in Henri J.M. Claessen and Peter Skalnik (eds), *The Study of the State*, 1981.

macy. It is trite to say that neither can really be employed without some admixture of the other, the prevailing amalgam of repression and legitimacy in any state depending, as Marxists would say, 'on the concrete historical situation'. However, between the poles of coercion and divine right there has always been another element which is clearly neither: consent, historically perhaps the least important type of obedience-eliciting relation between state and subject, but perhaps the most fertile of recent consequences, particularly unintended ones. In early states, one can think of consent as binding only some minute but special group of subjects to the locus of the state's will. The war gang's obedience to a tribal leader or that of the praetorian guard to the Emperor may be examples of consent which border on complicity. Whether it is augurs, priests or officers of the state security police, the obedience of such small groups of people is a condition of the state's tenure of power; like a pulley for lifting great weights by small force, it can set off the processes of repression as well as those, never assured of success, of creating legitimacy. Yet their complicity and collaboration with the state's ends derives as a rule neither from repression nor from legitimacy, but from an implicit contract with the state which *sets them apart from other subjects and rewards them at the latter's expense* in return for their willing obedience and consent to the state's power. Some intellectually quite intriguing, and in their effects most portentous, problems arise when the group thus set apart and rewarded, expands amoeba-like across society, with ever more people inside and less outside it, until in the theoretical limit everybody consents and everybody is rewarded for it but there is nobody left to bear the cost (cf. p. 238).

Consent for our purpose is best defined as an accord between state and subject, revocable with little advance notice by either party, whereby the subject adopts some appropriate and favourable attitude ranging from active militant support to passive allegiance, and the state furthers the subject's specific ends up to limits which are constantly renegotiated and adjusted in the political process. It is very much less than the social contract, if only because it creates no new right or power for the state. It is not 'social' because the civil party to it is never the whole of society, but merely the individual subject, group or class with motives and interests setting it apart from other individuals, groups or classes.

While the social contract treats the subject's life and property or (as in Rousseau) his general good, the contract of consent deals with his partial and piecemeal ends; both contracts attract the political hedonist, but in different ways. No continuing obligations are created by the contract of consent any more than by cash-and-carry transactions which do not bind the parties to repeat them.

Let us revert to the rewards of consent. When nanny and the children practise the politics of consent by agreeing that if the children will be good children this afternoon, there will be strawberry jam for tea, strawberry jam is within nanny's gift. In the short run, she can bestow it or not as she pleases. But the state has, generally speaking (and abstracting from such exotic and dated phenomena as strawberries grown on the royal domain) no rewards to bestow, no jam that is not already the jam of its subjects. Moreover, as I had occasion to point out in chapter 1, in the general case where its subjects are not unanimous in their conceptions of the good, the state can in the nature of the case only further *its* good which may, for all we know, be *its* conception of *their* good.

We have also noted that progressive assimilation of people's own ends to the ends selected and pursued by the state, i.e. the development of 'false consciousness', can erode and at least in principle fully dissolve this contradiction. As Professor Ginsberg puts it in his *Consequences of Consent*: democratic elections 'erode the adversary relationship between rulers and ruled ... encourage citizens to believe that expansion of the state's power meant only an increase in the government's *capacity to serve*,'[7] and 'modern democratic governments tend to increase their *control over the public's putative means of controlling* their actions.'[8] However, the spread of false consciousness is neither a strong nor a sure enough mechanism for always securing the allegiance the state requires. First, it is not something the state can be confident of engendering unilaterally, at its sole volition, and certainly not over a short enough period. After all, it took almost a century from Jules Ferry's vast reforms creating universal lay state education to the emergence of a socialist electoral majority in France, and over the intervening turns and byways the ultimate result was at best only rather probable, never certain. Where an ideologically not quite inept opposition exists, it can spoil the fresh growth of false consciousness as fast as the state is promoting it. Secondly, relying heavily on false consciousness is like 'doing it with

7   Benjamin Ginsberg, *The Consequences of Consent*, 1982, p. 24, his italics.
8   Ibid., p. 26, my italics, cf. also p. 197.

mirrors'. The people the least likely to be taken in could well be the tough and hard-nosed sort whose support the state most needs.

The common-sense perception that the state has no rewards to dispense that do not belong to its subjects anyway, so that it can only pay Paul by robbing Peter, is of course harmful for good-citizen false consciousness. By way of remedy, there stands the arguable assertion that the consent-generating transactions between state and subjects enhance social cooperation (and hence output, or harmony, or whatever good it takes social cooperation to produce) to the effect that the gains of the gainers exceed the losses of the losers. For well-rehearsed reasons, such an assertion is now generally taken to be a value judgement (it could be a statement of fact only in the special case where there are no losers, i.e. where all gains are net gains, and the latter are minor enough not to imply a significant change in the distribution of goods). It is the value judgement of the person who undertakes the adding up (with due regard to algebraic sign) of the gains and losses. No very good reason is on hand why his values should take precedence over anybody else's who might get a different sum from the same addition. Recourse to the value-judgements of the gainers and losers directly involved settles nothing, for the losers might well value their losses more highly than they do the gainers' gains, while the gainers are quite likely to do the opposite. Thus an impasse is reached. For equally well-rehearsed reasons, no gainer-to-loser compensation test seems possible which could 'factually', in a *wertfrei* manner prove the availability of a residual surplus of gains over losses, to be applied to the greater fulfilment of the gainers' ends. Without such a surplus, however, there is no fund, created by the incremental contribution of the state to some index-number of total social end-fulfilment, out of which the state could bestow bits of end-fulfilment to selected subjects without damage to others.

Nor would the production of a surplus of good and its bestowal be sufficient to earn consent for the state. If a given subject came to hold that the activities of the state do generate additional end-fulfilment for him, he would for that reason alone have no interest to support the state any more than he was already doing. As far as he was concerned, the state's bounty might be falling from heaven and changing his own conduct *vis-à-vis* the state could not make it fall any thicker. If he became a more docile subject and a more convinced supporter of the 'government party', he may have done so out of admiration for good government, or gratitude, but not out of rational self-interest in the narrow sense, on which political calculus can be based. This is possibly the abstract and general common element in the political failures of Enlightened Absolutism, the reformist good governments of Catherine the Great, the Emperor Joseph II and (less obviously) Louis XV, each of which met mainly with stony indifference and ingratitude on the part of the intended beneficiaries.

Rewards, to elicit self-interested support, must be contingent on performance. They must be embedded in implicit contracts of the 'you will get this for doing thus' kind. Consequently, it is difficult to envisage the politics of consent without a type or types of political markets joining rulers and ruled, to enable bargains to be struck and revised. Democracy might be regarded as one or both of such types of markets functioning side by side. One is the majority-rule, one-man–one-vote type of pure electoral democracy, where the state at intervals engages in a competitive auction with (actual or potential) rivals for votes. The other, much older and less formal type of market, now usually called 'pluralistic' or 'group interest' democracy, is an endless series of parallel bilateral negotiations between the state and what one could, vulgarly but tellingly, call the wielders of clout within civil society. Clout must be seen not only as the capacity to deliver votes, but also as any other form of support useful for maintenance of the state's power over its subjects, as a substitute for outright repression by the state itself.

I have no formal theory to offer which would take stock of and systematically organize the general causes inducing the state to aim at securing power more by consent and less by repression (or, what seems as yet much rarer, *vice versa*). Perhaps no such theory is really possible, at least not one which would deduce the state's chosen policies from the assumption that it will select the means which lead efficiently to its ends. For it is arguable that the state relies on consent basically out of short-sightedness, weakness of will and the corollary liking for the line of least resistance. It usually seems easier to give than to withhold, to extend and dilute rewards than to restrict and concentrate them, to please more rather than less and to wear a bland rather than a stern face. Repression, moreover, has in fact often involved close identification of the state with an ally in civil society, a group, stratum or (in Marxist sociology, invariably) a class such as the nobility, the landed interest, the capitalists. Rightly or wrongly, states tended to judge that close alliance with some such narrow subset of society made them a captive of class, caste or group and negated their autonomy. As kings from medieval times sought to lessen their dependence on the nobility by soliciting the support of town burghers, so did the state in more modern times emancipate itself from the bourgeoisie by enfranchising and buying the votes of successively broader masses of people.

Taking these democratic ways out of the predicament which repressive government represents for the state (rather like committing the moral fault by which the protagonist tries to escape his fate in a properly constructed tragedy), entails its own punishment. 'Punishment' for the state comes in the form of having to put up with political competition with rivals for power, whose consequences are ultimately destructive of the very ends the state was attempting to fulfil.

One logical issue out of this dilemma is resort to what is politely called people's democracy, where the state has ample means to repress political competition yet solicits a degree of its subjects' consent by raising expectations of future rewards once the building of socialism is sufficiently advanced. Some implications of open rivalry for state power, the multi-party system and of 'clout' in civil society which *may oppose the state unless bought off* or reduced, will be more systematically treated in chapter 4, 'Redistribution', and the state's rational response, principally the *reduction of civil society's clout,* in chapter 5, 'State Capitalism'.

When it is a question of obtaining tenure of the state in the first place, or not losing it, first things come first, with any considerations of how to *use* power *once it is secured,* coming obviously second in logical order if not in value. Assembling a broad enough base of consent can both earn power, and pre-empt the political ground which a narrower base would leave dangerously vacant and open for others to invade. Whether or not the rulers of a democratic society have the acuity to foresee the ultimately frustrating character of rule-by-consent (as compared to the disciplines of rule-by-repression, and the state of grace which is rule-through-legitimacy), the logic of their situation – drift – the politics of small steps drive them on in the democratic direction. They must deal with the immediate consequences of their previous weaknesses regardless of what the more distant future may call for, because, in the unforgettable phrase of a famous British consent-seeker, 'a week is a long time in politics.'

Some of these considerations may help explain why, contrary to the early schoolbook version of disenfranchised masses clamouring for the right to participate in the political process, the drive for widening the franchise often came as much from the ruler as from the ruled. This seems to me the realistic view to take of Necker's electoral initiatives for the French provincial estates in 1788–9, of the English reforms of 1832 and 1867 and of those of the Second Reich after 1871.

Rewards, finally, do not spontaneously grow on trees, nor are they generated and distributed to good citizens by good government. They are bargaining counters which the state *acquires* for distribution to its supporters *by taking sides*. A presumptive adversary of all in civil society, to obtain the support of some, it must become the actual adversary of others; if there were no class struggle, the state could usefully invent it.

Taking Sides

The rise of partisan democracy in the nineteenth century served to build both mass consent and a bigger and cleverer state apparatus.

In a republic of teachers, the capitalist ends up as the political underdog.

The foundations of the lay Western welfare state were probably laid in England's 1834 Poor Law, not because it was particularly good for the welfare of the poor (it was in fact bad in that it abolished outdoor relief) but because, at the same time as concerning itself with the poor, the state transferred the larger part of the administrative responsibility for them from the dilettante and independent local authorities to its own professionals in what was then starting to take shape as the civil service. The foremost author and promoter of this scheme of building state muscle and governing capacity was the great practical utilitarian Edwin Chadwick, without whose intense drive much of the intervention of the English central government in social affairs might have taken place several decades later than it did. However, there he was, his zeal speeding up historical inevitability by twenty years or so, clearly recognizing that if the state is effectively to promote a good cause, it must not rely on the goodwill of independent intermediaries whom it does not control.[9] when subsequently he addressed his energies to public health, he obtained the creation of the General Board of Health with himself as its first Commissioner, only to have the Board peter out on his retirement in 1854, demonstrating how much depended, at that incipient stage of historical inevitability, on the commitment of a single individual. It was not till 1875 that the state got round to re-creating an administrative body in the Public Health Act and in doing so, incidentally committing 'the largest invasion of property rights in the nineteenth century'.[10] It is surprising, in view of the authority the state was acquiring over the subject in other areas of social life, that education remained facultative until 1880.

On a lower level of eminence than Chadwick, the inspectors created by the first Factory Acts had a somewhat analogous role as spearheads, at one and the same time, of social reform and of the aggrandizement of the state apparatus. In supervising the observance of the successive Factory Acts, they in perfect good faith kept finding further social problems for the state to solve. As these problems were in turn tackled, they found that as an incidental by-product, their own authority and the number of their subordinates had also increased. There was, in fact, a first major wave of expansion of the state's concerns and, parallel with it, of its apparatus, from the Reform Act of 1832 to 1848, as if meant to secure the allegiance of the new voters; then followed a relative lull from 1849 to 1859, coinciding with the decade of conservative reaction on the Continent; and a rush of increasing activism ever since.

It has been estimated that over the period from 1850 to 1890 the number of British government employees grew by about 100 per cent and from 1890 to 1950 by another 1000 per cent; public expenditure in the nineteenth century averaged about 13 per cent of GNP, after 1920 it never fell below 24 per cent, after 1946 it was never less than 36 per cent and in our day it is, of course, just below or just above the half-way mark depending on how we count public expenditure.[11]

9   Chadwick did not think that he and his fellow civil servant pioneers were empire-building, promoting their own pet policies, fulfilling their own (selfless) ends or working for the (selfish) interests of a self-serving bureaucracy. No doubt sincerely, he felt that they were neutrally administering the law and thus, but only thus, serving the public. He did not see that they were largely making the law. In fact, he considered attacking a civil servant to be like hitting a woman – the analogy presumably residing in their common defencelessness!
10   Sir Ivor Jennings, *Party Politics*, 1962, vol. III, p. 412.
11   The estimates are those of G.K. Fry in his *The Growth of Government*, 1979, p. 2.

Statistical series over longish periods are rightly mistrusted because their context is liable to change in important ways. For similar reasons of non-comparable contexts, international statistical comparisons, say, of GNPs absorbed in public sector consumption and transfers, should be treated with some reserve. Nevertheless, where the relative numbers show vast differences either over time or between nations, one can safely draw at least the modest conclusion that government in England in the last century and a half increased several times over, or that among the major industrial countries, no government leaves as much of GNP for private purposes as the Japanese. It is perhaps appropriate at this point to recall again Walpole's lack of governing zeal and relate it to the fact that his government had all of 17,000 employees, four-fifths of them engaged in the raising of the revenue.[12]

I will not deal a second time with the irrefutable dialectic argument that when in a situation of conflicting class interests the state sides with the working class, it is *really* siding with the capitalist class, for whoever has at his command the invincible adjective 'real' must win any controversy over this, as over anything else. I merely note that in areas of possible concern which the earlier English state (the Hanoverian even more resolutely than its Stuart predecessor) largely ignored, the nineteenth century saw public policy playing an increasing role which was at least *prima facie* favourable to the many, the poor and the helpless. The passage from the state's absence and unconcern to its progressive predominance had (in part predictable) consequences for the freedom of contract, the autonomy of capital and how people came to view their responsibility for their own fate.

At least in the early part of the century, the anti-capitalist drift of the reform movement certainly did not come from some clever calculation on the part of the state that there was more support to be gained on the 'left' than lost on the 'right'. In terms of the pre-1832 electoral arithmetic, this would have been dubious reckoning anyway. Up to the 1885 electoral reform if not beyond it, the main political benefit of taking sides with the labouring poor was derived not from getting *their* votes, but those of the progressive professional middle class. The earliest pro-labour legislation pleased above all the squirearchy and beyond it those magnates who particularly despised the money-grubbing of the mill-owners and their unconcern

12   Ibid., p. 107.

for the welfare of the millhands and their families. Sadler, Oastler and Ashley (Lord Shaftesbury) were imbued with righteous animosity towards the manufacturers, Sadler's 1831–2 Select Committee on Factory Children's Labour producing one of the most virulent anti-industry tracts ever.

The capitalist defence was characteristically inept. With the passage of time, as and when state policy helped the poor at the expense of the rich, it was both to help the poor and to please some altruistic or envious third party – the concerned middle class reared on Philosophical Radicalism (and, once or twice, just a certain, inordinately influential Master of Balliol). Even when broad popular support became a more clearly recognized and avowed objective, the state may have often been pushed farther by articulate middle- and upper class opinion than could be warranted by the tangible political advantage to be reaped from some progressive measure. 'False consciousness', a ready acceptance (bordering on gullibility) of what the articulate *say* about the duty of the state in matters of social justice, was seldom absent from tentative forecasts of political profit and loss.

Perhaps the most intriguing feature of the relatively quick transformation of the near-minimal Georgian state into a Victorian partisan democracy, an adversary of capital, endowing itself with an autonomous bureaucracy (albeit to a more moderate extent than many other states that were, for various reasons, more powerful and autonomous to begin with), is the mute defeatism with which the capitalist class, instead of drawing confidence from the dominant ideology of the age as it was supposed to do, submitted to the role of political underdog, contenting itself with making good money. Germany had Humboldt, France had Tocqueville to think and express the thoughts that were becoming urgent about the proper limits of the state and the awesome implications of popular sovereignty. England had only Cobden, Bright and Herbert Spencer in this camp. Her major thinkers, in keeping with the utilitarian tradition, in fact prepared the ideological foundations of the adversary state. (Historical circumstance, which gave Jacobinism to France and an adulation of the nation state to Germany, was admittedly much less kind to statism in England, where its ideologists had a relatively hard row to hoe till the last third or so of the century.) Mill, despite his ringing phrases in *On Liberty,* his mistrust of universal franchise and his dislike of the invasion of liberty by popular government, had no doctrine of restraint upon the state. His pragmatism strongly pulled him the other way. For him, state intervention involving the violation of personal liberties and (to the extent that these are distinct) property rights, was always bad except when it was good. True to his broad utilitarian streak, he was content to judge the actions of the state 'on their merits', case by case.

The doctrinal impotence of the capitalist interest is nicely illustrated by the course of labour law. English law regarding trade unions went round full circle between 1834 and 1906, from forbidding combinations to restrain competition in both the supply of and the demand for labour, to ultimately legalizing combinations to restrain supply and also exempting them from having to keep contracts when it was inconvenient to do so. Much the same effect favourable to labour could have been achieved in less provocative ways. Violating the principle of equality before the law between capital and labour was, one might have thought, asking for it. Yet there was no worth-while doctrinal capitalist counter-attack, no appeal to first principles, nor to the as-yet uncontested verities of political economy.

The English state, twice almost disarmed *vis à vis* civil society in 1641 and 1688, regained its predominance over private interest on the back of social reform, accomplishing its partisan anti-capitalist turn tentatively and gradually over nearly a century. In Continental Europe, civil society never disarmed the state which remained powerful, in governing apparatus and repressive capacity, even where it was standing on clay feet. The anti-capitalist turn as a means of building a base of consent, came rather later in these countries, but it was accomplished more rapidly. The watershed years when capitalism became the political underdog (though very much the top dog financially, becoming acceptable socially and still capable, in the case of such eminences as the Pereira brothers, the James de Rothschilds, the Bleichröders or the J. P. Morgans, to bend back the state to serve capitalist purposes), were either side of 1859 in France, 1862 in the North German Federation and 1900 in the USA.

It was roughly in 1859 that Napoleon III, in his own eyes a man of the left, began really to rely on the Assembly and to practise the rudiments of parliamentary democracy, and of a particular sort at that: for Guizot and Odilon Barrot were gone from the scene, to be replaced by such men of the radical left as Jules Favre, Jules Ferry and Gambetta, with only the 'despicable Thiers' representing continuity of an unlovely kind with the bourgeois monarchy. Striking became legal in 1864 and a proper charter for labour unions, with fringe measures ranging from workers' pensions to price control on bread, was legislated in 1867, Napoleon III taking a sympathetic interest in the encouragement of trade unions. Perhaps coincidentally with his shift toward the politics of consent, he showed a fine disregard for the capitalist interest in throwing open the French iron and steel, engineering and textile industries to the more efficient English and Belgian competition. Sharing the widespread illusion that a nation of shopkeepers will pay for a commercial good turn with such political support as he needed for his transalpine ambitions, in late 1859 he sent Chevalier, an ex-professor of economics with the free-trade convictions that such a calling tends to engender, to Cobden in London; it took the two kindred spirits an hour to negotiate a whole new free-trader tariff, to the furious surprise both of the Minister of Finance and the manufacturers concerned. Though perhaps of no more than anecdotal interest (anyone with a little acquaintance with tariff negotiations can at least smile at the story), the incident is characteristic of the respect the French state had, then as ever, for the interests of its industrialists.

Another facet of the adversary state which started to matter under the Second Empire and became very important in the Third Republic, was the autonomous evolution of the bureaucracy. The French professional civil service, built by the labours of Colbert, Louvois, Machault, Maupeou and, in unbroken continuity, by Napoleon, was at first closely entwined with property and enterprise, both because of the negotiability and (initially) relatively high capital value of offices, and of the dual role most of the civil service dynasties played in the royal administration and in the chief capitalist trades of the time, army contracting and tax farming. At the fall of the July monarchy, in 1848, a regime which was less ambitious than most to dominate society, the civil service was more powerful than ever and, of course, more numerous (Marx noted, as a significant element in his characterization of the Second Empire, that there were 500,000 bureaucrats smothering civil society in addition to 500,000 soldiers), but no longer had much of a proprietorial stake in French industry and little property in general. The estrangement between capital and the bureaucracy was further accentuated in the Third Republic. While the top layer of the civil service was certainly upper-class (to Gambetta's indignation) and continued to be dynastic, such property as it had was mainly in *rentes,* and it had no understanding of, nor common interest with, entrepreneurial capitalism.

Moreover, when in 1906 the emoluments of a *député* were nearly doubled, the profession of legislator became overnight quite attractive as a living. Till then, whatever was the social and economic background of the civil service, at least on the legislative side, capital, industry and land were strongly represented. From then onward, however, the republic of *notables* rapidly became, in Thibaudet's oft-cited phrase, a 'republic of teachers' which, to judge by the occupational backgrounds of successive French legislatures, it has remained ever since.

Unlike France, Germany did not have its 'bourgeois' revolution (not that it is altogether evident how its history would have been different if it had). Nor did it have its July Monarchy, cheering on the German bourgeoisie to enrich themselves, though (despite their late start around the mid-century) they did not fail to do so for all that. Under the romantic anti-capitalism of Frederick William IV, (i.e. till 1858), the Prussian state, while resisting the national liberal ideas imported from the Rhineland, nonetheless cleared up much of the administrative clutter and pointless interference which used to encumber enterprise. This relative economic liberalism was an (albeit minor) enabling cause of the spate of new enterprise which characterized the 1850s. When Bismarck gained the highest office in 1862, the National Liberals had definitely to give up any serious hope of shaping state policy. If it is not too crude to regard them as the party of capital, one can say that their subsequent conduct really signified the acceptance by the capitalist interest of a politically quite subordinate role.

Both directly, and indirectly by harnessing William I's obsession with the army, Bismarck ensured that absolute priority be given to all-German and foreign affairs, almost regardless of the consequent tax burden on industry. The schematic explanation of his freedom of manoeuvre is, of course, his ably managed truce, at times amounting to a downright alliance, with the mainstream of the Social Democrats. A simple, but not for that reason wrong, way to grasp Bismarck's policy is that his remarkably advanced social security and welfare legislation was the price he compelled German capital to pay, to have the domestic calm and consent *he* needed for the effective pursuit of *his* priority objectives in foreign policy. The latter was of mixed benefit to German industry and finance. Perhaps more accurately, one might judge that German manufacturing, technically and commercially riding the crest of the wave, could have derived some benefit from almost any feasible foreign policy of passable competence and continuity, whether active or passive, at least as long as it produced the German customs union. It did not really need more to prosper. Achieving much more than that in foreign policy probably cost it more than it was worth.

Bismarck's fundamental bargain with a vital part of the socialist left and the fiscal exigencies of his foreign policy, however, were not the sole causes of the Prussian state, and later the Second Reich, turning a stern mien to capital. Another reason was the intellectual grip which *Kathedersozialismus* ('socialism of the professorial chair' and 'teachers' socialism' seem equally inadequate renderings) – took upon some of the most ambitious and devoted elements in the civil service, both through formal education and through the influence of the research done within the *Verein für Sozialpolitik*. If this *Verein* was more potent, and won its influence sooner, than the Fabians in Britain, its greater initial impact on legislation and regulation was in large part due to the excellence and policy-making latitude of the German civil service. It had a strong tradition, going back to Stein, of not only *serving* but of actually *defining, interpreting the good of the state,* and no false modesty about 'merely executing' the will of its political masters. If we remember, in addition, that it tended to have little or no fortune and its family roots were mainly in the austere East while those of the representative German capitalist were more to the West or North, we have enough elements for appreciating the Reich's adversary relationship to capital in the era of its greatest organizational and technical success. The breach with Russia, William II's febrile foreign policy and the collision with France and England in 1914 were the culmination of a half-century of policy choices, rational and competently executed at the outset and progressively less so as time went by, in which the narrower interests of German capital were unhesitatingly sacrificed to the state's own conception of the global national good. This was accomplished with the support of the bulk of social democracy and the labour union movement.

The reason, if ever there is a good reason for trying precisely to date historical turnings, for calling Theodore Roosevelt's accession to the Presidency the start of the adversary relation between American government and capital, is mainly that any earlier starting date would include the McKinley years at the White House, about the most obvious antithesis to the thesis I am putting forward. The McKinley–William Jennings Bryan contest was the last time that money alone, against all odds, could get its candidate elected. The closing years of the nineteenth century saw the executive power of the state depending for support, in a way never since seen, on the capitalist interest rather than on the popular appeal of its conduct of affairs. The political colour of Theodore Roosevelt's two terms is all the more of a contrast. His anti-trust, anti-railroad and anti-utility accomplishment is as wide by past standards as it is puny by those of most of his successors. It may be true that his bark was more fierce than his bite, that his true element was demagogy rather than unostentatious achievement, and that his administration in fact represented less of a populist and pro-union tilt, less of a stealing of the Democrats' clothes, than one would judge from its bluster. However, his bark was in the short run perhaps as effective as any bite could have been, to put distance between himself and big business in the eye of the public and to mobilize national support for his purposes.

It is probably fair to say that there has never been an American administration which did not almost exclusively rely on consent to get itself obeyed, unlike some British and Continental European regimes which did not rely on it or did so only a little. Lincoln's administration, having to take on in civil war the minority, might not otherwise have retained the consent of the majority (which is precisely Acton's point about the potentially tragic implications of democracy in a non-homogeneous society). Consent was either votes or clout. Champions of the people tended to rely directly on votes. Others relied in the first place on the clout of those concentrations of private power, be they men or organizations, which stand between the state and the amorphous mass of the citizenry and provide society with structure.[13] The alternance between the two types of organizing consent, the direct and the indirect, used to play much the same role in American political life as did (and do) the alternance of ideologically marked tendencies, conservative and progressive, Christian and lay, monarchist and republican parties in other societies. With

13 Leszek Kolakowski, the philosopher and eminent student of Marx's thought, holds that civil society cannot have structure without private ownership of the means of production (*Encounter*, Jan. 1981). If so, the democratic drive (noted by Tocqueville) to break down structure, bypass intermediaries and appeal to one-man–one-vote, and the socialist drive to abolish private ownership of capital, are more closely related than is apparent.

Theodore Roosevelt, alternance in this sense ended in the USA; two parties subsist but both have become champions of the people. If one is less of an adversary of capital and readier to make use of sheer clout than the other, the difference is but of slight degree, especially as clout is no longer well correlated with capital.

The American example, where material inequalities were for a long period more admired than resented and rich-to-poor and rich-to-middle-class redistribution has only recently become the central tool of consent-building, lends itself poorly to clarifying the relation of consent by vote to consent by clout. Take instead any 'country' which is perfectly repressive to begin with, say a concentration camp. For its successful functioning according to the purposes of its commandant, the allegiance or support of its cowed and emaciated inmates is immaterial, no matter how numerous they are; that of the less numerous band of well-fed trusties is relatively more important; and that of the handful of well-armed guards is essential. Even if he could, the camp commandant would be ill-advised to try and win over the inmates by promising to give them the guards' rations. The subset of camp society containing the commandant and the guards is essentially a pure electoral democracy in that, with all the guards about equally well armed, the commandant must find the support of a majority of them, and it is the head count that matters (even if there is no formal voting). If a larger subset including the trusties were carved out, the greater clout of the guards would have to be used to sway the 'vote' of the trusties and secure the consent of their majority to the commandant's way of running the camp. The implicit threat of throwing dissenters to the inmates would normally suffice. If, for some reason, the democratic subset were to be further enlarged and the rule of consent extended to the inmates, they would have to be divided and the support of one part obtained (if that was at all possible) by promising them the rations of another part. The less the clout of the guards and trusties or the less use one could make of it, the more the whole camp would approximate pure electoral democracy giving consent by headcount, with the majority getting the minority's rations.

It seems to be a strange confusion, and one suffered by many states no less than by their subjects, to want to have the state rely on consent *and* to be everybody's state, standing above classes and group interests, beholden to no group and impartially realizing its conception of society's greatest good.

When the state takes sides, not only is it building the required base of consent. Perhaps unconsciously and unwittingly, it is also 'learning by doing'. With every measure it takes to favour a subject or group of subjects, to modify the system of rewards and obligations which derives from past custom or voluntary contracts, to change social and economic arrangements that would prevail but for its intervention, it acquires more knowledge of its subjects' affairs, a better and bigger administrative apparatus and, hence, an added capacity both to imagine and carry out further measures. Two channels of unanticipated causation are dug in this manner, and end by forming a self-sustaining circuit. One leads from intervention to capacity for intervention, as physical labour leads to bigger muscle. The other leads from a larger state apparatus to an altered balance of interests in society, tilted in favour of more state intervention; for by self-aggrandizement the state increases the activist constituency.

These channels run *within* the state apparatus and not *between* it and civil society. Another and probably more potent circuit runs from state benefactions to a condition of dependence or addiction *in* civil society, calling for further benefactions. It is easier to grasp the mechanics of such circuits than to have confidence in their stability, in the capacity of built-in regulators ultimately to prevent them from getting out of control.

Tinker's Licence

Utilitarianism favours activist government mainly because it is constructed to ignore a whole class of reasons for hastening slowly.

Judging things on their merits with an open mind fatefully attracts open minds.

It would be unhistorical and worse to imply that the state will in general just up and do whatever most efficiently ensures its political survival and the fulfilment of such other ends as it may have. On the contrary, it is, time and again, liable to choose relatively inefficient means to its ends, and even retard or hinder their attainment, for its feasible choices are to some extent pre-set for it by the *Zeitgeist*, the ethos of time and place. It cannot, without endangering the often delicate compound of repression, consent and legitimacy which it is aiming at worst to maintain and at best to strengthen, resort to actions for which it has, as it were, no ideological licence.

At the same time, in one of the chicken-and-egg sequences which seem to govern much of social life, ideology will sooner or later providentially issue the licence for precisely the sort of action which it is efficient for the state to undertake. Thus when we speak of 'an idea whose time has come' (the development of the 'base' producing the corresponding 'dominant ideology'), we must also bear in mind the equally interesting inverted version, i.e. that the time has come because the idea has called it forth (the 'superstructure' bringing about a corresponding development of the 'base'). This preliminary is offered to help put in perspective the reciprocal relations of the adversary state and utilitarianism.

It is fairly conventional practice to discern three stages in the evolution of the state's functions (though they are better regarded as heuristic rather than as historical, real-time stages). In the first, a vaguely Hobbesian state resolves a basic prisoners' dilemma by enforcing respect for life and property, such enforcement being taken to include protection against a foreign state also. When political theory is handled as if it were economics, such a first-stage state can be assimilated to the single-product monopolistic firm making one public good, e.g. 'order'. The second or Benthamite sort of state would then resemble a multi-product firm which provides a diversified range of goods or services whose profitable free-enterprise production runs up against some prisoners' dilemma or at least a 'free-rider' problem, and consequently requires coercion to cover its costs. (Voluntary arrangements lacking coercion would by assumption produce either distant substitutes, or different, possibly smaller, quantities of close substitutes of such goods.) What additional goods or services the state shall provide, or what additional functions it should undertake, *is to be decided on their merits*. In the third stage of the evolution of its functions, the state will undertake to produce the range of public goods thus selected *and* social justice as well.

There is no such dividing line between these stages as there is between the state of nature and the state. Each stage contains all of the 'preceding' ones and is recognizable by the upsurge of one type of function without the abandonment of the others. When the balance of consent-seeking political advantage is in favour of the state restricting hours of factory work and laying down rules of safety, providing road signs, lighthouses and air-traffic controls, building sewers, inspecting abattoirs, obliging travellers to be inoculated, running schools and ordering parents to make their children attend them, teaching peasants how to farm and sculptors how to sculpt, adjusting a practice, reforming a custom, imposing a standard, the licence for undertaking these piecemeal improvements is provided by utilitarian doctrine. Its operation, by now often an unconscious habit of thought, is best understood as a sort of two-stroke argument, whose first stroke is a rejection of *a priori* conservatism, an implicit denial that existing arrangements contain a presumption in their own favour. Utilitarians reason, to pick up one of the pearls Michael Oakeshott is in the open-handed habit of casting before his readers,

> as if arrangements were intended
> for nothing else but to be mended[14]

as if everything *could* and *should* be looked at with an open mind, with a view to deciding whether it shall be tinkered with or not.

The second stroke of the argument (which could be so formulated as to subsume the first)[15] is that actions are good if their consequences are good. ('Act-utilitarianism' gets to this result directly, 'rule-utilitarianism' indirectly.) Therefore, we ought to alter any arrangement which would be improved thereby. Despite his non-interventionist reputation, this was precisely J. S. Mill's position. He held that a departure from *laissez faire* involving an 'unnecessary increase' in the power of government was a 'certain evil' unless required by 'some great good' – greater than the evil in order that the balance of good and bad consequences should be good. He at least had the virtue of making it explicit that the general form of the argument for tinkering must provide for the offsetting of a possible bad consequence (if only as an 'empty box'), a form which makes advocacy of reforming an arrangement a somewhat more exacting task, for the good consequence had then better be very good.

Judging actions by their consequences is a difficult and peculiar rule, as is easily seen by considering the intrinsic nature of consequences. If we do not know what consequences an action will bring,

---

14 Michael Oakeshott, 'Political Education', in Peter Laslett (ed.), *Philosophy, Politics and Society*, 1956, p. 2.
15 For example, it could be stipulated that no arrangement must be tinkered with unless doing so produced a greater gain in utility than the loss, if any, entailed in the act of tinkering, where utility would include the value that one may attach to *the mere non-disturbance* of an existing arrangement in addition to its utility in the customary, narrower sense.

the rule means that we cannot tell a good action from a bad one until *after* its consequences have been duly produced. Apart from the absurd moral implications, such an interpretation renders the doctrine quite unhelpful. On the other hand, if we know, or even think we know, 'for certain' what the consequences are, we do so because we think they must surely, predictably follow from the particular action. If so, they are functionally inseparable from it like death is from beheading. In such a case, if we were to say 'this action is good because its consequence is good', we would really be saying no more than the action is good because, taken as a whole, it is good. This would be tantamount to recommending those reforms which improve arrangements – a wholly empty rule.

Utilitarianism does not, however, allow us to consider an action (say giving alms) to be good if its consequence (the beggar gets drunk on the money and is crippled by a passing car) is bad. Conversely, it requires us to approve an action if we would approve of its consequence. Between the limiting cases of not knowing the consequence at all and of knowing it for sure, lies the huge problem area where utilitarianism is bound up with questions of imperfect foresight. Over this area, policies *appear* to have several *alternative chains of consequences* ('*ex ante*'), though only one of the alternative chains can materialize ('*ex post*'). The *ex ante* consequences appear to have greater or lesser probabilities. The proper guide to political action is thus no longer 'maximize utility', but 'maximize the expected value of utility'. The instant we say this, however, we let loose an avalanche of problems, each of which is insoluble except by *recourse to authority*.

Each alternative consequence can perfectly well appear to have different probabilities to different persons. These persons, in turn, may be (a) well- or ill-informed, and (b) astute or stupid in converting such information as they have into a probability assessment. Given the (Bayesian) nature of the probability in question, does it make any sense to say that they use the *wrong* probability assessment in valuing uncertain consequences?

On the other hand, it must seem hard to accept that a policy should be judged in terms of the possibly ill-informed, illusory, naive or biased probability assessments of the persons who are to enjoy or suffer its consequences. What if they have been misled by propaganda? And if several persons are affected by a policy, whose subjective probabilities should be used to value the alternative consequences? Should each person value the consequence *to him* by *his* assessment of its probability? It is obviously tempting to discard some of these probability judgements, retain the 'best' or calculate some weighted average of the several best ones, and use *it* in maximizing expected utility.[16] Whoever has authority to choose the 'best' judgement, or the method for calculating a composite one, is in effect implicitly choosing his own.

Moreover, as each alternative consequence is capable of affecting several persons, 'maximizing expected utility' would be an unhelpful rule even if the problems arising out of the term 'expected' were taken to have been resolved by resort to authority. The meaning of 'utility' must be resolved, too, so that it is agreed to represent a summation (no weaker method of ranking will go far) of the utilities of all the persons liable to be affected. In the language of the trade, it must be interpersonally integrated, 'social' utility. Interpersonal integration of utility is no less problematical than interpersonal probability. Some aspects of it are treated in the next section in order to show that it, too, depends on authority for its resolution.

When Bentham in the *Fragment on Government* defined 'the measure of right or wrong' as the happiness of the greatest number, he was manifestly conducting a discourse not on what was ethically right, but on how to choose between one action and another in the mundane business of legislation and government, and if such a distinction is on scrutiny hard to uphold, it is one practical men readily fall in with. (We may also recall, though it is perhaps no excuse, that Bentham wrote the *Fragment* in great part in order to fight Blackstone's doctrine of legislative inaction, which he saw as an apology for complacency and sloth.)

The utilitarian prescription, then, which the state and its leading servants made their own, was to investigate existing arrangements, to report upon them to Parliament and public opinion, and to prepare reforms from which good consequences would ensue. The proposed change would be either one for which 'effective demand' was already perceptible (though not always or mainly on the part of the prospective beneficiaries), or one for which such demand could be generated. It would seem that the more governments came to rely on popular

16   Frank Hahn, 'On Some Difficulties of the Utilitarian Economist', in Amartya Sen and Bernard Williams (eds), *Utilitarianism and Beyond*, 1982, pp. 195–8, has a particularly lucid exposition of this question. Cf. also P.J. Hammond, 'Utilitarianism, Uncertainty and Information', in the same volume.

support (in England in the last third of the nineteenth century), the more willing they became to arouse demands for change instead of letting sleeping dogs lie. (Neither the wholly repressive nor the fully legitimate state has a rational interest in waking up sleeping dogs.)

The piecemeal improving approach, which ceaselessly inspects arrangements of society, finds some that could be usefully 'mended', gains support first *for* and then *from* mending it and, with added strength, proceeds to the next one, is, as it were, purpose-built to isolate the proximate consequences of each action from the cumulative consequences of a series of them.[17] Though the sum of the trees is the wood, the tree-by-tree approach is notorious for its built-in bias to lose sight of the wood. One of the pitfalls of judging actions by their consequences is that the latter, properly considered, form a virtually never-ending chain most of whose length stretches into an indefinite future. In human society, perhaps even more hopelessly than in less labyrinthine universes, *ultimate* consequences are in general unknowable. In this lies the innocence, both touching and dangerous, of the standard utilitarian advocacy of active government.

Take, in this context, the textbook injunction regarding state action to deal with 'externalities': 'the presence of externalities does *not* automatically justify government intervention. Only an *explicit comparison of benefits and costs* can provide reasonable grounds for such a decision.'[18] The statement is impeccably cautious and disarming. What could be more innocuous, more unexceptionable than to refrain from intervening unless the cost–benefit comparison is favourable? Yet it treats the balancing of benefits and costs, good and bad consequences, as if the logical status of such balancing were a settled matter, as if it were technically perhaps demanding but philosophically straightforward. Costs and benefits, however, stretch into the future (problems of predictability) and benefits do not normally or exclusively accrue to the same persons who bear the costs (problems of externality). Therefore, the balancing intrinsically depends both on *foresight* and on *interpersonal comparisons*. Treat-

---

17 It is only fair to remind the reader that Sir Karl Popper, in his *Poverty of Historicism*, 2nd edn, 1960, approves of piecemeal (at least as opposed to large-scale) 'social engineering' on the grounds that the piecemeal approach allows being 'always on the look-out for the unavoidable unwanted consequences' (p. 67). Being on the look-out is certainly the proper attitude. It is effective when the consequences are easy to identify and quick to appear; it is not when they are not.

18 William J. Baumol, *Welfare Economics and the Theory of the State*, 2nd edn, 1965, p. 29.

ing it as a pragmatic question of factual analysis, one of information and measurement, is tacitly taking the prior and much larger questions as having been somehow, somewhere resolved. Only they have not been.

If it is as good as impossible to foresee all or the ultimate consequences of actions upon very complex social matter, while the proximate consequences are set out in a lucid piece of explicit cost–benefit analysis, the outcome of arguments is prejudged by their form. Advocacy of the action is conducted in the language of rational argument by open minds to open minds. If the visible good consequences are found to outweigh the visible bad, it is reason itself which calls for 'improving intervention'. Opposition to it has few precise facts, little positive knowledge to marshal. It is reduced to uneasy premonitions, vague surmises of roundabout side-effects, dark mutterings about the undefined threat of state omnipresence, creeping collectivism and where will it all end? Its argument, in short, will bear the odious marks of obscurantism, political superstition and irrational prejudice. Thus will the open-minded utilitarian sheep be separated from the intuitionist goat along progressive–conservative, rational–instinctual, articulate–inarticulate cleavages.

These are quite unintended and slightly absurd consequences of the state needing, as it were, a licence to tinker, a rational justification for the piecemeal gathering of votes and clout. They nonetheless supply a perfectly possible answer (though there are others) to the puzzle of why, for the last two centuries or so, most brainy people having (or at least being trained to have) an open mind, have felt more at home on the political left, though it is easy to think of some *a priori* reasons why they might prefer to congregate on the right instead.

An object lesson in unintended and unforeseen effects is the fate of Bentham himself. He meant to provide a charter for individualism, and he fought in the name of liberty against a sluggish, obscurantist and, to his mind, despotic civil service (which regarded him as a crank and a nuisance). Yet Dicey, for whom the period from the Reform Bill to about 1870 was still the phase of Benthamism *and* individualism, calls the last third of the century the phase of collectivism and makes a chapter title out of 'The Debt of Collectivism to Benthamism'.[19] Incontestably, at least in English-speaking countries,

19   A.V. Dicey, *Lectures on the Relation between Law and Public Opinion in England during the Nineteenth Century*, 1905.

Bentham has a stronger claim than the founding fathers of socialism to be the intellectual progenitor of the progress (as roundabout and occult as his parenthood of it was unintended) towards state capitalism.

The intellectual case for political utilitarianism rests on two planks. One, set lengthwise to link present action to future consequences, is the assumption of sufficient predictability. As a matter of day-to-day political judgement, the assumption of predictability tends to be replaced by the simple exclusion of the distant and the long term. Practical consideration is given to readily visible proximate consequences only ('a week is a long time in politics'). Of course, if the future does not matter, not dealing with it is as good as having perfect foresight *and* dealing with it. The second plank is, as it were, placed crosswise and lets one person's utility be balanced against that of another person. To this balancing we must now turn.

The Revealed Preference of Governments

Nothing distinguishes interpersonal comparisons of utility to determine the best public action, from the government 'revealing its preference' for certain of its subjects.

When the state cannot please everybody, it will choose whom it had better please.

While deriving the goodness of an action from that of its consequences is the feature that most visibly sets utilitarianism apart from explicitly intuitionist moral philosophies, I would argue that even this apartness is only virtual and that at the end of the day utilitarianism is swallowed up by intuitionism. The steps in this argument lead once more to the realm of unintended effects. The nominal priority accorded to individual values leads, through the subordination of the lesser utility of some persons to the greater utility of others, to the *exercise of state 'intuition' to compare utilities,* and to the enhancement of state power.

Defining good actions as those which have good consequences defers the question and asks at one remove, Which consequence is a good one? The received answer is partly dross: the word useful (utile) has pedestrian, mundane and narrowly hedonistic connotations which indicate a value system lacking nobility, beauty, altruism and transcendence. Some utilitarians, not least Bentham himself, bear the guilt for letting this false understanding get into the textbooks. Strictly, however, it ought to be discarded. In a suitably general form, utilitarianism tells us to regard a consequence as good if it is liked, no matter whether it is 'pushpin or poetry' and no matter why; certainly not exclusively, and perhaps not at all, because it is useful. The liked consequence is synonymous with the satisfaction of a desire as well as with the fulfilment of an end, and it is 'the measure of right or wrong'. The subject whose liking, desire or end qualifies a consequence, is always the individual. Arguments aimed at the good of the family, the group, the class or the whole society must first somehow satisfy individual criteria – they have to be derived from the several goods of the persons composing these entities. The individual person is sovereign in his likes and dislikes. No one chooses his ends for him and no one has a brief to dispute his tastes (although many utilitarians choose to restrict the domain of utility, in effect postulating that ends must be worthy of rational and moral man). Moreover, as it is clearly possible for individuals to like liberty, justice or, for that matter, divine grace, their attainment is productive of utility in the same way as, say food and shelter. It is, therefore, possible to treat utility as a homogeneous resultant, a general index of end-attainments in which their plurality is in some unspecified manner synthesized in the individual mind. Such a view presupposes that there are no absolute priorities, that for each person every one of his ends is continuous, and suitably small bits of it can be traded off at some rate against bits of any other end. Though convenient, this treatment is somewhat arbitrary and possibly wrong. Besides, merging such ends as liberty or justice into an index of universal utility would conjure away some of the important questions political theory wants to ask.

(With the pretentiousness which makes the language of the social sciences sometimes so tiresome, 'liking' is invariably transformed into its derivative 'preference'. Texts on 'social choice' usually talk of preferring, even when they do *not* mean liking *better*. This usage is now a *fait accompli* and I will conform to it as long as I do not also have to say 'betters' when I mean 'goods'. It would be a relief, though, if accepted practice did not oblige us to employ the comparative where the simple affirmative would suffice.)

Private actions, often, and public ones nearly always, have consequences for several persons, typically for entire societies. Since the unit of reference is the individual, the measure of their goodness is the *algebraic sum* of the utilities which they cause to accrue to each individual they affect. (Vaguer rankings of goodness can serve for very limited purposes only.) We are, in other words, dealing with the sum of the utilities gained by the gainers *less* that lost by the losers. If the public good is to maximized, the choice between mutually exclusive public policies must favour the one which causes the greater net positive utility. How do we tell?

The two easy cases, where we can simply ask all concerned and take their answer (or watch what they do in order to read off the preferences they reveal), are unanimity and so-called Pareto-superior choices, the latter being cases where at least one of the people concerned prefers (the consequences of) policy *A* and none prefers policy *B*. In all other cases the choice, whatever it is, could be disputed *either* because some of the people concerned would opt for *A* and others for *B or* – doubly open to dispute and more realistic as a description of political life – because there is no *practicable way of reliably consulting* everybody even on the most important choices that would affect them, nor of causing each person to reveal his preference in other convincing ways. Let me stress again in passing that the unit of rererence is still the individual; he alone has desires to satisfy and hence preferences to reveal.

To consign utilitarianism as a political doctrine to the *oubliette*, we can take the position that disputes arising out of conflicting views about the net balance of utility, are matters for knocking heads together, for there are no intellectually more acceptable means for resolving them. Consequently, unless some other doctrine is agreed for justifying its taking sides, the state ought to *lean over backwards to avoid putting itself in a position* where it *must* make choices pleasing some of its subjects and displeasing others. This leaning over backwards is, of course, the stance of the capitalist state which we have derived, from quite different premises, in chapter 1 (pp. 29–32).

The adversary state, on the contrary, positively needs occasions for taking sides, for reducing the satisfactions of some people, as this is the available coin with which to buy the support of others. To the extent that state policy and dominant ideology must advance more or less in step, dropping utilitarianism in the *oubliette* could have left the democratic state temporarily out on a limb, to be rescued eventually by the rise of substitute doctrines. It is not altogether clear whether this has, in fact, happened. Many strains of political thought, while protesting to have broken with utilitarianism, reason by what amounts to all practical purposes to the utilitarian calculus. Perhaps only properly trained socialists (who do not deal in satisfactions), are not unconscious 'closet utilitarians'. Many, if not most, liberals abjure interpersonal comparisons, yet advocate actions by the state on quintessentially interpersonal utility-maximizing grounds.

The uncompromising view of interpersonal comparisons that would deny the least place to political utilitarianism, is that to add one man's quiet contentment to the exuberant joy of another, to deduct a woman's tears from another woman's smile, is a *conceptual* absurdity which will not bear examination but, once stated, collapses of its own. When children learn that they must not try to add apples to pears, how can grown-ups believe that, if only they are performed carefully enough and buttressed by modern social research, such operations could serve as the guide to the desirable conduct of the state, to what is still fondly called '*social* choice'?

A revealing private confession by Bentham himself about the honesty of the procedure has been discovered in his private papers by Elie Halévy. Ruefully, Bentham declares, ''Tis in vain to talk of adding quantities which after the addition will continue as before, one man's happiness will never be another man's happiness . . . *you might as well pretend to add twenty apples to twenty pears* . . . This addibility of the happiness of different subjects . . . is a postulatum *without the allowance of which all practical reasoning is at a stand.*'[20] Amusingly, he was prepared to admit *both* that the 'postulatum of addibility' is logical wickedness *and* that he could not do without it. This might have caused him to pause and reflect on the honesty or otherwise of the 'practical reasoning' he wished to promote. However, there could be no question of letting 'practical reasoning come to a stand'. He accepted pretence, intellectual opportunism '*pour les besoins de la cause*', rather in the manner of the atheist priest or the progressive historian.

Conceding that the utilities of different persons are incommensurate, so that utility, happiness, well-being cannot be interpersonally integrated is, at the same time, an admission that social science operating with utilitarian premises cannot be invoked to validate

---

20 Elie Halévy, *The Growth of Philosophical Radicalism*, p. 495, quoted by Lord Robbins, *Politics and Economics*, 1963, p. 15; my italics.

claims about one policy being 'objectively' superior to another (except in the rare and politically almost insignificant case of 'Pareto-superiority'). Utilitarianism then becomes ideologically useless. If policies still need rigorous intellectual advocacy, they have to be argued for in some other, less convenient and less seductive doctrinal framework.

Against this intransigent position, three stands rehabilitating interpersonal comparisons can be discerned. Each is associated with the names of several distinguished theorists, some of whom in fact straddle more than one position. It is as arbitrary to confine them to a single stand as it is sharply to demarcate one stand from another. Partly for this reason, and partly to avoid giving offence through what can be little better than vulgarized capsules unfit to contain the whole of a subtle and complex treatment, I will refrain from attributing specific positions to particular authors. The informed reader will judge whether or not the resulting *roman à clef* represents fairly the thinly disguised real characters involved.

One stand restoring to utilitarianism its role of judging policy, is that interpersonal comparisons are obviously possible since we are making them all the time. Only if we denied 'other minds' could we rule out comparisons between them. Everyday linguistic usage proves the logical legitimacy of such statements as 'A is happier than B' (level-comparison) and, at a pinch, presumably also 'A is happier than B but by less than B is happier than C' (difference-comparison). A degree of freedom is, however, left to interpretation, which vitiates this approach. For these everyday statements can, for all their form tells us, just as well be about facts (A is taller than B) as about opinions, tastes or both (A is more handsome than B). If the latter, it is no use linguistic usage telling us that interpersonal comparisons are 'possible' (they do not grate on the ear), because they are not the comparisons utilitarianism needs to provide 'scientific' support for policies. An equally crucial ambiguity surrounds the piece of linguistic testimony that tends to be invoked in direct support of redistributive policies: 'a dollar makes more difference to B than to A.' If the statement means that the incremental utility of a dollar to B is greater than it is to A, well and good. We have successfully compared amounts of utilities of two persons. If it means that a dollar affects B's utility more than A's, we have merely compared the *relative* change in B's utility ('it has been vastly augmented') and in A's ('it has not changed all that much'), without having said anything about

B's utility-change being *absolutely* greater or smaller than *A*'s (i.e. without demonstrating that the utilities of two persons *are* commensurate, capable of being expressed in terms of some common homogeneous 'social' utility).

Another integrationist stand confronts the issue of heterogeneity, as it were head on, by proposing what I would call *conventions* for getting rid of it, rather as if Bentham had announced that he was going to feel free to call both apples and pears 'fruit' and perform additions and subtractions in terms of 'fruit-units'. These conventions can be regarded as non-empirical, not-to-be verified postulates introduced to round out a non-empirical circle of argument. It is, for instance, said that the utilities of 'isomorphic' persons, who are identical in all but one variable (e.g. income, or age) can be treated as homogeneous quantities, and it is further proposed to treat certain populations for certain purposes as isomorphic. A different convention would have us regard everybody's utility as inextricably bound up with everybody else's *via* a relation of 'extended sympathy'. Yet another approach transforms (roughly speaking) the utility functions of different people into linear transformations of one and the same function, by taking out of the parameters of preferences everything that makes them different, and putting back the differences 'into the objects of the preferences'. There is also a proposal (which I personally find disarming), to put in place of people's actual preferences the 'moral' preferences they would have if they all identified themselves with society's representative individual. A somewhat comparable convention is to regard different persons as 'alternative selves' of the observer.

These and related conventions are *an sich* harmless and acceptable alternative statements of what *would suffice* to legitimize the integration of different persons' utilities, happinesses or well-beings. They can be paraphrased to read: 'The welfares of different individuals can be added into a social welfare function if they are agreed not to be different individuals.' Such conventions may well command agreement as to the sufficient condition which *would* make the summation of personal utilities legitimate. They are, however, not to be mistaken for ways to legitimize the summation if it was not legitimate *to begin with*.

A (to my mind) diametrically opposed stand is fully to accept that individuals are different, but to deny that this must render social welfare judgements arbitrary and intellectually unclean. This stand, like the 'linguistic' one, seems to me to suffer from the ambiguity that the judgements it makes and the decisions it recommends (these being possibly two distinct functions) may be either questions of fact or matters of taste, without their form necessarily telling us which they are. If they are matters of taste – even if it is 'taste' educated by practice and enlightened by information – there is little else to be said. We are manifestly in the hands of the sympathetic observer and all depends on who has the power to appoint him. Claims that one policy is better for society than another will rest upon authority.

On the other hand, if they are to be understood as verifiable, refutable matters of fact, interpersonal comparability must mean that any difficulties we may have with adding up are technical and not conceptual; they are due to the inaccessibility, paucity or vagueness of the required *information*. The problem is how to get at and measure what goes on inside people's heads and not that the heads belong to different persons. Minimal, widely accessible information about Nero, Rome and fiddling, for example, is sufficient for concluding that, *for a fact,* there was no net gain of utility from the burning of Rome while Nero played the fiddle. Progressively richer, more precise information allows progressively more refined interpersonal findings. Thus we move forward from the non-addibility resulting from sheer lack of specific data to an at-least quasi-cardinal utility and its at least partial interpersonal comparison.[21] At least ostensibly, the contrast with proposals to ignore specificity and strip individuals of their differences, could not be more complete. The proposal here seems to be to start from admitted heterogeneity and approach homogeneity of individuals by capturing as many of their differences as possible in pairwise comparisons, as if we were comparing an apple and a pear first in terms of size, sugar content, acidity, colour, specific weight and so on through n separate comparisons of homogeneous attributes, leaving uncompared only residual ones which defy all common measure. Once we have found the n common attributes and performed the comparisons, we have n

---

21 A rigorous exposition of the types of interpersonal comparisons required for various types of 'social welfare functions' is provided by K.C. Basu, *Revealed Preference of Governments*, 1980, ch. 6.

   I have borrowed the title of this perfectly dispassionate book to head the present section because its unintentional black humour conveys so well what I take to be the irreducible core of the utilitarian solution. The only preference which is ever 'revealed' in the maximization of social welfare is *that of the maximizer*, of the holder of sovereign power over society.

separate results. These must then be consolidated into a single result, the Comparison, by deciding their relative weights.

Would, however the admission that this procedure for adding up utilities is intellectually coherent, suffice to make it acceptable for choosing policies? If the procedure were to be operated, a host of debatable issues would first have to be somehow (unanimously?) agreed by everybody whose utility gain or loss was liable to be compared in the operation. What distinguishing traits of each individual (income, education, health, job satisfaction, character, spouse's good or bad disposition, etc.) shall be pairwise compared to infer utility levels or utility differences? If some traits can only be subjectively assessed, rather than read off from Census Bureau statistics, who shall assess them? What weight shall be given to each characteristic in inferring utility, and will the same weight do for people of possibly quite different sensibilities? Whose values shall condition these judgements? If some 'equitable' way were unanimously agreed for delegating powers for taking comparative readings and setting the weights, the delegate would either go insane, or would just produce *whatever result looked right to his intuition.*[22]

The long and short of it is that objective and procedurally defined interpersonal comparisons of utility, even if they are modestly partial, are merely a roundabout route all the way back to irreducible arbitrariness, to be exercised by authority. At the end of the day, it is the intuition of the person making the comparison which decides, or there is no comparison. If so, what is the use of making intuitive interpersonal comparisons of utility so as to determine the preference ranking of alternative state policies? Why not resort directly to intuition for telling that one policy is better than the other? Intuitively deciding what had best be done is the classic role assigned to the sympathetic observer who has listened to the arguments, looked at the facts and then for better or worse exercised his prerogative. Who else is he, albeit at one remove, if not the state?

Failing unanimity on how exactly to perform interpersonal comparisons, different descriptions of the choice of policy are simultaneously possible. It can be said that the state, marshalling its

22 A non-unanimous (e.g. majority) agreement to perform interpersonal utility comparisons in certain ways, would confer the same logical status upon the utility-maximizing quality of the public action selected on the basis of such comparison, as upon those directly selected, without benefit of any interpersonal comparisons, by any sort of non-unanimous agreement (vote, acclamation or random choice).

statistical resources, its knowledge, sympathy and intuition, constructed measures of its subjects' utilities, enabling them to be added
to and deducted from each other. On this basis, it calculated the
effect of each feasible policy upon total utility, and chose the one
with the best effect. Alternatively, the state can be said to have simply
chosen the policy which it thought was the best. The two descriptions
are mutually consistent and one cannot contradict or refute the
other.

In an analogous manner, the two statements 'the state found that
increasing group *P*'s utility and decreasing that of group *R* would
result in a net increase in utility' and 'the state chose to favour group
P over group *R*' are *descriptions of the same reality*. Nothing
empirical distinguishes the two operations they refer to. Whichever
description is employed, by its choice the state will have 'revealed its
preference'. This is not to try and argue that all inquiry must stop at
this point, for it is not done to question the causes of a preference. It
is, however, a plea not to explain the state's partiality by some futile
hypothesis which can, by virtue of the irreducible arbitrariness of
interpersonal comparisons, never be falsified.

Interpersonal Justice

*Property and the freedom of contract (to be upheld) produce
unjust distributive shares (to be redressed).*

Free contracts are unfree if they are unfair.

In sketching the posture of the state consistent with letting people
sort out among themselves the bundles of goods they would rather
have (pp. 23–7), I described the capitalist state as one which,
subject only to the non-violation of third-party rights, respects
contracts entered into by consenting adults regardless of their status
and of the fairness of the terms agreed. This does not in the least
imply that such a state is impervious to ideas of fairness or justice or
that it lacks compassion for those whose lot, such as it emerges from
the interaction of contracts, is unhappy. It does imply, though, that
the state does not feel entitled to indulge its or anybody else's ideas of
fairness and feelings of compassion.

The liberal doctrine justifying the adversary state, on the other
hand, affirms (though at the outset it used to make relatively heavy

weather of the grounds for any such affirmation) that it is entitled to do so; that over a wide area of contractual relations it has licence and indeed an express mandate to do so; and that its moral entitlement and its political mandate are the twin sources of its right to employ the coercion without which the aims of fairness and compassion cannot be attained. This, in effect, is the ideology which calls upon the state to do what it would be induced to do anyway in the normal course of building and maintaining consent to its rule, 'dispensing distributive justice' being one way of describing such actions, 'buying votes, buying clout', another.

The progression from the Benthamite agenda of piecemeal improvements in social arrangements and additions to the range of public goods produced, to the liberal programme of doing distributive justice, is unbroken. In retrospect, once it is granted that a net interpersonal balance of good is not conceptual gibberish and special pleading, and that it can be brought about by promoting the (greater) good of some people at the expense of the (lesser) good of others, there is no difference in kind between forcing rich taxpayers to pay for prison reform, the eradication of cholera or a literacy campaign, and forcing them to supplement the standard of life of the poor (or, for that matter, of the less rich) in more comprehensive ways. As a matter of historical sequence, of course, there were differences of timing. The arguments for utilitarian tinkering with, say, public health or education were different, too, from those postulating the subordination of property rights to social justice or more generally to some conception of the greatest good of society. On the level of political practice, however, once the state, in a context of electoral democracy on a broad franchise, had made a habit of rewarding support, it was just a matter of cumulative consequences before relatively innocuous piecemeal tinkering proved inadequate for continuing political survival. Tenure of state power in competition with rivals came to require a progressively more systematic and consistent interference with contracts.

Interference can be of two broad kinds: *constraint*, which limits some of the terms which contracts are allowed to have (e.g. price control), and *overriding* which retroactively undoes the effect of contracts (e.g. redistributive taxes and subsidies).

When I say 'contracts', I am especially interested in their role as instruments in bringing about a certain pattern of social cooperation and the corresponding distribution of incomes. In the state of nature (in which social cooperation takes place without help or hindrance by the state), the freedom to contract has the effect that production and people's shares in the product are simultaneously determined by causes subsumed under such categories as the state of the art, tastes for goods and leisure, capital and people's capacities for various types of effort. (The reader is no doubt alert to the fact that this account of distribution glosses over formidable problems. Enterprise, what Alfred Marshall called 'organization', and labour are all put in the pot labelled 'capacities for various types of effort'. Explicit mention of the supply of labour and, above all, of the conceptually treacherous 'stock of capital' is avoided, as is that of the production function, though covertly both continue to lurk in the wings. Happily, the course of our argument does not oblige us to face these difficulties.) People in the state of nature 'get what they produce', more precisely they get the value of the marginal product of whatever factor of production they contribute. Instead of 'contribute', it is often more instructive to think of the factor they 'could but do not withdraw'. Either expression must be supplemented to allow for the quantity of the factor contributed or 'not withheld'. The capitalist, then, gets the marginal product of capital in proportion to the capital he owns. The entrepreneur, the doctor and the machine-minder get the marginal products of their various kinds of effort in proportion to their exertions. If under a regime of free contracts, all potential contracting parties follow their interest (or if those who do not – the rational altruists or the simply irrational – do not weigh too heavily), factor prices will be bid up or down to marginal value-products (and the nearer each market approaches perfect competition, the more closely will they correspond to the values of their marginal physical products).

But once we leave the state of nature, we confront an irreducible complication. The state, to live, takes a share of the total final product. Hence, outside the state of nature, marginal productivity theory can at best determine the pre-tax incomes of its subjects. Post-tax distribution becomes in part some function of the pre-tax one and in part that of the political process, the latter determining what the state shall get from each of us.

In particular, distribution will be shaped by two major activities of the state: its production of *public goods* (understood, broadly, to include law and order, public health and education, roads and bridges, etc.), and its production of *social justice* through income redistribution. On some definitions, the production of social justice becomes part of the production of public goods; this gives rise to difficulties we can safely and advantageously leave on the side. (There is a not too far-fetched sense in which the production of any public good at public expense is *ipso facto* redistributive, if only because there is no unique, 'right' way of apportioning the total cost to be borne, among members of the public according to the benefit derived by each from a given public good. Some can always be said to get a bargain, a subsidy, at the expense of others. Thus, the distinction between the production of public goods and explicit redistribution must be a matter of arbitrary convention.) Even the pre-tax pattern of distribution is, however, upset by the feedback effect which the post-tax one exercises upon it. Factors of production will, in general, be more or less readily supplied according to the price they can command and the situation of their owners (technically, the price- and income-elasticities of supply), so that if one or both are changed by taxes, there should be repercussions on output and on marginal products.

Apart from recognizing their logical possibility and indeed their likely importance, I have nothing specific to say on these repercussions. (In any case, they are difficult to come to grips with empirically.) I would, nevertheless, note a plausible *a priori* supposition regarding capital. Capital, once it has been accumulated and embodied in capital goods, cannot quickly be withdrawn. It takes time to 'decumulate' (what Sir Dennis Robertson liked to call 'disentangle') it by the non-replacement of capital goods as they lose value due to physical wear and obsolescence. The short-period supply of capital goods must, therefore, be rather insensitive to the taxation of rent, interest and profit. The suppliers of effort may or may not 'retaliate' against taxes on earned income by withholding their efforts. The suppliers of capital cannot, in the short period, retaliate against the taxation of unearned income, and it is the short period that is relevant to short-tenure politics. No immediate harm, then, is done to the economy by such measures as an excess profits tax, or rent control – an apartment block, once built, will not readily get unbuilt. It will fall down only after many years of non-maintenance. Though its neighbours might wish that it did so sooner, the resulting urban decay is at a politically safe distance away in the future.

Thus while the state can take the side of the many against the few and of the poor against the rich on the strength of arguments about the balance of total happiness or social justice, it can also favour labour over capital on grounds of economic expediency. It can, on the same ground, find arguments for favouring capital over labour as well. The availability of a diversified set of reasons for taking sides, even when some of them cancel each other out, is a great comfort to the state in assembling the system of rewards for consent upon which reposes its tenure of power. While these reasons may be regarded as mere excuses, as pretexts for doing what has to be done anyway to obey the imperatives of political survival, I think it would be wrong to suppose that for the rational state, they *must* be pretexts. The ideological commitment of the state may be perfectly sincere. In any case, it does not matter in the least whether it is or not, and there is no way of telling, as long as the ideology is the right one – by which is simply meant that it tells the state to do what the attainment of its ends calls for.

Classes which adopt an ideology telling them to do things contrary to their interest are said to be in a condition of 'false consciousness'. It is, in principle, quite possible for this to happen to the state as well, and historical examples can be found where the condition of the state fits this description. 'False consciousness' is, in particular, liable to mislead a state to relax repression in the illusory belief that it can obtain a sufficiency of consent instead, such misjudged relaxation being probably a frequent source of revolutions. Were it not for false consciousness or ineptitude or both, governments would probably last forever, states might never lose tenure. Plainly the broader, the more flexible and the less specific is an ideology, the less likely it is that false consciousness will bring to grief the state adhering to it. The liberal ideology with its malleability and plurality of ends is, from this point of view, a wonderfully safe one, in that adherence to it will rarely call for the state to stick its neck out and adopt a thoroughly risky line of conduct for its political survival. It is an ideology which typically offers many diverse 'options', each about as liberal as every other.

Reverting, after this digression about the concordance of ideology and rational interest, to the distributive shares which people, in entering into contracts, award to each other, there is of course no presumption for shares arrived at in this manner to be equal. The presumption for equality arises precisely out of the absence of valid reasons for inequality. If there are no reasons why people's shares should be such and such, or if we deny these reasons (so goes the egalitarian argument based on symmetry, on the avoidance of randomness), then they should all have equal shares. Theories of distribution, such as the marginal productivity theory, however, are coherent sets of such reasons. It is a very awkward condition for an ideology to incorporate both a positive theory of distribution and a postulate of equal shares.

Early liberal ideology, invented by T. H. Green and Hobhouse and mass-marketed by John Dewey, had not at first broken either with natural right (involving respect for existing relations of property for no other reason than that they were lawfully arrived at) or with classical and neo-classical economics (involving a disposition to consider wages and profits as any other price, a proximate effect of supply and demand). By and large, it accepted as both empirically true and morally valid, a set of reasons why the material well-being of various persons was what it was. At the same time, it was developing the thesis that relative (if not absolute) material well-being was a question of justice; that its actual distribution could be unjust; and that the state had somehow obtained a mandate to ensure distributive justice. The 'ought' was obviously destined to override the 'is'.

As it matured, the liberal ideology progressively emancipated itself from its early respect for the reasons that make distributive shares unequal. If these reasons are invalid, they cannot constrain distributive justice. Its doctrine can go where it will in all freedom. At the outset, however, this was far from being accomplished. Liberal thought sought both to accept the causes of relative well-being and to reject their effect. This *tour de force* was performed by T. H. Green, with his doctrine of a contract capable of being *apparently* free but *really* unfree.[23]

There are, in the marginal contribution type of theories of distribution, three reasons why one person's material well-being is different from another's. One is *capital*: some people, as a matter of

---

23   In the *Liberal Legislation and Freedom of Contract*, 1889, Green takes off from ground next door to the Manchester School, and lands on the Hegelian cloud. Property arises out of the conquest of nature by unequal individuals, hence it is rightly unequal. It is owed to society because without the latter's guarantee it could not be possessed. All rights derive from the common good. There can be no property rights, nor any other rights, against the common good, against society. The general will recognizes the common good.

The individual's *ownership of property, then, must be contingent on the general will approving of his tenure*, a result which is as much Jacobin as it is Hegelian. Green did not make this conclusion explicit. His successors increasingly do.

historical fact, own, and contribute to the productive process, more of it than others.[24] Another is *personal endowments,* whether innate or acquired by education, self-improvement and experience.[25] A third is work, *effort* measured in some way which can distinguish between various kinds of it. 'Organization' (in Marshall's sense), 'enterprise' (in Schumpeter's) might fit into the 'effort' category, though perhaps not very comfortably, while the reward for risk-taking must accommodate itself alongside the reward of the capital that is being risked. Taking these in reverse order, liberal thought even today (let alone a short century ago), does not strongly contest the justice of unequal shares due to unequal efforts, provided this is understood in the sense of 'hard work', carrying a connotation of *pain.* 'Hard work' in the sense of *fun,* or of passionate dedication, on the other hand, is a very much disputed ground for higher than average rewards.[26]

Personal endowments are a yet more controversial matter, for there has always been a strain of thought which implied that God-given talents, grace and beauty or the poise and assurance derived from a privileged background, were undeserved while advantages acquired by dint of application were deserved. By and large, however, earlier liberal thought did not seek to deny that people *owned their qualities* (though everybody was said to be entitled to equal opportunity to acquire at least those that education makes accessible to the ordinary plodder; there could be different views on what opportunities ought in equity to be provided for the brilliant person who gets more benefit out of the 'same' education – should he be taught less? – but those were relatively peripheral doubts). Their differential qualities, if they owned them, had to be reflected in differential rewards if marginal productivity theory, implying equal rewards to equal contributions, was to make sense. Finally, capital merited its remuneration, and though vast incomes accruing to the

---

24 'Owning' plainly excludes 'possessing *de facto* but unlawfully', and 'usurping'.

25 I find 'personal endowments' better to use than the 'natural assets' employed among others by Rawls, because it begs no unintended question of how a person has come by his endowments, 'naturally' or not – whether he was born with them, worked for them or just picked them up as he went. In my scheme, personal endowments differ from capital only in that they are not transferable; 'finders are keepers' rules out questions about their deservedness and 'provenance'.

26 Cf. Brian Barry, *The Liberal Theory of Justice,* 1973, p. 159, for the suggestion that there are enough people who enjoy, or would enjoy, doing professional and managerial jobs to enable the pay of these jobs to be brought down to that of teachers and social workers.

owners of vast amounts of capital were hard to swallow, it seemed harder yet at first to say that property is inviolable when you have only a little of it but can be violated when you have a great deal.[27] The temptation to gnaw at the edges of the principle of property's inviolability could not long be resisted. Property had to be socially responsible, it had to provide work for people, its fruits (let alone the principal!) ought not to be dissipated in extravagant spending. T. H. Green himself rather approved of industrial capital while detesting landed property, and many liberals were inclined to feel that though capital was owned by particular individuals, it was really held in trust to society, a feeling seldom offended by the archetypal turn-of-the-century capitalist who saved and reinvested all but 'the interest on the interest'.

Capital and personal endowments were thus, albeit grudgingly, admitted as legitimate causes for one person ending up with a bigger bundle of goods than another; yet the justness or otherwise of the relative bundles nevertheless became subject to public review, with the state legitimately proceeding to the adjustments deemed appropriate from such review. However, it was not the legitimate causes of inequality that produced the injustice – this would have been a patent absurdity – but the fact that some apparently free contracts were in reality (in T. H. Green's phrase) 'instruments of disguised oppression', hence their terms were capable of producing unjust distributive shares.

How to pin down this Hegelian distinction? At first sight, it looks as if it referred to the unequal *status* of the contracting parties. A contract between the strong and the weak is not *really* free. Reflection shows, though, that this will not do. When is a worker weaker than a capitalist? He must surely be weaker when he is unemployed and badly needs a job? Does it then follow that when there is a severe labour shortage, it is the capitalist who badly needs workers who is weaker? If this is the wrong symmetry to employ, what else can we say but that the worker is always weaker than the capitalist? Employment contracts are thus always unequal and it is always wages that are too low and profits that are too high.

As liberal thought did not really mean this, however, what did it

27   It is tempting to ascribe the early liberal respect for property to the Lockean tradition in Anglo-American political thought, with its close identification of property and (political) liberty. In a different culture, a different explanation would have to be found: why did the Abbé de Sieyès, a liberal in the Dewey mould who did not care a fig about Locke, think that everything should be equal except property?

mean? The more we try permutations of economic and social status, bargaining power, market conditions, the business cycle and so forth, the clearer it becomes that the operative distinction between 'strong' and 'weak' contracting parties is that the person making such distinction considers the terms agreed as *too good* for the one and *not good enough* for the other. No other ground is available for this diagnosis than his sense of justice. The *injustice of a contract,* in turn, serves as sufficient *evidence that it was entered into by unequal parties,* that it was an unequal contract. If it was unequal, it was unjust, and so we go around in circles.

When, then, is a contract unfree, an 'instrument of disguised oppression'? It is no good answering 'when it produces unjust distributive shares', i.e. when profits are excessive and wages are inadequate. This would stop us from saying 'distributive shares are unjust when they are produced by unfree contracts.' If we are to escape circularity we must find an independent criterion *either* for unfree contracts (so we can spot unjust shares) *or* for unjust shares (so we can identify unfree contracts). Pursuing the early liberal approach calls for the former, for an independent definition of the unfreedom of contracts, so we can argue *from* unfreedom *to* injustice.

The tautological criterion of the unfreedom of a contract is that it was agreed to under duress. But for such a contract to pass as *apparently free,* the duress must be unseen. If everybody could spot it, it would not be 'disguised oppression', it could not be mistaken for free. It takes a discerning eye to detect it.

The next best criterion for disguised duress, then, is that the discerning eye recognizes it as such. This, however, only defers our difficulties, for now we need an agreed independent criterion for identifying whose eyes are discerning. Who, in other words, shall have the quality of judging that a contract involves disguised duress, i.e. that it is really unfree? It is this kind of conundrum which arose in national socialist Germany over the muddled attempts in the Nuremberg laws to define who is or is not Jewish, and which Hitler is reputed to have cut through by declaring: '*Wer ein Jude ist, das bestimme ich!*' (*I shall decide who is a Jew!*).[28]

---

28 It is a gross fallacy to suppose that the rule 'it is public opinion, or the majority of voters, who shall determine whether somebody is a Jew' is morally or rationally of a superior order to the apocryphal Hitler rule. Note, however, that 'the majority of voters shall determine whether a contract is free, and whether distributive shares are just' is widely accepted by the general public.

It would seem, therefore, that for lack of independent criteria, interpersonal justice relies on the same intuitionist solution as inter-personal utility. Whoever commands power for mending the arrangements of society, and uses it, may be deemed to have assessed the effects on the utilities of all concerned, compared them and chosen the arrangement maximizing his estimate of interpersonal utility. It is meaningless to assert that he has *not* done so, or that he has falsified his *own* estimate, finding one result and acting on another. His choice will 'reveal his preference' in two equivalent senses: putting it simply, his preference for the gainers over the losers; putting it more awkwardly, his assessment of the utilities of the prospective gainers and of the prospective losers respectively, and his way of comparing the two.

This account of the finding of the balance of *utilities* goes, *mutatis mutandis,* for the discovery of distributive justice by finding the balance of interpersonal *deserts*. Whoever is using coercion to put constraints upon the terms contracts are allowed to have, and to tax and subsidize so as to correct contractual outcomes according to the just deserts of the parties, can be deemed to have sympathetically observed contracts, to have detected the instances of disguised op-pression of the weak and, in overriding such really unfree contracts, to have given effect to deserts and maximized justice as much as was politically feasible. It is futile to deny that he has done so, as it is to argue that he was *not* led by his true conception of justice. The standard liberal view is that the state which behaves as if it acted on interpersonal comparisons of utility or deserts or both, should be doing so in a framework of democratic rules so that there should be a popular mandate for its coercing the losers.

It is always comforting to ascribe coercion to a popular mandate, for everybody tends to approve more easily of a choice if 'the people wanted it' than if 'the despot wanted it'. There are, however, morally more ambiguous possibilities. Instead of the state's interpersonal preferences being the result of popular mandate, causation can be thought to run the other way. In a political system resting mainly on consent of the 'headcount' (electoral democracy) type, it is plausible to think of the state as organizing a popular mandate for its tenure of power by manifesting interpersonal preferences and promising to act in favour of selected people, groups, classes, etc. If it is successful in so doing, it can obviously be seen as balancing interpersonal utility or deserts and dispensing distributive justice along lines yielding the required result.

The attempt to tell which way round things 'really' work can hardly be subjected to empirical test. One could perhaps tentatively suggest that in 'the people's mandate directs the state' version, it is the subjects' sense of justice the state must satisfy, while in 'the state bribes people to get their mandate' it is their interest. But few people consciously believe that their interest is unjust. Unless they do, their interest and sense of justice will coincide and be satisfied by the same actions. Hurting their interest will strike them as an injustice. There will be no litmus test for telling apart a state pursuing social justice from one playing 'end-of-ideology', 'pluralist' interest-group politics.

If the state is 'merely obeying orders', carrying out the democratic mandate, responsibility for its actions lies with 'the people' whose tool it is. More precisely, it is the majority (of voters, wielders of clout, or a blend of the two, depending on the way the particular democracy works) which is responsible for the harm done to the minority. Things become more complicated if we must take the view that the state engineers a popular mandate and bears the same sort of responsibility for it as does the 'pusher' for his customers' demand for a habit-forming substance. The addict then becomes as much a victim as the person he mugs in order to feed his habit.

Obviously, if *all* contracts had been *really* free with no one made to accept unjust terms under disguised duress, the question of distributive justice would not have arisen, or at any rate not while property was still held inviolable. It was just as well for the muscular development of the democratic state that this was not found to be the case.

Unintended Effects of producing Interpersonal Utility and Justice

The constraints imposed on people by the state do not merely replace private constraints.

If people must always be bossed about and put upon, does it matter who does the bossing?

Whether it is conceived as pursuing interpersonal utility or distributive justice, the state provides a good for some of its subjects. Stretching words a little, it can be said that this good is the *intended effect* the latter were aiming at when lending their support to its policies. In the process of helping some (perhaps most) people to more utility and justice, the state imposes on civil society a system of interdictions and commands. This operation has inherent self-feeding characteristics. People's conduct will get adjusted, habits will be formed in response to the state's aids, interdictions and commands. Their adjusted behaviour and new habits create a demand for additional aids, needs for commands and so on, in a presumably endless iteration.[29] The system becomes progressively more elaborate and requires an increasing apparatus of enforcement in the widest sense. Regularly or spasmodically, the power of the state over civil society will increase.

Incremental power accruing to the state in this way is a kind of second growth, over and above the accretion of state power engendered by its expanding role as the producer of more putative interpersonal utility and justice. These servitudes impinging to varying degrees on all subjects, and the enfeebled relative position of civil society as a whole, are the *unintended effects* of the state promoting the good of its subjects.[30]

This observation is not original, the less so as the rise of state power, the modification of people's behaviour towards it (and towards each other) and the mutually reinforcing character of some of these developments belong to that momentous class of unintended effects which are not wholly *unpredictable,* yet remain largely *unforeseen.* The process is typically one within which prophecy has every chance of being disbelieved. Tocqueville saw it before any of it really happened, and Acton saw it about as soon as it started to gather momentum. When it was going strong, the liberal ideology had to find a place for it.

It did so by nurturing three separate strands of argument. The first basically denied that anything untoward was going on, that there were large and possibly ominous unintended effects piling up both in

29 I am indebted to I.M.D. Little for the suggestion that 'endless iteration' is not the unavoidable fate of this social process. Convergence towards a state of rest is logically just as possible. Nor is there an *a priori* presumption that endless iteration is more *likely* to be the case. However, the historical experience of actual societies supports the hypothesis of endless interation and does not support that of convergence towards an equilibrium where no new state commands, prohibitions and aids are forthcoming.
30 The reader may think that between the above lines there lurks a dim shadow of some 'social trade-off between justice and liberty' which, side by side with the other trade-offs between pairs of society's plural ends, is at the base of 'pluralist' political theory. No such shadow is intended. As I fail to see how a *society* can be thought of as 'choosing', I would object to a *social* trade-off intruding its woolly head here.

front and in the wake of social progress. The truth of this argument is an empirical question, the answer to it seems to me tediously evident and I do not propose to discuss it.

The second is that the hypertrophy of the state, while possibly real, is not malignant, at least not *per se*. It is what the state *does* with its increased weight and power that should condition our judgement of it. The view that great state power is intrinsically bad because it magnifies the harm individual subjects, or all of civil society, would suffer *if* the state chose for whatever reason to use it harmfully, is arbitrary and biased. The correct liberal view must be that democracy ensures that state power will not be used in ways harmful to the people. As the source of the increase in state power is precisely the extension of democracy, the very mechanism which breeds the unintended effects the reactionaries pretend to fear also breeds the safeguard against their purported dangers.

A priceless instance of this argument, unearthed by Friedrich von Hayek, figures in an 1885 speech by the very liberal Joseph Chamberlain: '*Now* government is the organised expression of the wishes and wants of the people and *under these circumstances* let us cease to regard it with suspicion. *Now it is our business* to extend its functions and to see in what ways its operations can be usefully enlarged.'[31] The validity of this argument, like all arguments using the idea of a popular mandate, depends on the proposition that the state securing the consent of enough people to its tenure of power *is tantamount to the people having instructed the state* to do what it found expedient, necessary or desirable to do. If someone can see the popular mandate as corresponding to this equivalence, he can at least hold that democracy *is* a safeguard against the state's power harming *its own supporters*, say the majority, whose will and wish it was that it should act in certain ways and adopt certain policies.

The corollary of this is that *the greater is state power, the more exacting the demands of the majority can become* and the greater the harm the state may have to do to the minority in conforming to the

---

31   F.A. Hayek, *The Constitution of Liberty*, 1960, p. 444, my italics. The quotation repays study. First, we learn that what may have been true *then* is not true *now* that *we* control the state. Second, we are encouraged to embrace unintended effects, to make them into intended ones, positively to will second, third and *n*th rounds of state expansion and deliberately to push along the process of iteration engendered by the self-feeding feature of these effects. Used as we are to the contemporary state being overwhelmed by demands for 'extending its functions' and 'enlarging its operations' to help deserving interests, it may well strike us as funny that Joe Chamberlain saw a need for whetting people's appetites for the state's benefactions.

popular mandate. Along this route, we thus finally reach a perfectly Actonian conclusion about the morality of majority rule, with which liberals could not possibly agree.[32] This is perhaps why the argument about democracy being the *ipso facto* safeguard against the dangers of overmighty government is not, as a rule, pressed too hard.

The third liberal argument in defence of the state doing inter-personal good despite unintended effects which may be bad, is more viable but also more sombre. It does not seek to deny that liberal policies do cause a continuous increase of the state, of its bulk, power and penetration of many aspects of the life of civil society. Nor does it contest that being surrounded by the state on all sides can be a bad, a disadvantage to some or to all to varying degrees, primarily in terms of lost liberty but, at least for some, in terms of utility or justice, too. It would assert, though, that this ought not to deter us from soliciting the state to maximize 'total', 'social' utility or justice or both. For the loss of liberty, utility and justice which is its unintended side-effect is not a net loss.

The interpersonal balances of utility and of justice produced by state intervention are *ex hypothesi* positive, after all effects are duly accounted for, *if* they are being maximized; all the losses, including unintended ones, must be outweighed by the gains if the hypothesis of the state producing interpersonal good is to hold. But if liberty is a distinct end, separate from, say, utility, its loss may not be taken care of by the maximization of utility. It may also be that unintended effects are by their nature ill-adapted to be included in any utilitarian calculus (cf. pp. 93–4), because they always have a dimension of unpredictedness. Be that as it may, it would be foolish to deny that some liberty may be lost through the multiplication of the state's commands, its widening coercive intervention in arrangements people reach among themselves and its substitution of *just* terms for *negotiated* ones in their contracts.

What the more sophisticated versions of the liberal ideology intimate is that this is not really the replacement of freedom by unfreedom. It is, instead, the substitution of rational and systematic interference for the arbitrary, random interference with people's lives occasioned by 'the social Darwinist sweepstakes that masquerade as

---

32   The corollary could, for example, take this form: 'The stronger the blows it can deliver to smash the class enemy, the better the state of the dictatorship of the proletariat can fulfil its historic function.' Needless to say, the liberal ideology is quite unready to accept a corollary of this sort.

a free market-place'. The saving difference is that while the 'social sweepstakes' occasion interferences 'inadvertently', the state causes them 'intentionally' which, it is implied, is for some reason less bad.[33]

Some care is needed in handling this argument, which is less transparent than it looks. It would be invalid if it meant that because people are being bossed about anyway, a bossy state cannot be all that objectionable. This would be like saying that since people keep getting killed in road accidents, we might as well retain or restore the death penalty (which is at least intentional). It may be valid, however, if it means that by submitting to systematic state interference (say, the death penalty for careless driving), people escape from chance-directed private interference (say, road accidents). Three conditions must be used to make it valid.

One is empirical. Greater state interference must, as a matter of *fact,* lead to lesser interference by the forces of unplanned chance. Enlisting as a soldier, with all found, for instance, must mean that in the barracks one is really less exposed to the accident of circumstance and the whim of others than if one were picking up a living in the bazaar. Those who hold that this is in fact so usually have, in the forefront of their minds, the pursuit by the partisan state of diverse egalitarian objectives, whose realization reduces the material risks and rewards of life relative to what would prevail in the state of nature, or in my hypothetical 'policyless' capitalist state.

The second condition is that people should effectively prefer *systematic* interference by the state to *random* interference by the chance interaction of circumstances and other people's whim, provided they know both from equal experience. This must be so in order to ensure that life has not biased their preferences, inducing addiction or allergy to the situation they know better. Plainly, this condition is rarely if ever satisfied, for soldiers know the soldier's life and street traders know that of the street trader, but seldom each other's. If one prefers the barracks and the other the bazaar, we might want to say that each would have preferred the other place if only they had had a broader experience. Similarly, if the welfare state breeds people dependent on state welfare, and if given the chance they ask for more of the same (which seems to be a standard finding

33   Benjamin R. Barber, 'Robert Nozick and Philosophical Reductionism', in M. Freeman and D. Robertson (eds), *The Frontiers of Political Theory*, 1980, p. 41.

of contemporary opinion surveys), we might contend 'dialectically' that they never had the chance to develop their 'real' preferences.

Finally, the 'if we must be interfered with, better let the state do it' argument must meet a third condition. Granted that state interference can replace and relieve private interference, the rate at which it can accomplish this must (in some widely acceptable sense) be 'cheap', a favourable one. If it takes a crushing system of state coercion to get rid of a mildly irritating dose of private arbitrariness, the state coercion would not be worth accepting, almost regardless of people's preferences between a safely regimented and a chance-ridden life. The converse is obviously the case if the rate of substitution works the other way. A formal bit of theory could be made to rest upon this condition, along 'diminishing returns' lines borrowed from economics. At the start of the liberal state, a 'small amount' of public constraint could liberate people from a 'large' private one, with the rate of exchange between regular and irregular constraints steadily worsening as more and more private arbitrariness and accidents of circumstance were eliminated by the state's pursuit of interpersonal utility and distributive justice until, with every nook and cranny of social relations combed for arbitrary inequalities, the unintended effects of the state doing good became excessively large and only a tiny amount of further private servitudes and unfreedoms could be got rid of at the cost of a large extension of public constraints. At some point, the 'amount' of additional public constraint needed to replace a marginal 'amount' of private constraint would, as a matter of social and historical fact, become equal to the 'amount' with which a given individual would only just be prepared to put up, in order to be relieved of a marginal 'amount' of private constraint. We might, for a guilty moment, suppose that the individual in question was representative of his whole society. Feeling by definition more comfortable at this point of the liberal evolution than at a more (or less) 'advanced' point, society would choose to stop awhile. Such a point would stand for the stage of social progress where we would wish the state to pause, the equilibrium 'mix' between public direction and private liberty, public goods and private consumption, mandatory price and income 'policy' and free bargaining, public and private ownership of the 'means of production' and so forth. (Cf. also pp. 241–2 on rolling back the state.)

Before investing the least mental effort in thinking in terms of such a construction, one would have to feel confident in assuming that people really have some substantive choice in the matter. The idea of *'stopping the state'* at the equilibrium point, or anywhere else for that matter, must be a practical one. On both theoretical and empirical grounds, it looks sheer fancy instead. However, if it were a practical possibility, one would have to give up the artifice of a representative man standing for society (which corresponds to the very special case of unanimity). We should have to admit the general case where at a given time some people want a more- and others a less-extensive state. Failing unanimity, what do we make of the amount of state bossiness which 'people' are only just prepared to accept in exchange for reduced private arbitrariness, especially since *some* people are liable to get more of the relief and *others* to bear more of the cost?

Like any other attempt to construct a collective choice theory on the back of heterogeneous preferences and interests, the problem has no spontaneous solution. It requires the assignation, by some sovereign authority, of weights to the diverse preferences in place, to enable an interpersonal balance to be struck. There we go round and round, falling back upon the state (or an authority very much like it) to decide how much state would suit people best.

Whichever way the resultant of these arguments is taken to point, there is always a fallback position which would simply maintain that since people differ, no advice can be tendered on whether 'on balance' they feel better or less put upon in the barracks than in the bazaar; hence, if there is something in the very mechanics of consent to state power which *makes* their life progressively more like the barracks and less like the bazaar, so be it.

There is, nevertheless, room here for a prior consideration, on which prudential advice may not be out of place. The problem of putting up with the *unintended* effects discussed here bears some analogy with the problem of the *intentional* bargain the political hedonist, seeking to escape alleged Hobbesian lawlessness, concludes in entering into the social contract (cf. p. 43). *Mutatis mutandis*, it also resembles the abdication of power by the capitalist class to the state for a more efficient oppression of the proletariat (cf. pp. 53–4). In either case, the contracting party is relieved of conflict with his like, man with man and class with class; his conflict is assumed, his battle is fought by the state instead. In exchange, the political hedonist, whether a person or a class, is disarmed and in this helpless condition is exposed to the risk of conflict with the state itself.

In conflict with his own kind, he would have the faculty of appeal, of *recourse to a superior instance*. Freedom from conflict of like with like, however, puts him in potential *conflict with the higher instance*. In opting for the latter, the possibility of recourse is given up. The state cannot be seriously expected to *arbitrate* conflicts to which it is an interested party, nor can we invoke *its help* in our quarrels with it. This is why accepting private interference, no matter how much it resembles 'Darwinist sweepstakes', is a risk of a different order from that of accepting state interference. The prudential argument against putting public in place of private constraints is not that one hurts more than the other. It is the somewhat indirect but no less powerful one that doing so makes the state unfit to perform the one service for civil society which no other body can render – that of being the instance of appeal.

3

Democratic Values

Liberalism and Democracy

Divisive policies which democratic competition forces the adversary state to adopt are promoted by the liberal ideology as contributing to universally agreed values.

Democracy is not the good life by another name.[1]

It may help in grasping some of the essential features of the liberal ideology and of the practice of the adversary state, to reflect briefly on democracy as a *procedure* and as a *state of affairs* (presumably the result of adopting the procedure). When looking at the rationale of submission to the state, I argued that political hedonism involved the acceptance of coercion as the counterpart of a benefit conferred by the state. The functioning of the state facilitated self-preservation according to Hobbes, or the attainment of a broader range of ends, according to Rousseau; the realization of these ends required co-operative solutions which (or so went the contractarian contention) could not come about without non-cooperation being deterred. The most basic role of the state was to transform non-cooperation from an irresistible option (in game-theory language, a 'dominant strategy' which the player must adopt if he is rational) into a prohibitive one. It could perform this role in diverse ways, depending on how it combined the three ingredients which make up the obedience-inducing compound of statecraft, namely repression, consent and legitimacy.

---

1 I am alluding to S.M. Lipset's frequently quoted *cri de coeur* (*Political Man*, 1960, p. 403), that democracy is not a *means* to the good life, it *is* the good life.

The expectations of the hedonist could conceivably be fulfilled even by a state pursuing *its* ends while securing the compliance of civil society by repression alone. Provided *his* ends were limited in scope and modest in extent, and those of the state did not directly compete with them (for instance, if the political hedonist wanted protection from muggers and the state wanted national greatness), both ends could be simultaneously furthered by stern government.[2] Nor would the capitalist state necessarily require consent for carrying out its unambitious programme, i.e. to impose upon society the cooperative solution of respect for life and property, to keep out 'non-minimal', 'non-capitalist' rivals and to pursue such meta-political ends as it may fancy; while if it did heavily rely on consent, it is doubtful whether it could confine itself to as modest objectives as these.

The legitimate state, admitting that time and its own good conduct and good luck did earn it this rare status, could bring about cooperative solutions to a possibly wide range of otherwise unattainable ends over and above the preservation of life and property. It could do so by simply asking its subjects to behave accordingly. However, the more it asked, the more it would use and strain its legitimacy. Even if its own ends were perfectly non-competing with those of its subjects – an obviously hard condition to fulfil – such a state would still have to consider the scope of any social contract as limited (if indeed it saw its services to society in contractual terms). Such cooperative solutions as it was prepared to ask for would, therefore, be confined within narrow bounds.

Political obedience resulting predominantly from consent, on the contrary, not only allows the social contract (or its Marxist equivalent, the transfer, by a class, of power to the state in exchange for the latter repressing another class), to be virtually open-ended in scope, but actually thrives on its ceaseless enlargement. The reason is that a state which needs its subjects' consent to its tenure of power, is *by virtue of its non-repressive nature exposed to the actual or potential competition* of rivals who solicit the withdrawal of consent from it and its award to themselves. To secure its tenure, the state cannot confine itself to the imposition of cooperative solutions where

---

2   Notably by the state drafting potential muggers into the army and leading them to pillage rich foreign towns in the manner of Bonaparte in 1796. The conflict arises later, in the follow-up: Bonaparte soon came to require, as he put it, 'an annual revenue of 100,000 men' ('*une rente de 100,000 hommes*').

there were none before, since its rivals, if they know their business, will offer to do the same *and* something more in addition.

Having done or agreed to do all the things that make some people better off and nobody worse off (which is how cooperative solutions are usually regarded), the state must go on and make some people *even better off* by making others worse off. It must engage in the wide range of policies apt to win over classes or strata, interest groups, orders and corporations, all of which involve, in the last analysis, interpersonal balancing. Specifically, it must give or credibly promise benefits to some by taking from others, for there are *no benefits left which do not 'cost' anybody anything*.[3] In this way, it must obtain a favourable balance between consent gained and consent lost (which may or may not be the same as the balance between the consent of the gainers and that of the losers). This balancing of political advantage is factually indistinguishable from the balancing of interpersonal utility or justice or both, which is supposed to underlay the maximization of social welfare or distributive justice.

I propose to call 'democratic values' the preferences subjects reveal in responding to interpersonal balancing by the state. These are likings for ends which can only be realized at another party's expense. If the other party is an unwilling loser the attainment of such ends typically requires the threat of coercion. They are realized in the course of the imposition of a particular kind of equality in place of another kind, or in place of an inequality. These imposed equalities can be thought of as primarily political or primarily economic. Though the distinction between the two is often spurious, it is always confidently made. Gladstone's England or the France of the Third Republic are, for instance, regularly berated for having achieved political without economic equality. Conversely, sympathetic critics of the Soviet Union, Cuba or other socialist states believe that they have progressed towards economic equality to the neglect of political equality.

3 Cooperative solutions are best understood as outcomes of *positive-sum* games with *no losers*. A game, however, may have losers as well as gainers and yet be considered to have a positive sum. In helping some by harming others, the state is supposed to be producing a positive, zero or negative sum. Such suppositions in strict logic imply that utilities are interpersonally comparable.

It may be said, for instance, that robbing Peter to pay Paul is a positive-sum game. If we say this, we affirm that the marginal utility of money to Paul is higher. Instead of saying this, it is perhaps less exacting to assert that it was only just or fair to favour Paul; that he deserved it more; or that he was poorer. The last argument may be an appeal *either* to justice *or* to utility, and thus has, like fudge, the strength of shapelessness.

A step is made toward the maximization of democratic values when the state reduces its capacity for repression and increases its reliance on consent; when it leans less heavily on the consent of the powerful and clever possessors of clout and more heavily on sheer numbers, for example by broadening the franchise and making the ballot really, safely secret; and when it redistributes wealth or income from the few to the many. Now do not these examples, which stretch across the breadth and length of 'political and economic' democracy, show that it is quite redundant to talk of 'democratic values'? It is the usual and sensible convention to regard everybody as preferring more power to less (at least the power to resist others, i.e. self-determination, if not the power to dominate others) and more money to less. If a move gives more power to many and less to a few, or more money to many and less to but a few, more will like than dislike the move. That is all there is to it. What is the point of baptizing the simple consequence of an axiom of rationality a 'liking for democratic values'? The objection would have to be upheld, and democracy would be seen as a mere euphemism for 'the conditions under which the self-interest of the majority overrides that of the minority' or words to that effect, were it not for the possibility of people valuing arrangements which do not serve *their* self-interest (altruism) or, what may well be more important, valuing arrangements in the mistaken belief that they do. The latter may be due as much to honest ignorance of the unforeseen or unintended effects of an arrangement (Do egalitarian policies really give more money to the poor after *all* or *most* effects on capital accumulation, economic growth, employment and so on, have been counted? Do the masses determine their own fate with one-man–one-vote?) as to dishonest manipulation, political 'marketing' and demagogy. Whichever source it springs from, Marxists would quite reasonably label it 'false consciousness', the adoption of an ideology by someone whose rational self-interest would in fact be served by a different one. A preference for democratic values, divorced from his self-interest, is the mark of many a liberal intellectual.[4]

Democracy, whatever else it may be, is one possible procedure a set of people, a *demos*, can adopt for 'choosing' among *non-unanimously preferred collective* alternatives. The most spectacular and

---

4   Is the liberal intellectual better off in the state of nature, or under state capitalism? If he just cannot tell, and if he is the sort who must nudge society, which way should he nudge it?

portentous of these choices is the award of tenure of state power. How this award is made to a contender or to coalitions of contenders, and indeed whether it can in all circumstances be made and rendered effective at all, depends on the direct or representative features of the democracy in question, on the interrelation of the legislative and executive functions, and more generally on custom. These dependences are important and interesting, but not central to my argument, and I intend to leave them on one side. All democratic procedure obeys two basic rules: (a) that all those admitted to the making of the choice (all members of a given *demos*) have an equal voice, and (b) that the majority of voices prevails over the minority. Defined in this way, members of the central committee of the ruling party in most socialist states constitute a *demos* deciding matters reserved for it in conformity with democratic procedure, each member's vote weighing as much as every other's. This does not prevent inner-party democracy from being, effectively, the rule of the general secretary, or of the two or three kingmakers in the general secretariat and the political bureau, or of two clans or two patron-and-client groups allied against the rest, or any other combination political science and gossip can think of. More extensive forms of democracy can include in the *demos* all party members, or all heads of households, all adult citizens and so on, the acid test of democracy being not who is in and who is not, but that all who are in are *equally* so.

This can have paradoxical consequences. It makes multiple, 'weighted' voting undemocratic while letting pass Athenian democracy, or that of the typical Renaissance city-state where all adult male citizens had the vote but up to nine-tenths of the residents were non-citizens. It virtually guarantees the bypassing, underhand 'fixing' or overt breach of democratic rules by calling for the same weight to be given to the voice of Cosimo de' Medici as to that of any other Florentine citizen of the 'little people', the same importance to the general secretary as to any cock-on-the-dungheap *oblast* chief. These reflections are not to be read as a complaint that democracy is not democratic enough (and ought somehow to be made more so), but as a reminder that a rule flying in the face of the facts of life is liable to get bent and to produce perverse and phoney results (though this is not sufficient reason for discarding it). Perhaps there is no conceivable rule which does not violate some important fact of life to some extent. But a rule which seeks to make anyone's vote on any matter equal to anybody else's is a *prima facie* provocation of reality in complex, differentiated communities, let alone entire societies.[5]

The other basic rule of democratic procedure, i.e. majority rule within a given *demos,* also has more and less extensive applications. The most extensive is widely considered to be the most democratic. Applied this way, majority rule means that the barest plurality, and in two-way Yes/No splits the *barest majority,* gets its way on *any* issue. Constitutional restrictions upon majority rule, notably the exemption of certain issues from the scope of choice, the barring of certain decisions and the subjection of others to qualified instead of simple majority rule, violate the sovereignty of the people and have clearly to be judged undemocratic *unless* one were to hold that the state, being *incompletely controlled* by the people, ought to have its sovereignty restricted precisely in order to enable democratic rules (or what is left of them after constitutional restrictions) to operate without fear.

I shall have occasion briefly to come back to the fascinating problem of constitutions in chapter 4 (pp. 188–95). In the meantime, suffice it to note that the logical limiting case of majority rule is where 50 per cent of a *demos* can impose their will on the other 50 per cent on any matter, it being a toss-up *which* 50 per cent does the imposing. (This is equivalent to Professor Baumol's suggested most-democratic criterion of *maximizing the blocking minority.*)[6]

Though it is not one of its essential rules, democracy is for sound practical reasons also identified in the public mind with the secret ballot. Admittedly, some democratic modes of operation like coalition-forming and log-rolling are hampered by secrecy. Trades of the 'I vote with you today if you will vote with me tomorrow' kind run up against a problem of enforcing performance if the vote is secret. The same non-enforceability would frustrate the purpose of the direct buying of votes if the sellers sold in bad faith and did not vote as they had agreed to. By far the most important effect of the secret ballot, however, is in reducing or removing altogether the risks

5   A simple, undifferentiated community in this context means not only that all its members are equal (before God, before the law, in talents, influence, wealth or other important dimensions in which equality is customarily measured), but that they are all about *equally concerned by any of the issues* which come up to be democratically decided on behalf of the community. A community of equals in the customary loose sense may have members of different occupations, sex and age groups. They will not be equally concerned by issues which impact occupations, sex or age groups differentially; most issues do.

6   It is an interesting fact that German and French company law make important provision for 'blocking minorities' (*Sperrminorität, minorité de blocage*), while British company law and American corporation law do not.

the voter runs by voting against the eventual winner who gains power and is enabled to punish him for it.[7]

Where does this leave democracy seen as the *result* of collective decisions rather than as a particular *way* of reaching them? There is no 'rather than', no meaningful distinction if we simply agree to call democracy the state of affairs, whatever it turns out to be, that results from the democratic procedure (along the lines of regarding as justice whatever results from a just procedure). But the democratic rules are not such that, provided only they are applied, reasonable men would be bound to agree that what they produce *is* democracy. Many reasonable men, in fact, consider the German Nazi electoral victory of 1933 as anti-democratic, although it resulted from reasonable observance of the democratic procedure.

Whether it is a democratic result for the majority to invest with power a totalitarian state whose avowed intention is to suppress competition for power, hence voiding majority rule, voting and all other democratic ingredients, is a question which has no very obvious answer. Like the right of the free man to sell himself into slavery, the majority's democratic choice to abolish democracy should be judged in its causal context, in terms of the feasible alternatives and the motives of the choice rather than just in terms of its anti-democratic consequences, grave as the latter may be. Whichever way the judgement may fall, even if in the end it were to find it democratic to choose totalitarianism, it is clear that its dependence on a factual context precludes the 'democratic *because* democratically arrived at' type of simple identification-by-origin.

If a state of affairs resulting from the application of recognized democratic rules is not necessarily democracy, what is? One answer, implicit in much of twentieth-century political discourse, is that 'democratic' is simply a *term of approbation* without any very hard specific content. Democracy becomes the good life. If there can be two views about what constitutes the good life, there can be two views, too, about what is democratic. Only in a culturally very homogenous society is it possible for the state and its rivals for power to share the same conception of democracy. If a contender for power believes that his gaining power is conducive to the good life, he will tend to regard political arrangements which favour his accession as

---

7   Cf. Thomas C. Schelling, *The Strategy of Conflict*, 2nd edn, 1980, p. 19. For Schelling, the secret ballot protects the voter. This is undoubtedly true. However, it is also true that it transforms him into a bad risk. Corrupting, bribing him becomes a sheer gamble.

democratic, and those which hinder him or favour the incumbent as anti-democratic. The converse holds for the tenant of state power.

Failure to understand this leads people to brand as cynical any resort to a practice that is condemned as anti-democratic when employed by a rival. A nearly perfect instance of this is the tight state control and ideological *Gleichschaltung* of French radio and television since 1958 or so, indignantly attacked by the left before 1981 and by the right since. There is no reason to suppose that either is being cynical in regarding control by the other as anti-democratic, since control by oneself is for the better and control by the others is for the worse, and there is nothing insincere in arguing from this basis.

It follows also from the conception of democracy as the good life, the desired state of affairs, that it may be necessary and justified to violate democratic *rules* in the interest of the democratic *result*. Only Marxist–Leninists go all the way in following this logical implication. Once in power, distrustful of the short-sightedness and false consciousness of the voter, they prefer to make sure in advance that elections will have a really democratic outcome. However, in non-socialist countries where the means of making sure are not in hand or are not employed, and elections take place more or less according to the classical democratic rules, the loser often considers that the result was rendered undemocratic by some undue, inequitable, unfair factor, e.g. the hostility of the mass media, the mendacity of the winner, the lavishness of his finances, etc. The sum of such complaints amounts to a demand for amending and supplementing the democratic rules (e.g. by controlling the mass media, equalizing campaign finances, forbidding lies) till finally they yield the right result, which is the sole test that they have become sufficiently democratic.

Neither as a particular procedure, nor as the political good life – the arrangement we approve – is democracy sufficiently defined. If we would narrow down a little the use of the term, this is not because we grudge the equal rights of Outer Mongolia, Ghana, the USA, Honduras, the Central African Republic and Czechoslovakia to call themselves democracies. It is rather because the attempt at formulating a tighter conception should illuminate some interesting relationships between democratic values, the state that produces them and the liberal ideology. These three elements could, for instance, be loosely linked thus: democracy is a political arrangement under which the state produces democratic values, and the liberal ideology equates this process with the attainment of ultimate, universal ends.

As defined above, democratic values are produced by the state as a result of interpersonal calculus; for instance, it will democratize the franchise or the distribution of property, if and to the extent that it expects to reap a net gain of support from such a move. But it would have engaged in the same policies if, instead of rational self-interest, it had been motivated by a liking for equality. Empirically, then, there is no test for telling apart the enlightened absolutism of the Emperor Joseph II and of Charles III of Spain from the populism of Juan Peron or of Clement Attlee; they were all, on the face of it, producing democratic values. We have good reasons for thinking, though, that the former two, relying for their power hardly at all on popular support, did not *have* to do what they did, and chose it out of a liking, a political conviction. Causality, then, runs from the monarch's preferences to the political arrangement and its democratic features. On the other hand, we might strongly presume that whether or not a Peron or an Attlee had egalitarian convictions and a desire to raise the working man (and they both had both), the exigencies of consent for their accession to and tenure of power would have obliged them anyway to pursue the sort of policies they did. If so, we would suppose causality to be running round a circuit composed of the state's liking for power, its need for consent, the rational self-interest of its subjects, satisfaction for the gainers at the expense of the losers, and the justification of this process in terms of uncontested, final values by the liberal ideology – the whole interdependent set of factors taking the form of a political arrangement with democratic features.

The two types of causation, one operating in enlightened absolutism and the other in democracy, can be told apart in an *a priori* sense by having either one, as it were, act in a 'society of equals', where all subjects (except, where applicable, the praetorian guard) are equal at least in such respects as political influence, talent and money. The enlightened absolute monarch, liking equality, and seeing his subjects equal, would be broadly content with political arrrangements as they are. The democratic state, however, would be competing with rivals for popular consent. A rival could attempt to divide society into a majority and a minority by finding some dimension like creed, colour, occupation or whatever, with respect to which they were unequal; he could then bid for the support of the majority by offering to sacrifice to them some interest of the minority, e.g. its money. Since everybody has equal political influence (one-man–one-vote, simple majority rule), if everybody followed his self-interest, the democratic incumbent would lose power to a democratic rival unless he, too, proposed *inegalitarian* policies and offered to transfer, for instance, more of the minority's money to the majority.[8] (The equilibrium conditions of this competitive bidding are sketched in chapter 4, pp. 200–5.) In a society of equals, then, democracy would act in the opposite sense to the levelling we associate with it; using some convenient criterion for separating some subjects from others, it would have to carve out a majority and sacrifice the minority to it, the end-effect being some new inequality. This inequality would then function as a democratic value approved by the majority. If democracy ever created a 'society of equals', it is possibly along such lines that it might then develop *further,* calling for an ideological adjustment which does not look unduly difficult.

In the last such historical adjustment, which began roughly when the present century did, and which replaced government as nightwatchman by government as social engineer, the ideology of the advancing state has changed in almost everything but the name. Owing to the breathtaking transformation which the meaning of 'liberal' has undergone in the last three generations, the original sense of the word is irretrievably lost. It is no use any more shouting 'Stop, thief!' at those who stole it. Speaking of 'classical' liberalism or trying to resuscitate the original meaning in some other form would be a bit like saying 'hot' both when we mean hot and when we mean cold. My use of the term 'capitalist' is, in fact, intended to avoid such misleading usage and to stand in for at least the hard core of the original sense of 'liberal'.

Hoping that this might help thin out some of the prevailing

---

8 Majority rule, with votes cast entirely according to interest, would inevitably produce some redistribution, hence some inequality in a society of *equals*. In a society of *unequals*, there would likewise always be a majority for redistribution. As Sen has remarked, a majority could be organized for redistribution even at the expense of the poor. 'Pick the worst off person and take away half his share, throw away half of that, and then divide the remainder among the rest. We have just made a majority improvement.' (Amartya Sen, *Choice, Welfare and Measurement*, 1982, p. 163.) Competition, however, ensures that the majority has more attractive, richer redistributive alternatives to vote for, i.e. that redistribution will *not* normally be at the expense of the poor. Given the choice, egalitarian redistribution would be preferred to the inegalitarian, because the potential pay-off is always greater in rich-to-poor than in poor-to-rich redistribution.

semantic fog, I will employ 'liberal' as the modern shorthand symbol for political doctrines whose effect is to subordinate individual good to the common good (leaving no inviolable right) and to entrust its realization to the state ruling mainly by consent.[9] The common good consists for the most part of democratic values, which are whatever the exigencies of consent require. In addition, however, the common good also calls for the fulfilment of an evolving variety of further goals for which there is, at any given time, no majority support. Present-day examples of such goals include racial desegregation, abolition of the death penalty, banishment of nuclear energy, affirmative action, homosexual emancipation, aid to underdeveloped countries, etc. These goals are deemed progressive, i.e. expected to become democratic values in the future.[10] Liberal doctrine holds that civil society is *capable of controlling the state* and that the latter is therefore necessarily a benign institution, the observance of democratic procedure sufficing to confine it to the subordinate role of *carrying out society's mandate* which, in turn, is some kind of sum of society's preferences.

Given this nature of the state, there is a certain unease in liberal doctrine about *freedom as immunity,* a condition which can negate the priority of the common good. Where immunity is conspicuously a privilege not shared by all, as it patently was in most of Western Europe up to at least the middle of the eighteenth century, liberalism opposes it. Its remedy is as a rule not to extend privilege as much as possible if that is not sufficient to create equality, but to abolish it as far as possible. Tawney, a most influential developer of the liberal ideology, waxes eloquent on this point:

> [Freedom] is not only compatible with conditions in which *all men are fellow-servants,* but finds in such conditions its most perfect expression.[11]

---

9 Wiser heads would perhaps judge me foolhardy for advancing a definition of liberalism, considering that 'it is an intellectual compromise so extensive that it includes *most of the guiding beliefs* of modern Western opinion.' (Kenneth R. Minogue, *The Liberal Mind,* 1963, p. viii, my italics.)

10 Liberals do *not* espouse these goals today because they expect the majority of people to espouse them tomorrow. Rather they expect the majority to do so because these goals *are* valuable. Either reason would be sufficient for boarding the bandwagon before it started rolling. The second reason, however, tells liberals that the bandwagon is morally worthy of being boarded.

11 R.H. Tawney, *Equality,* 1931, p. 241, italics in text.

What it excludes is a society where *only some are servants* while others are *masters*.[12]

Like property with which in the past it has been closely connected, liberty becomes in such circumstances the privilege of a class, not *the possession of a nation*.[13]

That freedom is most perfect when all are servants (more perfect even than if all were masters) reflects the presumption in favour of levelling down. It is not the condition of *servitude* which contradicts freedom, but the *existence of masters*. If there are no masters yet there are servants, they must be serving the state. When servitude is to the state, freedom is at its apogee; it is better that none should have property than that only some should have it. Equality and freedom are, albeit a shade obscurely, synonymous. We could hardly have come farther from the idea of the two being competing ends.

Even if it were not yet one more dimension of people's existence, like money or luck or breeding, in which equality can be violated, freedom as immunity would still have to be opposed by the liberal. *Even when we all have it,* the immunity of some curtails the state's ability to help others and consequently its production of democratic values; even *equal* freedom-as-immunity is inimical to the common good.[14]

This is strikingly manifest in the way liberal thought looks upon property. Private property, capital as the source of countervailing power, reinforcing the structure of civil society *versus* the state, used to be considered valuable both to those who owned some *and to those who did not*. Liberal thought no longer recognizes such value. It considers that democratic procedure is the source of unlimited sovereignty. It can rightfully modify or override title to property.

12   Contrast the diagnosis of Tocqueville: '*on semblait aimer la liberté, il se trouve qu'on ne faisait que haïr le maître*.' (C.A.H.C. de Tocqueville, *L'ancien régime et la révolution*, Gallimard, 1967, p. 266. English translation, *The Ancien Regime and the French Revolution*, 1966.)
13   Tawney, *Equality*, p. 242, my italics.
14   In his classic *Origins of Totalitarian Democracy* (1960), J.L. Talmon, having postulated that there is now a liberal and a totalitarian democracy but that at one time these two were one, is at a loss to locate the schism. He looks for it mainly in and around the French Revolution without claiming that he has found it. Perhaps it is impossible to find the schism; perhaps there never was one.
   Talmon seems implicitly to lean to this view in characterizing democracy as a fundamentally unstable political creed, a potential monster which must be firmly *embedded in capitalism* to be safe. He does not address the question of how this can be accomplished. As the reader who got this far will have gathered, it is part of my thesis that no such thing is possible. Democracy does not lend itself to be 'embedded in capitalism'. It tends to devour it.

Choices between private and public use of private incomes, as well as between private and public property in the narrower sense, can and in fact ought to be made *and subjected to continuous review* in pursuit of such aspects of the common good as democratic values or efficiency.

These criteria must primarily govern the scope and manner of state interference with private contracts in general. For instance, a 'prices and incomes policy' is good, and ought to be adopted regardless of the violation of private agreements it entails, if it helps against inflation without impairing allocative efficiency. If it does impair it, it ought still to be adopted, in conjunction with a supplementary measure to rectify the impairment. Liberal thought is rarely at a loss for additional measures to complete the first one, nor for policies to take care of any unintended effects the latter may produce, and so on in an apparently infinite regress, in hopeful pursuit of the original aim. (Arguably, a measure taken today is the nth echo of some earlier measure in that the need for it, in that particular shape and form, could not have arisen without the preceding measure(s); and as the echo shows no signs of dying down, n has a fair chance of growing into a very large number.) The fact that a measure brings a cascade of consequential measures in its train is a challenge to imaginative government, not an argument against it. The fact that imaginative government needs to override property rights and the freedom of contract is neither an argument against it nor for it, any more than the breaking of eggs is an argument for or against the omelette.

This exploration of some sensitive tenets of liberal doctrine may invite a parallel analysis of socialism. The reader, who incidentally would have no difficulty in doing this for himself, is likely to note a few vital points of incompatibility between the two, despite the large extent of surface resemblance which has long nourished the facile and ambiguous thesis of the 'convergence of the two world systems'. The crucial incompatibility, in my view, lies in their treatment of power and hence of property. The liberal is relatively relaxed about power. He trusts the majority to direct the state in society's best interest, which is tantamount to trusting it to award state power more often than not to him, to his friends, to the party of liberal inspiration. Consequently, while he may interfere with private property for a number of reasons, he will not do so out of a perceived *need to weaken civil society's ability to take state power away from an incumbent.*

For the socialist, however, power is a cause for deep anxiety. He sees majority rule as a licence for the rule of false consciousness, involving an unacceptable risk of relapse into reaction, due to the defeat of progressive forces by the ballots of a mindless electorate. He must have public ownership of the commanding heights of the economy (and as much as possible of the slopes and the plains, too) for public ownership (both in itself and as the corollary of *no significant private ownership*) is the best guarantee of the *security of tenure of power*. Private ownership loosens the state's control over the livelihood both of the capitalist and of the worker (in the widest sense) whom he may choose to employ. It is thus an enabling cause of opposition by both. The socialist state, less trusting than the liberally inspired one and more knowledgeable about power, thus feels a far more vital concern about property, even though its view about the relative efficacies of planning, the price mechanism, allocation or incentives may be no different from that of most non-socialist states.

The surface compatibility of liberal and socialist doctrines, however, is such that discourse in terms of one can inadvertently get caught up in the strands of the other. The ensuing cross-breeding of ideas can produce startling progeny. One area where ideological miscegenation is apt to happen is the concept of liberty, its refractoriness to definition and its nature as an ultimate, self-evident good. Not for nothing does Acton warn us to be wary: 'But what do people mean who proclaim that liberty is the palm, and the prize, and the crown, seeing that it is an idea of which there are two hundred definitions, and that this wealth of interpretation has caused more bloodshed than anything, except theology?'[15] Any political doctrine must, in order to look· complete, incorporate liberty among its ultimate ends in some fashion. The rules of ordinary speech guarantee that it is a solid value: it sounds as absurd to say 'I dislike liberty, I want to be unfree' as to assert that good is bad.[16] Moreover, one is safe to feel dispensed of any obligation to derive the goodness of liberty from some other value, to which liberty may lead as a means leads to an end, and which may turn out to be contestable. Happiness

---

15   Lord Acton, *Essays on Freedom and Power*, 1956, p. 36.
16   There must be an 'out' for the man who likes it in boot camp; some prisoners too, like the relief from responsibility and are said to prefer inside to out. To accommodate this, we can always have recourse to the dialectic understanding of freedom. The man under military discipline attains *real* freedom. Civil society governed by the state is a prerequisite of *genuine* freedom as opposed to the *virtual* freedom offered by the state of nature. Many people actually do use such arguments.

(freely translated as 'utility') and justice are on the same footing. It is impossible to say 'I am against justice', 'there is a lot to be said for unfairness' and 'utility is useless'. Such ultimate, uncontested ends can be made to play a particular role in *validating other ends* that an ideology seeks to promote.

Equality is the prime practical example. The problem of inserting it in the value system is that it is not self-evidently good. The statement 'there is a good deal to be said for inequality' may provoke vigorous disagreement; it may require backup argument; it is in any case not nonsensical. Ordinary speech tells us that it is possible to contest the value of equality. If we could see that it is derived, by a chain of propositions we accept, from the value of another end which we do *not* contest, we would not contest equality either. Utility and justice have alternatively been employed in elaborate attempts to establish equality as an uncontested end in this way. The next three sections of this chapter are intended to show that these attempts, like the squaring of the circle, are futile; equality can be made into a valuable end if we explicitly agree to put value on it, but it is not valuable *by virtue of our liking for something else.*

I know of no systematic argument trying to derive the goodness of equality from our liking for liberty in the way attempts have been made to derive it from utility or justice, perhaps because the very idea of liberty lends itself poorly to rigorous argument. On the other hand, it positively invites the muddling up of pieces from incompatible ideologies, whose result is some strange proposition like 'freedom is equal servitude' or 'freedom is enough food.' Such conceptual miscegenation, by coupling equality to freedom, gives it a piggyback ride. Carried on the back of liberty, it is smuggled in among our agreed political ends.

This is the drift of thinking of liberty (as Dewey would have us do) as 'the power to do': as material sufficiency, food, money; as an empty box unless filled with 'economic democracy'; as some fundamental condition not to be confused with the 'bourgeois' or 'classical' liberties of speech, assembly and election, all of which are totally beside the point to the 'really' (economically) unfree. (It is surely possible to interpret history as 'proving' the contrary. Why else did the English Chartists agitate for electoral reform rather than higher wages? By the same token, one can plausibly present the formation of workers' councils, the call for a multi-party system and free elections in Hungary in 1956, and of the wildfire spread of a nationwide autonomous trade union in Poland in 1980, as demands for the classical bourgeois freedoms by the 'economically' unfree. In fact, the opposite interpretation looks grossly implausible. We cannot seriously be asked to believe that it was the happy accomplishment of 'economic liberation' that has engendered the demand for bourgeois freedoms in these societies.)

It is to show up the deceptive ease with which equality rides piggyback on freedom past the most watchful eyes, that I choose a text by the usually so lucid Sir Karl Popper, who is as prominent a critic of totalitarianism as he is a distinguished logician:

> Those who possess a surplus of food can *force* those who are starving into a 'freely' accepted servitude.
>
> A minority which is economically strong may in this way exploit the majority of those who are economically weak.
>
> If we wish *freedom to be safeguarded,* then we must demand that the policy of unlimited economic freedom be replaced by the planned economic intervention of the state.[17]

The use of the word 'force' is, of course, poetic licence. What Popper is saying is that those with a surplus of food just sit back and do not volunteer to share it with those who are starving; to eat, the latter must come forward and offer to work for them. Since they cannot 'really' choose to starve, their offer to work is an acceptance of servitude. It is 'free' but not 'really' free choice. Note also that it is the minority who do this to the majority, which makes their conduct somehow even more reprehensible than if it were the other way round. Our democratically conditioned consciences have thus one more reason to approve the 'planned economic intervention of the state', though it is a little bewildering that in defence of the Open Society, we are proffered the *Gosplan*.

Poetic licence or not, the multiple confusion which finally gives us the *Gosplan* as a condition of freedom, needs sorting out. First, Popper asserts that there is an analogy between the strong bully enslaving the weaker man by the threat of force, and the rich exploiting the economic weakness of the poor.[18] But there is no such analogy. There is a plain distinction between *taking away* a man's

---

17   Karl R. Popper, *The Open Society and its Enemies*, 1962, vol. II, pp. 124–5, my italics.
18   Ibid., p. 124.

freedom (by threatening to beat him up) and *not sharing* our 'freedom' (=food) with a man who lacks it in the first place.

Second, there is confusion between the availability of choice (between servitude and starving) which is a matter of *liberty*,[19] and the equity, fairness, justice of a situation where some people have a lot of food and others none, which is a matter of *equality*. Third, confusion is spread by leaving unstated a number of assumptions which are needed to stop this situation from ending up as a normal neo-classical labour market equilibrium, where those owning a lot of food compete to hire those who own none and who compete to get hired, until hirers and hired are all earning their respective marginal (value) products.

The assumptions under which the outcome is starving or servitude are quite strong ones, though they may have some realism in particular kinds of societies. In such societies, the minority's offer of food in exchange for the majority's servitude is at least 'Pareto-superior' to letting them starve while redistribution through 'planned intervention of the state' would have generally unpredictable results, one likely possibility being that much of the food goes bad in government warehouses.

Finally, although freedom is not food, and liberty is not equality, equality may yet help justice, or be otherwise desirable, but this does *not go without saying*. Before anyone can state that the coexistence of a minority with a surplus of food and of a starving majority ought to be redressed, he has to show, either that greater equality in this respect would *contribute to other ends* in such a way that self-interest will make rational people opt for the equality in question, or that people's sense of justice, symmetry, order or reason demands it to the exclusion of contrary considerations. The endeavour to show this constitutes much of the ideological *Begleitmusik* of the development of the modern state.

To sum up and to restate some of the preceding argument. The democratic state is unable to content itself with providing benefits to its subjects that may make some better off and none worse off. In democracy, tenure of state power requires consent, revocably awarded to one of several competitors by an agreed procedure. Competition involves offers of alternative policies, each of which

---

19 For a different and much more complete formulation of this point, cf. Robert Nozick, *Anarchy, State and Utopia*, 1974, pp. 263–4.

promises to make designated people in society better off. These policies can be produced only at the cost of making other people worse off. In an unequal society, they tend to be egalitarian (and in a society of equals they should tend to be inegalitarian), to attract a majority. The majority's 'preference' for one of the policies on offer 'reveals' that its proximate effects represent the greatest accrual of democratic values. People may opt for it whether or not their interests are served thereby. The dominant ideology, liberalism, coincides with the interest of the democratic state and predisposes people under its influence to like democratic values. It calls upon the state to do for ethical reasons what it would have to do anyway to maintain its tenure. It tells people that the policy agreed to by the majority contributes to ultimate ends they all share. It also promotes additional policies, showing that they are conducive to the same ends and recommending that people opt for them when they are offered. In doing so, it both promotes and responds to the growth of the state.

Through Equality to Utility

The rule 'to maximize society's utility, equalize incomes' gains validity once incomes have been equal for long enough.

No man has more than one stomach, but this is a thin basis for holding that the more equally all goods are shared, the better.

It is part of our intellectual heritage that whatever else it may do which we hold for or against it, equalization of incomes will maximize their utility. The intuitive support which helps this proposition over the more obvious obstacles is that an extra dollar *must* mean more to the poor man than to the rich. On reflection, all that intuition really strongly supports is that a given absolute sum increases the poor man's utility relatively more (say, ten-fold) than that of the rich (say, by a tenth). Nothing in these 'cardinal' comparisons of the poor man's initial utility with its increase, and the rich man's initial utility with *its* increase, enables us to compare the two utilities, or the two increases, *between* them either 'ordinally' (in terms of bigger or smaller) or 'cardinally' (by how much bigger).

One view of this problem (with which, as chapter 2 has shown, I can't help but concur) is that we cannot do this because conceptually it just cannot be done, because interpersonal comparisons are intrinsically misdirected enterprises. If they are undertaken, all they can possibly *be known* to express is the preferences of whoever is making the comparison, and that is the end of the matter. Pursuing it beyond this point can take us into the analysis of these preferences. We will then be dealing with questions of ideology, sympathy, compassion, party politics, *raison d'état* and so forth. These or other elements can perhaps explain why the comparison fell out the way it did. They will not shed any further light on the utilities purported to have been compared.

However, the contrary view seems also to be tenable. It must be, if only because it is held by some of the most incisive minds who have addressed this problem. Thus, Little feels able to make 'rough-and-ready', and Sen 'partial', interpersonal comparisons of utility. The positive case, as distinct from the normative one, for giving some of the rich man's money to the poor man is that the same money, differently distributed, has more utility. Unless it is granted, for argument's sake, that such comparisons make sense, there is no factual case to prove, only moral judgements to be set one against the other and, as Bentham ruefully put it, 'all practical reasoning is at an end.'

Yet the intellectual tradition of discovering in equality an enabling cause of greater utility, is a positive one. Central to it is a conviction that we are dealing with matters of fact and not of sympathy. Some such conviction, albeit unconsciously and implicitly, conditions an important strand of the liberal argument about the distribution of the national income and optimum taxation.[20] It seems to me worthwhile to meet it on that ground, as if utilities could be compared and added up to social utility, and as if it was social *science* which told us that one distribution of income was superior to another.

Let me recapitulate – 'retrieve from the political subconscious' would be a truer description – the reasoning behind this conviction. It goes back at least to Edgeworth and Pigou (the former taking a more general, and also more cautious, view) and provides a robust example of the capacity of a dated theory to inspire practical contemporary thought with undiminished vigour.

At bottom the theory rests on a basic convention of economics which gives rise to fruitful theories in various branches of it, labelled

20 Other liberal arguments about redistribution are not positive but normative; they deal with *values*, not *facts*; their recommendations are supported by appeals to social *justice* rather than social *utility*.

the Law of Variable Proportions. The convention consists in assuming that if different combinations of two goods or factors yield the same utility (in consumption) or output (in production), the increments of utility or output obtained from combining increasing quantities of the one with a constant quantity of the other, are a decreasing function of the variable, i.e. each increase in its quantity will yield a smaller increment of utility or output than the preceding one. In theories of consumers' behaviour, this is also described as the 'principle of diminishing marginal utility', 'the convexity of indifference curves' or 'the falling marginal rate of substitution' of the fixed for the variable good.

Now if a person is given more and more tea while his other goods do not increase, the utility, satisfaction or happiness he derives from successive doses of tea diminishes. The intuitive support for presuming this resides in the fixity of his bundle of other goods. ('Presumption' is employed advisedly. A hypothesis framed in terms of utility or satisfaction must be a presumption, as it cannot be disproved by experiment or observation unless the context is one of uncertain alternatives, see below). The same presumption stands for any single good when all the other goods stay fixed. However, it cannot be aggregated. What is presumably true of any single good is not even presumably true of the sum of goods, i.e. income. As income increases, all goods potentially or actually *increase*. What, then, is the relevance of 'knowing' that the marginal utility of each good falls if the quantity of the others remains *fixed*? The diminishing marginal utility of *tea* conditions the mind to acceptance of the diminishing marginal utility of *income,* but the temptation to argue from one to the other is a trap.

A presumption can be established for the falling marginal utility of income by defining income as all goods *except one* (which stays fixed when income rises), e.g. leisure. It is possible to suppose that the more income we have, the less leisure we would give up to earn additional income. However, if the falling marginal utility of income is a consequence of excluding one good from income, then it cannot be applied to a concept of income which excludes no good. If any good can be exchanged at some price against any other including leisure, which is by and large the case in market economies, income is potentially any and all goods, and none can be supposed fixed to give rise to falling marginal utility for the sum of the rest.

It is well established that the realm of certainties – where we are sure to get a pound of tea if only we ask for it and pay the shopkeeper the price – does not lend itself to observation of the marginal utility of income. Meaningful observation of the rate of change of utility as income changes, however, is conceptually possible in the face of risky choices. The pioneer study of lotteries and insurance, as evidence relevant to the shape of the utility function, strongly suggested that the marginal utility of income may be falling in certain income brackets and rising in others, consistent with a hypothesis that changes of income which leave a man in his class have, in a sense, a lesser value than changes giving access to a quite different kind of life: '[a man] may jump at an actuarially fair gamble that offers him a small chance of lifting him out of the class of unskilled workers and into the "middle" or "upper" class, even though it is far more likely than the preceding gamble to make him one of the least prosperous unskilled workers.'[21] We must note (and mentally carry forward to the next two sections of this chapter) that this is the precise obverse of the type of valuation of income which is supposed to induce rational people to adopt a 'maximin' defence of their interest in Rawls's *Theory of Justice*.[22]

Now anyone who carelessly reasons as if there could be a means, independent of the observation of choices involving risk, for ascertaining the marginal utility of income, is apt to say that some positive or negative utility may attach to the taking of risks, so that what risky choices measure is the marginal utility of income *plus/minus* the utility of being at risk, of gambling. Whether we would like it to mean more, or less, to say that there is positive utility in exposure to risk *means* to say that the marginal utility of income is rising. That a person is adverse to risk (declines fair gambles or is willing to bear the cost of hedging), is no more, and no less, than evidence in support of the hypothesis that the marginal utility of his income is falling. No other proof, over and above the evidence drawn from risky choices, can be produced for it. People's answers to hypothetical questions about how much 'utility' or 'importance' they attach to successive tranches of their actual (or prospective) income, are not admissible

21 M. Friedman and L.J. Savage, 'The Utility Analysis of Choices Involving Risk', in American Economic Association, *Readings in Price Theory*, 1953, p. 88. First published in *Journal of Political Economy*, 56, 1948.
22 J. Rawls, *Theory of Justice*, 1972, p. 156. The second and third 'features' invoked by Rawls to explain why his people do what they do mean, respectively, that a rise in his 'index of primary goods' (which is stated to be co-variant with his income *tout court*) would not make the Rawls man significantly better off, and a fall would make him intolerably worse off.

evidence.[23] It is baffling to be told that the observable evidence (risk-avoidance, or risk-taking) somehow adds to or subtracts from the inferred condition (the falling or rising 'marginal utility of income') of which it is the sole symptom and whose existence it alone affirms.

There is no 'law' of the diminishing marginal utility of income. Educational and career choices, financial and other futures markets,[24] insurance and gambling provide abundant evidence that all shapes of utility functions may occur, falling, constant or rising; that one and the same person's marginal utility may change direction over different ranges of income, and that there is no obvious predominance of one type of function, the others being freaks. Not surprisingly, no theory of utility maximization by promoting a particular distribution of income could be built on so general and shapeless foundations.

The Edgeworth–Pigou theory in fact stands on a better basis than this, though this goes often unrecognized in bowdlerized accounts. Satisfaction derived from income in the properly stated, full theory depends on income itself *and* on the capacity for satisfaction. Its dependence on income alone does not really yield the standard conclusion usually associated with the theory; if all goods vary with income, the marginal utility of income need not be falling and we cannot say anything much about what an egalitarian redistribution of incomes would do to 'total utility'. Its dependence on the capacity for satisfaction, on the contrary, looks like leading to the desired result. As income rises in the face of a *fixed* capacity for satisfaction, the makings of a law of diminishing returns are all there, with intuitive support provided by the concept of satiety. If we have, then, two forces acting on the marginal utility of income and the effect of the first can go either way without any obvious bias, while the second makes marginal utility diminish, the tendency for a falling marginal utility of income could be taken as established in a probabilistic sense.

The remaining pieces fall easily into place. Only goods which can be brought into relation with the 'measuring rod of money' are taken

---

23 'Not even the chooser himself knows his preference until he is confronted with an actual choice, and his understanding of his own preferences is to be doubted unless he is in a real choice situation.' (Charles E. Lindblom, *Politics and Markets*, 1977, p. 103.) If this stand looks a little too severe with regard to the simplest, tea-rather-than-coffee preference relation, it is no more than properly cautious when applied to whole modes of life.
24 I say 'other' futures markets to stress that financial markets are *ipso facto* markets in futures, e.g. in future interest and dividends.

into account. People have the same tastes and pay the same prices for the same goods, hence spend a given money income the same way. For purposes of 'practical reasoning', they have the same 'appetites', 'intensity of wants', 'capacity for enjoyment' or 'temperament', as the capacity for satisfaction has been interchangeably called. Inherent in the concept of capacity was the idea that it could get filled up. Successive units of income would yield successively smaller increments of utility or satisfaction as the ceiling of capacity was getting closer. Given the total income of society, total utility must obviously be the greater the more nearly equal is the marginal utility of everybody's income, for the total can always by augmented by transferring income from people having a lower marginal utility to people having a higher one. Once marginal utilities are equal all round, no further utilitarian good can be done by income transfers; total 'social' utility has been maximized. Utility, satisfaction are intangibles, attributes of the mind. The visible evidence of the all-round equality of marginal utilities is that there are no rich and no poor any more.

This evidence is persuasive if we admit the requisite meaning of interpersonal comparisons (which I have decided to do for purposes of argument, to see where it gets us) and if we interpret the capacity for satisfaction (as it used to be interpreted) as physical appetite for standard goods, or as 'the lower order of wants' which are the same for rich and poor, for 'nobody can eat more than three meals a day', 'no man has more than one stomach', etc. When, however, the capacity for satisfaction is not, or no longer, viewed in the early textbook sense of a few basic physical needs, all bets are off.[25] Though it came straight from the horse's mouth, opinion-makers and utility-maximizers never took enough notice of Edgeworth's warning: 'The Benthamite argument that equality of means tends to maximum happiness, *presupposes a certain equality of natures*; but *if the capacity for happiness of different classes is different*, the argument leads not to equal, but to unequal distribution.'[26]

With the admission that capacities for deriving satisfaction from

---

25   Thus Robert Wolff in *Understanding Rawls*, 1977, p. 173: 'A full belly of beer and pizza requires very little money, but a cultivated, tasteful, elegant lifestyle, rationally managed in order to "schedule activities so that various desires can be fulfilled without interference" costs a bundle.'
26   F. Y. Edgeworth, *The Pure Theory of Taxation*, 1897, reprinted in Edgeworth, *Papers Relating to Political Economy*, 1925, p. 114, my italics.

income may well be widely different, what is left of the injunction to take money, say, from rich fat white men and give it to poor thin brown men? Equality ceases to be the direct command of rationality, for it can no longer be identified as the road to maximum utility. Admittedly, redistributive policies could be based on differential patterns of the capacity for satisfaction while rejecting elusive utility as the end to be maximized. In the well-known example of the manic-depressive cripple, utility-maximization would call for taking money away from him since he does not get much satisfaction out of it. An alternative *maximand* might require throwing a million dollars at him, because it would take that much to raise his satisfaction to the level of that of the average sane and healthy person. The latter policy has the *equalization* of happiness (and not its maximization) as its end. It makes sense if (in order to rise to the rank of an end) equality need not be *derived from* the good, but is postulated to *be* the good.

Under the utility-maximizing tradition, two possible positions seem to remain open. One is to posit that the capacity for satisfaction is a random endowment like the ear for music or the photographic memory, and there is no sensible way to reason about where in a population it is most likely to be concentrated. If so, there is also no sensible way to judge which distribution of income is most likely to maximize utility.

The other position is to assume that although the capacity for satisfaction is not spread evenly, it is not distributed randomly either, but forms patterns which can be inferred from people's other, statistically visible characteristics, e.g. it is concentrated in the under-eighteens, in the old, in those having *and* in those not having an academic education, etc. Discerning the pattern restores the utilitarian rationale of recommendations to distribute society's income one way rather than another. Happily, scope is thus found again for social engineers to devise redistributive policies which increase total utility and political support for the proponent of the policy, though the coincidence of the two is probably less assured than it would be in the straightforward and classic case of rich-to-poor redistribution.

Is it not, however, reasonable to act on the assumption that the young, with their appetite for leisure, clothes and travel, music and parties have more capacity for satisfaction than the old with their weaker lusts and saturated wants? A policy of making tax rates progressive not only with income, as at present, but also with age, might be a good one both for social utility and for getting the youth vote. By the same token, since the old, with their mature culture and greater experience, are *cet. par.* likely to have a greater capacity for satisfaction, tax rates declining with age could both increase utility and earn the senior citizen vote. There may also be a case, on plausible grounds, for increasing the income of teachers and decreasing that of plumbers as well as for proceeding the other way round.

Moreover, it stands to reason that the intensity of wants is liable to increase with exposure to temptation, so that total utility could probably be enhanced by subsidizing, for example, readers of Sears Roebuck catalogues. On the other hand, since their enhanced capacity for satisfaction is to some extent its own reward, it would also be a good idea to tax the subsidy and distribute the proceeds among non-readers of advertisements. On balance, benefits in terms of welfare and political consent could perhaps be drawn from adopting *all* of these policies at the same time or in turn, although careful sample surveys would be required to make the underlying social engineering really precise.

This of course is just being unkind to the kind of earnest and well-meaning officiousness which the majority of politically aware people used to indulge in until quite recently and which some, for a variety of reasons, still practise. It deserves being made fun of. However, more serious reasoning remains to be done.

The rule 'to each in proportion to his wants' as a sufficient condition of utility maximization, does not simply translate into the equalization of incomes. People's wants run to many things money can buy over and above bread and dripping, beer and pizza. It is preposterous to interpret their capacity for satisfaction in the physical sense of one man, one stomach. They are much too different for the levelling of their incomes to represent a plausible approximation to solving any maximum problem. Is there any other simple redistributive policy which would look more plausible?

Waiting in the utilitarian wings for this stage of the play are such notions as 'learning by doing', *'l'appétit vient en mangeant'*, 'tastes depend on consumption' or, perhaps, 'the utility of income is an increasing function of past income.' They strain the conventional limits of economics, just as the notion that preferences for political arrangements are heavily conditioned by the very arrangements that actually prevail (cf. p. 17), strains those of political theory. The usual and time-tested approach of these disciplines is to take tastes, preferences as given. Treating them as part of the problem may, nevertheless, be worth an occasional attempt.

Rather than assuming, too implausibly, that capacities for satisfaction are given and are much the same all round, let us therefore assume that they are conditoned by people's actual satisfactions, their culture, experience and habitual standards of living which taught them to cut their coat to their cloth, to adjust their wants and to feel relatively comfortable with the things that go with that standard. The greater have been people's incomes for some learning period, the greater will have become their capacity to derive satisfaction from them, and *vice versa,* though it might be wise to suppose that in the reverse direction, the learning period needed to reduce the capacity for satisfaction is much longer.

If interpersonal comparisons were 'on', the impartial spectator might find that there was little to choose between the happiness gained by giving a dollar to the representative underprivileged man and the happiness lost by taking a dollar from the representative well-to-do one (before counting the happiness the one loses by being coerced and the other gains by feeling the state's helping hand under his elbow, and the impartial spectator, to do his job properly, must count these gains and losses, too). Barring the *new poor* and the *new rich,* at the end of the day there is probably no utilitarian case left for tampering with the incomes people actually have. If any policy conclusion can be supported by abstract reasoning of this sort, it may well be that the existing distribution of income, if it has prevailed for some time, is more likely than any other to maximize total utility (and if such issue to the argument disgusted people sufficiently to make them stop thinking, however unconsciously, about how to maximize social utility, the quality of political debate would no doubt improve).

Stated otherwise, if income distribution were a means to a society's greater or lesser aggregate satisfaction, the least harmful policy rule to adopt would be that every society 'ought' to get the income distribution to which its members are geared by past experience. An egalitarian society, the sort Tocqueville resignedly expected to issue from democracy, where people's natures are similar, their tastes and thoughts conform to agreed norms and their economic status is uniform, 'ought' in all probability to be given an egalitarian income distribution – except that it has already got it.

Levelling in a society which was inegalitarian to begin with would quite probably violate the utility-maximization criterion which it was supposed to serve. This is not, in itself, a very good argument against levelling unless one were to take social utility maximization seriously, and despite its great influence on the public subconscious, there is no really strong case for doing so. Whether for or against, arguments about the merits of levelling seem to me to need some other basis. Democratic values cannot be derived, as it were, from the rational man's guide to utility; equality is not rendered valuable by virtue of its purported contribution to the greatest happiness of the greatest number. Whether the democratic values are contained in the rational man's guide to social justice, is the question to be addressed next.

How Justice Overrides Contracts

If rational people wish the state to override their bilateral contracts, they must be arguing from equality to justice rather than the other way round.

A 'scheme of social cooperation' need not be bought twice, first with rewards for burdens, second with a social contract to redistribute the rewards.

Let us revert to the idea of a society where individuals have title to their property and to their personal endowments (capacity for effort, talents) and are free to sell or hire them out on voluntarily agreed terms. Production and distribution in such a society will be simultaneously determined, in the proximate sense, by *title* and *contract*, while its political arrangements will be at least closely constrained (though not wholly determined) by the freedom of contract. Only the capitalist state, with the meta-political ends we attribute to it to keep it in its place, can be comfortable within such constraints. The adversary state, whose ends compete with those of its subjects and which relies on consent to gain and keep power, must proceed by breaking them down. In the limiting case, it may substantially abolish title to property and the freedom of contract. The systematic manifestation of this limit is state capitalism.

Short of this, the state will override people's bilateral contracts in the name of a social contract. The policies effecting this will, as far as the coincidence is feasible, serve the state's own ends and help realize democratic values. Broadening the franchise and redistributing income are two typical policies of this sort, though others, too, may achieve a degree of the desirable coincidence. At all events, such policies will in general be capable of being interpreted as maximizing social utility or justice or both, and since these *maximands* are recognized as ultimate ends (requiring no justification or supporting argument in terms of *other* ends), the policies will claim to be rational for society as a whole.

The interpretation of a policy as *ipso facto* a maximizing one is a tautology *if it depends on the underlying interpersonal comparisons having been favourable to it*; for such an assertion is by its nature incontrovertible. By contrast, when it takes the risk of being more than a tautology and invokes conformity to some substantive rule (which cannot be twisted and 'interpreted', but can be *seen* to be either observed, or breached) like 'to maximize utility, *equalize incomes*', 'to maximize justice, override contracts in favour of *the least advantaged*', 'to maximize liberty, give *everyone* the vote' or more cautiously phrased variations on such themes, the claim that the corresponding policies are rational stands or falls with the theory that yielded the rule.

Moved by such considerations, I shall now attempt to try out some implications of one democratic theory that was elaborated over the 1950s and 1960s by John Rawls and finally set out in his *Theory of Justice*. My choice is dictated, among other reasons by its being, to my knowledge, the only fully fledged theory within the liberal ideology of the state as the prime instrument of the justice of rewards and burdens.[27] *The state receives an irrevocable mandate from the parties to the social contract, and hence has unlimited sovereignty, to give effect to the principles of justice.*

One way of characterizing Rawls's *concept* of justice and approaching his *conception* of it (for the distinction, see his p. 5) is to suppose that at the end of any particular day people have become parties to all the feasible contracts they would like to enter into. Some will then sit up and reflect as follows:[28]

So far, I have done as well as circumstances allowed. Others more fortunately situated have done better, though those less fortunate have

---

27 Rawls's principles serve to help design 'practices' or 'institutions' which 'determine (the) division of advantages' and underwrite 'an agreement on the proper distributive shares' (*A Theory of Justice*, p. 4). (Page references in parentheses are all to this work.) He considers institutions on a high level of abstraction and generality, but it is clear, either from the context (esp. pp. 278–3) or from analysis of his arguments that the one institution that has 'bite' and that can 'underwrite' anything at all, is *the state*.

28 There is no ground for supposing, at this stage, that *all* will. The position *does not make for unanimity.*

done worse. Tomorrow, circumstances will have changed and I might do better or worse with new contracts. Some of my old contracts may work out nicely, but others might not look too good under changed conditions. Would it not be 'rational to insure (myself) and (my) descendants against these *contingencies* of the market'? (p. 277, my emphasis). I would then have an 'out' for each time I thought that my contracts were not treating me right.

As a matter of fact, I do think so now, for I feel disadvantaged by having less property and personal endowments than some others. I should like to see institutions of justice which would ensure that when my contracts provide me with 'rewards and burdens, rights and duties' which I consider less than fair, they should be adjusted in my favour. It is true, come to think of it, that every one of my contracts has another party to it, and if a contract is overridden in *my favour*, it is overridden in *his disfavour*. Now why should he agree to a 'background institution' which deals with his contracts in this way just when they are the fairest to him and he is happiest about them? Would I agree to it in his place? I would need some inducement, and surely so does he; I am quite happy to offer him something and I hope we can work something out, because without his consent, which must remain binding forever, the background institution I covet will not click into place.

This looks a candid paraphrase of that part of Rawls's theory which ought to lead to his 'contract situation', i.e. to cause the parties in the state of nature (who are assumed to be self-interested, non-altruistic and non-envious) to solicit each other *to negotiate* a social contract, a sort of omnilateral super-contract ranking above and, in case of conflict, overriding bilateral contracts.[29] Even before starting to wonder about what might be the next step, the substantive content ('the principles of justice') of the social contract, it is pertinent to ask how to create a 'contract situation' if someone, *whether or not fortunately situated,* declines to see the point of negotiating at all? Can this not happen? Can he not argue, (a) that he is doing all right

---

29 I believe it is fair to interpret Rawls as meaning that the *social contract* is a unanimous (omnilateral) agreement on principles for a state which will, by overriding ordinary (bilateral) contracts whenever the principles so require, ensure a *just* distribution. The *state of nature* is a network of ordinary contracts giving rise to a *'natural* distribution' with *no 'institutions' (no state) for making it conform to a conception of justice.* Aspects other than the distributive aspect of justice do not seem to enter into the distinction between 'social contract' and 'state of nature' in an important and explicit manner. A society equipped with *a state concerned with the preservation of life and property only,* would from the Rawlsian point of view *still be a society in the state of nature.* As he would be the first to admit, Rawls's social contract descends from Rousseau and not from Hobbes.

as it is, and *will not try to do better* under a social contract at the risk of having to accept to do worse? and (b) that the moral position to take about the justice of social arrangements (of which the division of labour is one) is *for everybody to keep his word,* whether or not it would be to his advantage to go back on it?

Argument (b), for all its Old Testament flavour, is at least consistent with Rawls's requirement that people must have a sense of justice (p. 148). The two arguments (a) and (b) seem to me to provide a quite Rawlsian rationale for prudently staying put and refusing any negotiation which would, in exchange for advantages or inducements to be defined, *release others from their contractual commitments.* The alternative is the state of nature, with 'finders are keepers' in place of the 'principles of justice'. At this stage, we cannot infer from anything that one is juster than the other, for the sole criterion of the justice of principles on offer is that, given the appropriate conditions, they would be unanimously chosen. However, appropriate conditions will not evolve through voluntary cooperation, and therefore people will not all wish to negotiate a social contract, if some have rational cause for abstaining.

Rawls's key assertion, that 'willing social cooperation' yields a net advantage, might perhaps prevent the theory from stopping short in this way. The advantage must manifest itself in an increment of society's index of 'primary goods' (provided no one makes a fuss about problems of aggregating such 'primary goods' as authority, power and self-respect) for no other advantage would be recognized under Rawls's theory of the good. Unless reflected in an increase in primary goods, there are no such advantages as 'greater social harmony' or 'no class hatreds'. This increment could presumably be distributed so that nobody was worse off and some were better off than under the distribution that is mutually agreed as plain, *de facto* cooperation unfolds.

Let us, therefore, revert to the ambition of a person B who wants to induce another person A to negotiate a social contract with power to override bilateral contracts. Under the latter, A and B (like everyone else) are already engaged in a scheme of social cooperation, producing a volume of primary goods and sharing them according to what Rawls calls a 'natural distribution' (p. 102). Each scheme of cooperation is predicated on a distribution, meaning that the resulting volume of primary goods must be wholly distributed to call forth the sort of cooperation in question. The natural distribution corresponds to *de facto* social cooperation.

Might not, however, another distribution call forth not merely *de facto*, but also *willing* social cooperation, of a sort that would yield an increment of primary goods, compared to the *de facto* one? This can, perhaps, be expected 'if reasonable terms are proposed', on which 'those better endowed, or more fortunate in their social position, neither of which we [sic] can be said to deserve, could expect the willing cooperation of others' (p. 15). Now if B wants to create a 'contract situation', he must convince A that if he were assured more reasonable terms than he is, or is liable to be, getting in the natural distribution, he would cooperate more willingly; his greater cooperation would yield an increment to pay for his 'more reasonable' (in the sense of more favourable) terms; and there would be a little something left over for A, too. But can he really deliver the required increment?

If he is not bluffing, i.e. if he is both capable and prepared to deliver it, *and* if the special terms he demands for doing so do not cost others *more* than this increment, *he would already be producing it* and *he would already be getting the special terms* under ordinary, bilateral contracts, for straightforward reasons of market efficiency. He *would* already by cooperating *more* willingly for *better* terms. That he is not, and his contracts do not already incorporate such better terms, is proof that the social contract, interpreted as redistribution in exchange for *greater* social cooperation, cannot be the *unanimous* preference of rational persons already cooperating and having agreed to a natural distribution.

Whether those better endowed deserve it or not is, in Rawls's system of choice criteria, irrelevant. The 'advantages of social cooperation' are looking very much like something of which everybody is already getting as much as he chooses to pay for. They are insufficient bait to lure him away from the mutually agreed natural distribution and into the social 'contract situation'. The extra quantity of primary goods that *greater* social cooperation with its attendant just-distributional requirements, is claimed to yield, can only be forthcoming by redistributing *more* than the extra quantity obtained (so that at least some must lose).

What are we to make of Rawls's contrary assertion that 'representative men do not gain at one another's expense ... since only reciprocal advantages are allowed' (p. 104)? In a reasonably functioning market, prevailing terms reflect all the reciprocal advantages that can be got. How, by acting on what parameter, does the social contract, with its terms which 'draw forth willing cooperation', alter this? If Rawl means the assertion to be one about facts, it is either wrong or unverifiable. (It is the latter if it depends on the purported distinction between *willing* cooperation and *de facto* cooperation being what we wish it to be; for instance, *willing* cooperation would mean a dream world of doubled productivity, no strikes, no inflation, pride in workmanship, no alienation and no command–obedience relation, while *de facto* cooperation is the poor, shoddy, muddled, unproductive, futile and alienated world we know.) If, on the other hand, it is to be an arbitrary frontier of the area within which the argument is applicable, the theory shrinks to total insignificance.

Still less can the theory get going on the strength of the mere desire of some people to persuade others effectively to let them out of this unattractive situation, though it is the best they could have chosen, and concede more attractive terms under an overriding super-contract. Whichever way we turn it, it is impossible for everybody both to have *and* not to have conflicting interests, to choose a set of contracts and unanimously to prefer another.

Why, however, should we accept the (historically quite unsupported) postulate that the yield (in primary goods) of social cooperation increases as better-than-market terms are offered to the less-advantaged? Why do the better-endowed *have* to propose 'satisfactory terms', in the form of redistribution topping up the rewards afforded by the market, seeing that they are already getting all the cooperation which 'terms' can advantageously buy them?[30]

And if special, better-than-market terms have to be offered by someone to somebody else to draw forth his 'willing' cooperation – which seems totally unsubstantiated – why is it the better-endowed who must do the offering? Nozick took a machine-gun to shoot this sitting duck to shreds, showing that if there is any argument about

---

30 Richard Miller, 'Rawls and Marxism', in Norman Daniels (ed.), *Reading Rawls*, 1974, p. 215, argues that willing cooperation can be maintained 'for centuries' by ideological institutions and the coercive apparatus of the state (paid for out of the workers' taxes!) without any social contract about principles of distributive justice.

Interpreted in a Marxist framework, Rawls's better endowed would agree on better-than-the-market terms for workers when they feared that the centuries referred to by Miller were drawing to their historically inevitable close, and reformist remedies were the order of the day. Although they would, I believe, be hastening their demise, and be suffering from 'false consciousness' in choosing the means to their end, the argument is at least genuinely based on self-interest. Rawls's argument altogether fails to establish a basis in self-interest.

this, it must be symmetrical and cut both ways.[31] Maybe, if cooperation, or its degree or extent, is in doubt or jeopardy for some unexplained reason, it is the worse-endowed who would have to offer special terms to get the better-endowed to go on cooperating with them (for, as the bitter joke goes, the one thing worse than being exploited is not being exploited at all).

Rawls's book provides no answer why *new* terms should be necessary or, which seems to amount to the same thing, why rational non-altruists would all accept, let alone seek to negotiate, about distributive justice. It does have a curious answer to why, if overriding terms are necessary, it is the rich who will concede them to the poor rather than the other way round or in some other, more sophisticated and complex redistributional patterns: 'Since it is impossible to maximize with respect to more than one point of view, it is *natural*, given the ethos of a *democratic* society, to single out the least advantaged' (p. 319, my italics). The principles of justice, then, are what they are because society is democratic, rather than society being democratic because it has been found just for it to be such. The democratic ethos comes first and the requirements of justice are deduced from it.

Here, moral philosophy is standing on its head and first principles come last.[32] Principles for designing a state which will make rewards and burdens different from what they would otherwise be, must necessarily be in the relative favour of somebody. Whom should they favour? Rawls singles out the least advantaged. This might have been a random choice, but as we now know, it was not; it was derived from democracy. Making the state take the side of the least advantaged has the great convenience that the consent-dependent state is by and large inclined to do it anyway for reasons inherent in competition for getting and keeping power. The imperatives of the 'democratic ethos' which make it 'natural' to bias distribution one way rather than the other, are *prima facie* a code word for the exigencies of majority rule. If not, they must express a belief that

---

31   Nozick, *Anarchy, State and Utopia*, pp. 192–5.
32   In fairness to Rawls, he provides an account (para. 9) of what moral philosophy is about, which (if correct) would make his stand right end up. His parallel with the theory of syntax is revealing. The way people speak is the source of knowledge about language. People's moral judgements are the source of substantive knowledge about justice. If it is democratic to like equality, this tells us something about justice – though nothing as crude is implied as that the principles of justice derive from opinion polls.

there is some (democratic) value anterior or superior to justice (for if there were not, it could not give rise to a principle of justice).

One suspects, having got this far, that some notion of equality might be this value; we could in that case argue *from* equality and recommend a distribution as more just than another *because* it favoured the least favoured, without having to demonstrate that favouring the least favoured *is* just (which would be an argument *for* equality rather than *from* it).

The irony of it all is that had Rawls not tried and failed to prove in the doing, that a theory of distributive justice is possible, it would be much easier to go on believing the universalist claim for democratic values, i.e. (in essence) that equality is valuable because it is the *means to the undisputed final ends* of justice or utility or perhaps liberty, too, and hence it is rational to choose it. Rawls had made it easier for non-democrats to cry that the Emperor has no clothes.

In the basic, 'justice as fairness' version of his theory, Rawls (to my mind successfully) showed that rational self-interested people would concede special terms to each other to regulate the permissible inequalities of burdens and rewards *if the only available alternative on offer* were their equality. It is self-evident that under his key 'difference principle' (inequalities must benefit the least advantaged or else they must go) the corresponding unequal distribution, if there is one, is better for everybody. If it makes the worst-off better off than they would be under equality, it must *a fortiori* make the best-off even better off, as well as everybody in between. (If the facts of life, production functions or elasticities of supply of effort or whatever, are such that this is in practice not possible, inequalities fail to get justified and the principle commands the distribution to revert to equal.) *In an egalitarian distribution,* an egalitarian distribution tempered by the difference principle will be regarded as 'just', i.e. chosen.

Taking equality as the base case (Rawls also calls it the 'initial arrangement' and it is the 'appropriate status quo' from which his theory can get going) – *the natural presumption* – and departures from it as requiring the Paretian justification of unanimous preference,[33] is in unison with *arguing from democracy* to justice. That no

---

33 'Strong' preference at that; to justify the inequality, even the least advantaged must be better off than they would be under equality, and other groups, strata or classes (or whatever representative men represent) must be better off than the least advantaged, for otherwise there

one seems to protest that here the cart is before the horse, simply shows that Rawls is, at least on this point, quite at one with the evolving liberal ideology. (The critics who, declaring for liberalism or socialism, attack Rawls's ideological content, so to speak, 'from the left', accusing him of being a Gladstonian relic, a disciple of the despised Herbert Spencer and an apologist of inequality, seem to me to have well and truly missed the point.)

But no majority vote can settle questions of justice. In the spirit of the liberal ideology, which considers people's rewards as subject to political review purportedly guided by some ultimate value, a change in distribution which favours someone at the expense of somebody else raises a question of justice. Answers can be sought by intuitionist or utilitarian arguments. (The latter, as I have contended in chapter 2, p. 102, are really intuitionist ones at one remove.)

---

would be no inequalities to justify. (I take it that people *always* 'prefer' to be 'better off' and prefer *only* that.) The two formulations 'inequalities must be to the advantage of *every* representative man' and 'of the *least advantaged* representative man' respectively, become equivalent *vis à vis* equality as the alternative, but not *vis à vis* the general case of all possible distributions.

This is easily seen by comparing how three representative men, *A*, *B* and *C fare under three possible distributions, o, p* and *q*; total income to be distributed increases with inequality, which is the case the 'difference principle' was invented for:

	o	p	q
A	2	5	7
B	2	4	5
C	2	3	3
	—	—	—
	6	12	15

Everybody is better off in both *p* and *q* than in *o* (equality), but only *A* and *B* are better off in the more unequal *q* than in the less unequal *p*; the additional inequality of *q* is of no benefit to the least advantaged *C*, and he is merely indifferent between them (being neither envious nor altruistic). Hence *q* will be ruled out as violating at least one of the principles of justice, though it would yield three more primary goods at nobody's expense.

This perverse result of the difference principle has been spotted early on by A.K. Sen, *Collective Choice and Social Welfare*, 1970, p. 138n. Rawls, ever conveniently, can rule it out by his strange assumption of 'close-knitness', under which the improvement in the situation of *A* and *B* when placed in *q* rather than *p*, entails an improvement in the situation of *C* also (and vice versa). In other words, 'close-knitness' asserts that *p* and *q* cannot *both* be possible, so we do not have to worry about which would be preferred and which is just.

Should close-knitness fail, Rawls has recourse to a more complex 'lexicographic' difference principle (p. 83), under which inequalities are permitted if they maximize the situation of the next-least-advantaged (in this example, of *B*) once that of the least advantaged (*C*) cannot be further improved.

Close-knitness is very hard to make sense of in a scheme where the difference principle requires that some people be made worse off so the least advantaged can be made better off (e.g. by redistribution of income). *Taxing A makes C both better off* (he gets a transfer payment) *and worse off* (as close-knitness requires).

Intuitionist arguments are irrefutable and do not rise above the rank of affirmations. Rawls could have put forward his principles as deductions from the given end of equality qualified by Pareto-optimality. Equality (its ultimate goodness) would then have the status of an intuitionist value-affirmation, while Pareto-optimality would tautologically follow from (non-envious) rationality. However, in his ambition to square the circle, Rawls appears to want to deduce 'the standards whereby the distributive aspects of society are to be assessed' entirely from rationality (p. 9). His justice must consist of 'principles that free and rational persons concerned to further their own interests would accept in an initial position of equality' (p. 11). What the 'initial position', the 'appropriate status quo' needed to get the theory going really amounts to is this: Rawls, in the *formal* core of the argument, takes out equality as an end and puts it back in as the rule imposed for playing the rational decision game.

He is plainly entitled to fix any rule he likes, but he cannot oblige rational people (or any other, for that matter) to join in the game and accept its outcome forever, *unless they already share his commitment* to the article of faith that unequal endowments of property and talent must not be allowed to shape a distribution if it is not to be unjust. Agreement on the justice of a certain principle of distribution will be the consequence of this shared commitment. Despite appearances, and the insistence that it is an application of decision theory, the argument is still dependent on the intuitionist affirmation (however disguised) that equality is prior and can give rise to justice. The 'appropriate status quo' is the moment when the rabbit is safely in the hat, ready to be pulled out.

Unlike any other status quo, it is one where there is no social cooperation at all to start with, hence no 'natural distribution' based on bilateral contracts, and where people can have no rational reason to suppose that if there were a 'natural distribution', their share in it would be larger or smaller than their neighbours'. This is the effect of the much-discussed 'original position', where complete ignorance of their own particulars (the 'veil of ignorance') enables people to choose a distribution (which is what choosing principles to design institutions which will shape the distribution, really amounts to) out of interest unsullied by any consideration which could make one person's interest diverge from another's. Behind the veil of ignorance (which blots out not only morally arbitrary personal particulars, but also society's particulars, except for certain general sociological and economic causalities), whatever principles people, henceforth moved by interest only (for their sense of justice is incorporated in the original position), choose in order to get some social cooperation, will give rise to a just distribution. The design of the original position ensures that whatever any person chooses every other person will choose, too, since all individual differences have been defined out of it. With unanimity, no occasion for interpersonal comparisons can arise.

It is one thing to acknowledge as formally unassailable the analytic statement that principles chosen in the original position will be those of justice, given that this is how they have been defined. It is another to agree that it is Rawls's principles that would be chosen; and yet another that what Rawls's principles represent is really justice. Each of these different questions has a contentious literature, most of which I cannot even acknowledge here. Nozick (*Anarchy, State and Utopia,* Part II, section II) seems to me to deal more thoroughly and devastatingly than most with the justice of Rawls's justice, while a rigorous (and to my mind convincing) argument that rational people in the 'original position' would not choose his principles, is offered by Wolff in *Understanding Rawls,* chapter XV. (I shall be addressing a few supplementary remarks to this effect in the next section.)

Rawls's core arguments are protected by a tissue of less formal discourse designed, in the spirit of 'reflective equilibrium', to enlist our intuitive agreement, appeal to our sense of the reasonable, and often to intimate that his justice is really little more than our plain prudential interest. Social justice is to be agreed to in part because, to be sure, we *ought* to be just, and because we *like* justice but in any event because it is a good idea, and because that is what elicits social peace. Such arguments echo those that champions of the 'third world', despairing of the generosity of rich white states, have lately been resorting to: give more aid to the teeming underdeveloped millions lest they go on multiplying, and drown you in their multitude, and rise up and burn your hayricks, or at the very least become clients of Moscow.[34] Also, give more aid so you may do more trade. The use of bribe or threat to induce us to do the right thing is hardly less blatant in Rawls. As Little puts it in his pithy paraphrase: (in the

---

34 If this were so, it ought surely to be taken by nations opposed to Moscow as a potent foreign policy reason for *not* increasing aid, in order to hang all these teeming millions around Moscow's neck.

original position) 'each participant would agree that anyone who is going to be rich in the society he votes for must be coerced to aid the poor, because otherwise the poor may upset the applecart and he would not choose to be an apple in so unstable a cart. This sounds to me more like expediency than justice.'[35]

Moreover, to read Rawls, coercion hardly enters into it and if it does, it need not hurt. The operation of the principles of justice lets us have our cake and eat it, have capitalism and socialism, public property and private liberty all at the same time. Rawls's blandness on these deeply contentious points is astounding: 'A democratic society may choose to rely on prices in view of the advantages of doing so, and then maintain the background institutions which justice requires' (p. 281). Considering that 'relying on prices' is synonymous with letting rewards be agreed between buyer and seller, to maintain background institutions which prejudge, constrain and retroactively adjust these rewards is, to put it no higher, to send contradictory signals to Pavlov's dogs. It is, in any case, an attempt to mislead the market about 'relying on prices'. In common with mainstream liberal opinion, Rawls must feel that there is no inconsistency; first, a market economy can be got to deliver its advantages 'and then' the background institutions can do distributive justice while leaving the said advantages somehow intact. There is no inkling in any of this of the possibly quite complex unintended effects of having the price system promise one set of rewards and the background institutions causing another set to be delivered.[36]

Lastly, we are to rest assured that a social contract which is powerful enough to override property, and which mandates the quintessential 'background institution' (the state) to ensure distribu-

---

35 I.M.D. Little, 'Distributive Justice and the New International Order', in P. Oppenheimer (ed.), *Issues in International Economics*, 1981.
36 Among such unintended effects, a fairly obvious one is the growth of the 'black economy' and of voluntary unemployment. These, in turn, set off a self-reinforcing tendency to place an ever-weightier burden on the ever-shrinking 'legal' and gainfully employed proportion of society which lets the 'background institution' batten on it, instead of its battening on the 'background institution'.
    However, other less conspicuous unintended effects may be more powerful in the long run. I am chiefly thinking of the ill-understood ways in which the characteristics of a society change as the behaviour of one generation slowly adapts to the kind of 'background institution' implanted by the preceding generation. The lagged sequence is, in principle, capable of bringing about a steady (or why not a variably paced, or accelerating?) degeneration both of society and of the nature of the state. It may, of course, be impossible ever to agree objective criteria for telling that such degeneration is going on, let alone for judging its pace and the no doubt very involved functional relations controlling it.

tive justice, does not invest the state with noticeably more power. Power continues to rest with civil society and the state develops no autonomy. Nor has it a will to use it in pursuit of its proper purposes. No genie is let out of any bottle. Politics is just vector geometry. To quote Rawls: 'We may think of the political process as a machine which makes social decisions when the views of representatives and their constituents are fed into it' (p. 196). We may indeed, but it would be better not to.

Egalitarianism as Prudence

Uncertainty about the share they will get is supposed to induce rational people to opt for an income distribution which only the certainty of getting the worst could make them choose.

A bird in the hand is best if we must have one and if two would be too many.

If the core of Rawls's *Theory of Justice* was vulgarized *à outrance*, it could perhaps be summed up thus: Devoid of the vested interests bred by self-knowledge, people opt for an egalitarian society allowing only such inequalities as improve the lot of the least advantaged. This is their prudent option, because they cannot know whether they would do better, or worse, in an inegalitarian society. Refusing to gamble, they take the bird in the hand.

Any sophisticated intellectual construction is inevitably reduced to some easily communicated vulgarization by the time it takes root in the broad public consciousness. Only the most robust arguments, whose core is of one piece, do not in such a process get reduced to pathetic fallacies. An author who needlessly invokes complex solutions to problems which have been assumed away to begin with, soon finds that for example he is publicly reputed to have 'proved by game theory' that maximin (maximizing the minimum among alternative outcomes) is the optimal life-strategy for 'prudent men', that 'the conservative decision rule is to agree to moderately egalitarian social policies' and other words to this effect. Given the value of such terms as 'prudent' and 'conservative', myths of this type are liable to sway many minds for some time to come, albeit for reasons which Rawls would be the first to disavow.

In his system, the characteristics of the 'original position' (ignorance about one's vital particulars coupled with some selective general knowledge of economics and politics), and three psychological assumptions, together determine what people would decide if put in such a position. They will choose Rawls's second principle, notably the part of it enjoining the maximization of the minimum lot in an unknown distribution of lots, or 'difference principle'. (The case for saying that they will also choose the first principle concerning equal liberty, and bar any more-of-one for less-of-the-other type of compromise between liberty and other 'primary goods', is much less open-and-shut, but we will not concern ourselves with that.) The first point at issue is whether the psychological assumptions leading to the maximin choice can properly be made about rational men in general, or whether they represent the special case histories of somewhat eccentric persons.

The end postulated for the rational man is the fulfilment of his life-plan. He ignores its particulars except that it takes a certain sufficiency of primary goods to fulfil it; these goods, then, serve needs and not desires.[37] However, it is hard to see *what else* makes a fulfilled life-plan into a worth-while end if it is *not* the expected enjoyment of the very primary goods which go into its fulfilment; they are the means but they must also be the ends.[38] The latter is really implied in their being *goods* whose index we seek to *maximize* (rather than merely bring to a level of *adequacy*) for the least-advantaged. Yet we are told that people are not anxious to have more of them once they have enough for fulfilling the plan. They show no interest in its over-fulfilment! This position is ambiguous, if not downright obscure.

To dispel the ambiguity, one could suppose that people want to fulfil the life-plan, not because of the lifelong access to enjoyable primary goods for which it is a shorthand symbol, but as an end in itself. The life-plan is like climbing Piz Palu which we just want to do, and primary goods are like climbing boots, of no value except as tools. The life plan either succeeds, or it fails, with no half-way house. It is not a continuous variable, of which it is good to have a little and better to have a lot. It is an either/or matter; we do not want

37   John Rawls, 'Reply to Alexander and Musgrave', *Quarterly Journal of Economics*, 88, 1974.
38   Cf. the diagnosis of Benjamin Barber, 'the instrumental status of primary goods is compromised' (Benjamin Barber, 'Justifying Justice; Problems of Psychology, Measurement and Politics in Rawls', *American Political Science Review*, 69, June 1975, p. 664). His reason for finding this, though, is different from mine.

to climb Piz Palu a *little*, nor can we climb higher than its peak. The lack of interest in more than a sufficiency of primary goods would then make sense, too, for who wants two pairs of boots for climbing one mountain?

This logical consistency between the end and the means (a necessary condition of rationality) would, however, be bought at the price of imputing to rational men much the same absolute view of the life-plan that saints have of salvation. Damnation is unacceptable; salvation is exactly sufficient and nothing else matters besides; it is nonsense to want *more* salvation. The life-plan is an un-analysable whole. We do not and need not know what the good is of fulfilling it. However, it seems meaningless to wish to more-than-fulfil it, and utter hell to fall short.

There is nothing irrational *per se* in imputing an uncompromising, saintly mentality to people engaged in devising distributive institutions; saints can be as rational or as irrational as sinners. The problem is rather that, unlike salvation which has profound meaning and content for the believer, the life-plan is emptied of content if it must be abstracted from command over primary goods (i.e. if the latter are to be stopped from serving as ends); can it still be sustained that it is the goal of the rational man to fulfil it, though it looks an unexplained eccentricity to want to do so? Besides this, it is hardly worth mentioning that interpreting the life-plan as an ultimate end, and an all-or-nothing affair at that, is forbidden by Rawls's own view that it is a mosaic of sub-plans which are fulfilled separately and perhaps also successively (see chapter VII), i.e. not an indivisible goal in which you either succeed or fail.

The significance of this question resides in the role three specific psychological assumptions are called upon to play in making rational people 'choose maximin'. Take the last two first. We are told (1) that 'the person choosing ... cares very little, if anything, for what he might gain above the minimum stipend' (p. 154), and (2) that he rejects alternative choices which involve some probability, however minute, that he might get less than that, because 'the rejected alternatives have outcomes that one can hardly accept' (p. 154). If these two assumptions were to be interpreted literally, the choosers would behave as if they had the single-point objective of climbing to a chosen mountain-top. They would go for a critical quantity (index number) X of primary goods like for a pair of nailed boots; less would be *useless* and more *pointless*.

If, in addition, they knew that opting for a society with a maximin-governed distribution of primary goods (income) would in fact produce for its least-advantaged members the critical stipend X, they would choose it regardless of the relative probabilities of getting a bigger, equal or smaller stipend in other kinds of societies. If worse alternatives are simply unacceptable and better ones leave you cold, it could not possibly matter *how probable* they are. Your *maximand* is discontinuous. It is the single number X. If you can get it at all, you take it. Talking of a 'maximin' strategy and of 'choice in the face of uncertainty' is the very paradigm of the red herring.

(What happens if a maximin-principled society turns out not to be rich enough to assure for everybody a high enough minimum stipend, such as X, sufficient to let them fulfil their life-plans? Rawls is satisfied that since such a society is both reasonably just and reasonably efficient, it can safely guarantee X for everybody (pp. 156 and 169); the certitude of X, then, is a preferred alternative to facing incertitude.

This, of course, is as it may be. A society may be efficient, yet quite poor – the successive Prussias of Frederick William I *and* of Erich Honecker would probably both fit this bill – and people in the original position have no clue whether the efficient and just society they are about to devise might not be quite poor, too. James Fishkin takes the view that if a society can guarantee everybody's satisfactory minimum, it is a society of abundance 'beyond justice'.[39] On the other hand, if the stipend guaranteed by enacting maximin fell short of the critical X, people could not both regard the meagre guaranteed stipend as one they 'can hardly accept' yet rationally choose it in preference to non-guaranteed, uncertain but more acceptable alternatives.)

If uncertainty is to be something more in Rawls's theory than a redundant catch-word, a passport to the fashionable land of decision theory, his life-plan and his two psychological assumptions about the minimum stipend (i.e. that less is unacceptable and more unnecessary) must not be taken literally. Though primary goods fulfil 'needs and not desires', we must firmly recall that they are consumable goods and not tools; that no matter how little or how much of them people have, they are never indifferent to having more; and that there

39 James Fishkin, 'Justice and Rationality: Some Objections to the Central Argument in Rawls's Theory', *American Political Science Review*, 69, 1975, pp. 619–20.

is no significant discontinuity, no void above and below the satis-factory minimum stipend, but rather an intense 'need' for primary goods below and a less intense 'need' above it, so that the index of primary goods becomes a proper *maximand*, a fairly closely spaced schedule of alternative numbers, fit to be ordered consistently, instead of one lonely number. Rawls wishes the theory of justice to be a particular application of the theory of rational choice; if his assumptions are taken at face value, all occasion for choice is shut out in advance; we must interpret them more loosely so that they leave room for genuine alternatives.[40]

Having done so, we find that we have in fact glimpsed the outline of the utility function of the people concerned (despite Rawls's protestations that they behave as if they had none). It conforms to the conventional supposition of diminishing marginal utility at least in the neighbourhood of a level X of primary goods. (There is a presumption, arising from Rawls's remarks, that it conforms to it in more distant ranges, too.) If people were oblivious of this, they could not be conscious of the greater or lesser acceptability of various stipends of primary goods, and would not feel an imperative 'need' to get at least so much, nor a much less compelling 'need' to get more. Unless they had some such awareness of the relative intensity of their 'needs' (or desires?), they could not *rationally* evaluate mutually exclusive uncertain prospects of getting different lots of primary goods, except for judging that one prospect was infinitely valuable and the others were worthless.

Consider next Rawls's first psychological assumption about 'sharply discounting estimates . . . of probabilities' (p. 154). People (still in the original position) are required to choose between prin-ciples which determine types of society, which in turn entail particu-lar income distributions, under each of which they could find themselves drawing any one of the different lots of primary goods which reward differently situated people in that type of society. They can, as we know, choose an equal distribution, or maximin (likely involving some inequality), or one of a possibly large number of feasible distributions, many of which will be more inegalitarian than

---

40 Formally a believer faced with the alternatives of going to heaven or to hell (and who knows neither purgatory, nor degrees of heaven from first to seventh), would be exercising rational choice by opting to go to heaven. However, the surrounding assumptions render the choice problem trivial, or rather phoney.

maximin.[41] We also know that maximin dominates equality,[42] i.e. that no rational and non-envious person will choose the latter if he can choose the former. Other than that, however, the mere requirement of rationality leaves the remaining choices wide open as between maximin and more unequal distributions. People are uncertain what their own lot would be in each, and have no objective data at all for guessing. They are, nonetheless, said to choose one and take their chances under it.

Since they are rational, the distribution they do choose must have the property that the utilities of the alternative lots that can be drawn under it, each multiplied by the probability $(0 \leqslant 1)$ of drawing that particular lot, yield a larger total sum than would any other feasible distribution. (For 'yield' one may wish to substitute 'are thought to yield'.) This is merely a corollary of the definition of rationality. In technical language, we would say 'it is analytic that the rational man maximizes the mathematical expectation of utility.'[43] The limiting case of uncertainty is certainty, where the probability of drawing a given lot is 1 and that of drawing any other lot is 0. The rational man can then be said to be simply maximizing utility and never mind its probability.

Rawls is free to assert that his parties are 'sceptical' and 'wary of probability calculations' (pp. 154–5). If they do choose in the face of uncertainty, which is what they have been put in the original position to do, *their choices amount to imputing probabilities* to outcomes, no matter whether they do it sceptically, confidently, anxiously or in any other state of emotion. We are even free to insist that they do no

41 This must obviously remain the case no matter how much Rawls's first principle (equal liberty, whatever that may mean) and the second part of his second principle (positions open to talents) restrict the set of feasible distributions by hindering the occurrence of very small and very large incomes (pp. 157–8) – a hindrance we may well admit for purposes of argument, without conceding that Rawls has established its likelihood.
42 For completeness, we may add that if maximin dominates equality, it must also dominate income-distributions intermediate between maximin and equality, i.e. all distributions more egalitarian than itself.
43 A frequently committed howler is to confuse the mathematical expectation of utility with the utility of the mathematical expectation. (The coincidence of the two would permit the statement that the marginal utility of income was constant.) A related howler is to double-count the utility function and the attitude to risk, as in 'he does not maximize utility because he has an aversion to risk', *as if risk-aversion were not just a more colloquial term for characterizing the form of his utility function.* Cf. Rawls's version of the argument in favour of maximizing average utility: 'if the parties are viewed as rational individuals who have no *aversion to risk*' (p. 165, my italics), '*prepared to gamble* on the most abstract probabilistic reasoning in all cases' (p. 166, my italics), but not otherwise, they will maximize the mathematical expectation of utility calculated with the help of Bayesian probability. But in behaving

such thing. All that matters is that their behaviour would make sense if they did. If their conduct cannot be described in such terms, the assumption of their rationality must be given up. We can say, for instance, that people attach a probability of 1 to drawing the worst lot and probabilities smaller than 1 but greater than 0 to drawing each of the better lots; but we cannot in the same breath say that they are rational. If they were, they would not implicitly contradict the axiom that the odds of drawing all the lots add up to one.

It is easy enough to accept that if rational people were certain of drawing the worst lot under any income distribution, they would choose the one which had the 'best worst' (maximin). This would always be the best play in a game where they could choose the distribution and the opposing player (their 'enemy') could assign them their place within it, for he would be sure to assign them the worst one.[44] Rawls says *both* that people in the original position reason as if their enemy was going to assign them their lot (p. 152), *and* that they should not reason from false premises (p. 153). Presumably, the fiction of an enemy is intended to convey, without quite saying so, that people act as if they imputed a probability of 1 to the worst lot. In fact, maximin *is* designed to deal with the assumed certainty that our opponent will make moves that help him most and hurt us worst, but conveying this without saying so does not make the idea sensible in a situation where there is no enemy, no competing player, no opposing will, in short, where there is *no game*, only gratuitously introduced game-theory language.

Each person in the original position knows without a doubt that

---

at all sensibly, they must be doing this anyway! If they are averse to risk, they will take one gamble and if they are not, they will take another. If 'refusing to gamble' is purported to be rational, it must be capable of being described as the gamble where the sum of the utilities of the possible outcomes, multiplied by their probabilities (which are all zero except for one outcome whose probability is unity), is the highest. It is virtually impossible so to describe the refusal to accept the very small probability of losing a very small sum for the sake of the remaining very high probability of gaining a very large sum, i.e. the requirement is not an empty one.

Probability, as the context should have made clear, is the 'subjective' kind of which it is meaningless to say that it is *unknown*. Only 'objective', frequency-type probability tolerates being described as 'known' or 'unknown', and it tolerates it badly at that!

There is one other way in which people can be represented as 'refusing to gamble': we can suppose that they just sit down and cry.

44 This is analogous to the 'fixed-sum game' of dividing a cake among n players where the nth player does the dividing and the n-1 players do the choosing. The nth player is sure to be left with the smallest slice. He will try to make it as big as possible, i.e. divide the cake into equal slices. This is his dominant strategy. If the n-1 players are blindfolded, n has no dominant strategy.

any unequal distribution of lots must by its nature contain *some* lots that are better than the worst one, and that *some* people will draw them. What can make him sure that *he* won't? He has 'no objective ground', nor any other cause for reasonable belief, that he has no chance of being one of these people. But if the better lots *do* have non-zero probabilities, the worst one *cannot* have a probability of 1, or else the odds would not add up. Hence whatever rational people may choose in the original position, they do not choose maximin except by a fluke (in the course of 'randomizing' in a mixed strategy?), so that the likelihood of unanimous choice is as good as nil and the theory is aground.[45]

A straightforward way to refloat it would be to jettison rationality. This would be all the more tempting as real people are not obliged to be rational. They are quite capable of tying themselves up in amazing logical inconsistencies. They can both accept and contradict a given axiom (such as the one that if one outcome is certain, the others must be impossible). Freed of the harsh and perhaps unrealistic discipline of rationality, they can be supposed to behave any way the theorist may fancy. (For instance, in his numerous writings on the theory of risky choices, G. L. S. Shackle substituted poetic and pretty suggestions about human nature in place of the arid calculus of probability and utility. The 'liquidity preference' of Keynesian economics is at bottom also a resort to suggestive poetry. Many theories of producers' behaviour rely on assumptions of non-rationality – full cost pricing, 'growth' and market share objectives, rather than profit maximization, are well-known examples.) Once conduct need no longer conform to a central maximization assumption, 'anything goes', which is precisely the weakness of such approaches, though this need not prejudice their suggestiveness and teachability.

It takes only a modicum of poetic licence to impart the idea that it is a sensible thing to vote for a type of society in which you would not

45   With people knowing no more than that *every* lot has *some* non-zero probability of being drawn and all the lots together have a probability of 1 (i.e. *one*, and *only* one, of the lots is sure to be drawn), any further logical inference being 'discounted' (which is how Rawls expects his parties to reason) it is hard to see what will make their choice determinate, let alone unanimous. The plausible hypothesis seems to be that they will behave like particles in quantum mechanics, and never (short of eternity) reach agreement on a social contract.

If they were allowed to grasp a less inchoate conception of probabilities, e.g. if they could apply the principle of insufficient reason and suppose tht failing any indication to the contrary, they were as likely to draw one lot as another, they would have a better chance of reaching agreement on a distribution – which would presumably be more inegalitarian than the one ruled by the maximin 'strategy'.

come to great harm even if your particular place in it were designated by your enemy. Thus is a non-rational, impressionistic case established for maximin, the egalitarian bird in the hand as the counsel of conservatism, prudence and moderation.

Perhaps without realizing that he has moved on to non-rational territory, Rawls bolsters this case, in the spirit of his reflective equilibrium, by two related arguments. Both appeal to our intuition and he seems to regard both as decisive. One is the *strain of commitment*: people will refuse to 'enter into agreements that may have consequences they cannot accept', especially as they will not get a second chance (p. 176). This is a puzzling argument. If we play 'for real', we may of course lose what we stake. We do not get it back to play with again. In this sense, we *never* get a second chance, though we keep getting *other* chances in subsequent plays. They may be worse ones, in that we enter them *weakened* by the loss of our stake in the first play. Poker and business do have this cumulative character, where nothing fails like failure and chance favours the longest purse; pure games of chance and games of skill do not. Admittedly, if we draw a poor lot of primary goods, under the assumptions of the *Theory of Justice,* we will not get a chance to draw again in our and our descendants' lifetime. Social mobility is ruled out. Yet there is still a multitude of other gambles ahead, where we can be lucky or unlucky. Some of them, such as the choice of wife or husband, having children, changing jobs, may be as decisive for the success or failure of our 'life-plan' as the 'stipend of primary goods' we have drawn. Naturally, a low stipend may affect our chances in these gambles.[46] Gambling for the lifetime stipend is, therefore, sure to be one of the most important gambles we ever face, which should by rights be an argument for, and not against, applying to it the rules of rational decision making.

If we know at all what we are doing, the term (for a lifetime, for all posterity) over which a given lot of primary goods, once drawn, is to last us, must of course be built into our valuation of each such lot from the worst to the best. It is precisely its lifetime term which explains why it is our entire life-plan which determines the relative

---

46   Unlike poker or business where a previous loss tends to worsen present chances, certain other risky choices may not be adversely affected. For instance, a low lifetime stipend may not worsen the odds against marrying the right person or having good children.

The very question whether Swiss families are happier than Russian ones is fatuous, although the person who has agreed to draw lots for a place in Russian society does not get a second chance to draw lots for a place in Swiss society.

intensity of our 'need' for various-sized lots of primary goods. If drawing the lot of a dim-witted, idle beggar means living his life till we die, we are bound to weigh the risk of it very carefully. Our mathematical expectations of the utility of the lots among which there is such a repulsive one, must already reflect all our dread of this prospect. It seems double counting that, re-baptized 'strain of commitment', it must reflect the same dread a second time.[47]

No doubt we weigh the risk of death seriously. Death, whatever other prospects it may hold, in our culture is taken to exclude a second chance at earthly life. But it is obviously wrong to assert that the 'strain of commitment' to an unacceptable outcome makes us refuse the risk of death. Our everyday peacetime life is abundant proof that we do not refuse it. Why would the risk of living a dim, idle and beggarly life be different in kind? It must all depend on our assessment of the probabilities characterizing the risk and of the attractiveness of the possible rewards we can earn by taking the risk. The 'strain of commitment', if there is one, is a legitimate consideration entering into these assessments. As a separate and overriding consideration, it is at best poetry.

Finally, it is incomprehensible to be told that *good faith* would stop us from accepting the strain of commitment, since if we took a given risk and lost (e.g. voted for a very inegalitarian income distribution and found ourselves in bottom place), we might not be *able or willing* to pay up (i.e. to accept the bottom place). If someone lets me bet him a million dollars which (unlike 'Bet-a-million Gates') I do not have, I am acting in bad faith and he is acting rashly. But the 'original position' of Rawls is not credit betting. If I turn out a dim bottom-person in the society I chose and which treats such persons badly, there is no obvious way in which I can 'default'. How do I refuse to honour my bet and play my allotted role of a dim bottom-person given that I am one? How do I extort from the more privileged members of my inegalitarian society a satisfactory minimum stipend and an agile brain? Considering that I could not if I would (and that as a dim person I may not even want to), the fear of my own default

---

47   The prudent man's finding that risk-taking is difficult, especially if it is a risk of losing your stake, is not unlike Sam Goldwyn's celebrated profundity that forecasting is difficult, especially if it is about the future.

'Refusing to gamble' is itself a gamble, and 'not making forecasts' is a particular forecast as long as it is unavoidable for today's future to become tomorrow's present. You do not avoid exposure to it by *not* adjusting to what it might or might not be like. Your adjustment may not be successful. Not adjusting is even less likely to be successful.

will not stop me. Good or bad faith, weakness of will and shame at not honouring my bet do not enter into it.

A separate informal argument contends that people will choose maximin, i.e. a tempered egalitarian distribution favouring the worst-placed, in order to make their decision '*appear* responsible to their descendants' (p. 169, my italics). Now it is one thing to *be* responsible and another to *appear*, to be seen to be so (though the two may overlap). If I want to do what I think *is* best for my descendants and never mind how my decision will *look* to them, I am acting as if I were a principal. In seeking to do as well for them as I would for myself, I might allow for their utility (say, the time-pattern of their 'need' for primary goods) to be different from mine. My rational decision, however, must still correspond to the maximization of expected utility, except that it is my best guess of their utility I will try to maximize. If maximin is not rational for me, it does not become rational for my descendants either.

If, on the contrary, my concern is how my decision will *look*, I am acting as an employee or a professional adviser would rationally act for his principal. In addition to the latter's interest, he would consider his own. It is difficult to devise conditions in which the two are certain to coincide. For example, if he made a gain for his principal, his own reward, fee, salary or job security might not increase proportionally. If he made a loss, his own loss of job or reputation as a responsible treasurer, trustee or manager might be more than proportional. As his assessment of the *ex ante* risk entailed in an *ex post* gain need not be the same as that of his principal, it cannot even be said that if instead of acting selfishly, he tried to maximize his principal's gains he would be acting (i.e. taking the same gambles) as would the principal.[48] In general, it is unlikely that if he maximized *his* expected utility, he would also be maximizing that of his principal, or *vice versa*. The two *maxima* will tend to diverge, the decisions of the employee being usually biased to ward off possible blame and to conform to conventional wisdom; the principal for whom he is acting cannot *know* that this conduct does not maximize his utility but only that of the employee.

---

48 Anyone who has had his investments handled by a bank trust department is probably familiar with the phenomenon of 'managing wisely but not well'. Anyone who has observed the functioning of financial markets dominated by institutions rather than by principals, knows what it means that paid portfolio managers 'do not want to be heroes' and 'do not stick their necks out', buying when everybody else is buying and selling when everybody else is selling.

If maximin, a bird in the hand and selling your *uncertain* birthright for a guaranteed mess of pottage were asserted often enough to be the responsible thing to do, the employee would rationally have to opt for them if his *maximand* was best served by *appearing* responsible to his principals, like Rawls's contracting parties who want to *appear* responsible to their descendants. Here, then, is a fairly successful deduction of moderate egalitarianism from rationality. Rawls has accomplished this at the cost of having parents arrange the future of their children with a view, not to the latter's best interests, but to what would probably make them look prudent in their children's eyes. Some parents no doubt do behave like this, and some might even help install the welfare state in order that their children should praise their forethought;[49] but on the whole the argument hardly looks strong enough to explain the terms of a unanimous social contract and to support a whole theory of justice.

Love of Symmetry

Wanting equality for its own sake is no reason for wanting one equality rather than another.

One-man–one-pay and one-man–one-vote are not rules providing their own justification.

Everybody is bound to like ultimate goods like liberty, utility or justice. Not everybody is bound to like equality. If the democratic state needs consent and obtains some by producing some equality (a rather summary description of one type of political process, but it will have to do for my present purpose), it is the function of liberal ideology to inculcate the belief that this is a good thing. The high road leading to harmony between state interest and ideological prescription is to establish a deductive link, a causal relation or a reciprocal implication between ends which nobody disputes, such as liberty, utility and justice on the one hand, and equality on the other. If the latter produces the former, or if the latter is indispensable for

---

49 If parents thought that children were going to grow up less able, less provident and less resilient than themselves, they might consider that a welfare state would be genuinely better for them than an inegalitarian state. The parents might then want to install it straightaway, either because they could not trust their children to recognize their best interests, or because the choice of state had to be made right now for all posterity. However, Rawls does not use this line of paternalistic argument.

producing the former, it becomes a simple matter of consistency, of plain common sense, not to dispute equality any more than one would dispute, say, justice or well-being.

Hearsay has it that there *are* such deductive links: that freedom presupposes an equal sufficiency of material means; that social welfare is maximized by redistributing income from rich to poor; or that rational self-interest induces people unanimously to mandate the state to look after the least privileged. On examination, however, the detailed arguments from which the hearsay is distilled, prove unsuccessful. Like most hearsay, they have influence without quite silencing controversy and doubt. Far from establishing its universal validity to which men of good will cannot help but agree, it leaves the ideology vulnerable just as a religion which has the misplaced ambition of claiming the validity of logical deduction or scientific truth for its beliefs, is vulnerable. A less ambitious way, invulnerable to refutation, is to postulate that people do like equality for its own sake (so that its desirability need not be *deduced from* the desiredness of anything else), or at least they would if they recognized its essential character.

People love symmetry, their senses expect it, they identify it with order and reason. Equality is to a system of rules as symmetry is to a design. The essence of equality *is* symmetry. It is the basic presumption, it is what people visually or conceptually expect to find. For asymmetry as for inequality, they naturally look for a sufficient reason and are disturbed if there is none.

This line of reasoning tells people that it is inherent in their nature to approve of such rules as one-man–one-vote, to each according to his needs and the soil to him who tills it. In each of these rules, there is a clear symmetry which would be spoilt if some men had two votes and others one or none, if some (but only some) were given more than their needs and if some land belonged to the tiller and other land to the idle landlord.

However, if the choice is not between symmetry and asymmetry but between one symmetry and another, which is it inherent in human nature to prefer? Take the design of the human form, which must accommodate two arms and two legs. The arms can be placed symmetrically on either side of the spine, or symmetrically above and below the waist, and so can the legs. Between vertical and horizontal symmetry, which is right? A human figure with two arms on the right shoulder and hip and two legs on the left shoulder and hip would strike us as rather off-putting, not because it was asymmetrical (it would not be), but because its symmetry violated another to which our eye has become accustomed. Similarly, the preference for one order over another, one rule over another, one equality over another does not in any obvious manner spring from the depths of human nature, even if the preference for order over disorder may be plausibly held to do so.

The choice of a particular order, symmetry, rule or equality over its alternatives needs either habit, custom, or the force of substantive argument to explain it; if it is the former, political theory gets swallowed up in history (which might be a well-deserved fate) and if it is the latter, we will be back to square one, making *derivative* cases for a liberty-securing, a utility-maximizing or a justice-dispensing equality rather than proving the claim that equality *for its own sake* is intrinsically desirable.

It is worth spelling out that one equality crowds out another and that, as a corollary, the resulting inequality can always be said to have some equality as its reason and indeed its justification. (The adequacy of such a justification may have to be established, but this is very different from establishing the superiority of equality over inequality.) Take, for example, one of the central preoccupations of egalitarianism, the relations of symmetry or otherwise that prevail between workers, work, pay and need. One possible relation is equal pay for equal work, an equality which can be extended into the proportionality that more or better work should earn more pay.[50] If this rule is good, it is a sufficient reason for inequality of remunerations. Another rule which suggests itself is to keep symmetry, not between work and pay, but between work and the satisfaction of the worker's needs; the more children a worker has or the further away he lives from his place of work, the more he should be paid for equal work. This rule would yield unequal pay for equal work. Further 'dimensions' can always be invented so that symmetry in one implies asymmetry in some or all the others, e.g. the importance or responsibility of the work done. Equal pay for equal responsibility will then (except for cases of purely accidental overlap) generally displace the

---

50   Also called 'Aristotelean equality'. If the extension is denied, the rule becomes 'equal pay for equal work *as well as for unequal work*', which seems contrary to the intention of the proposer. If he did *not* want proportionality, he would have proposed 'one man, one pay' regardless of the quantity or quality of the *work*.

equality between any two of the remaining characteristic dimensions of the relationship between worker, work, pay and need.

This logic is agreed by Marx to be valid up to and including the 'first phase of communist society' (though, to cheer up last-ditch egalitarians it ceases to be valid in the second phase):

> The right of the producers is proportional to the labour they supply. ... This *equal* right is an unequal right for unequal labour. It recognizes no class differences, because everyone is only a worker like everyone else; but it tacitly recognizes unequal individual endowment and thus productive capacity as natural privileges. *It is, therefore, a right of inequality, in its content, like every right.* Right by its very nature can consist only in the application of an equal standard; but unequal individuals (and they would not be different individuals if they were not unequal) are measurable only by an equal standard in so far as they are brought under an equal point of view, are taken from one definite side only, for instance, in the present case, are regarded *only as workers* and nothing more is seen in them, everything else being ignored. Further, one worker is married, another not; one has more children than another, and so on and so forth. Thus, with an equal performance of labour, and hence an equal share in the social consumption fund, one will in fact receive more than another, one will be richer than another, and so on. To avoid all these defects, right instead of being equal would have to be unequal.
>
> But these defects are inevitable in the first phase of communist society. ... I have dealt ... with 'equal right' and 'fair distribution' ... in order to show what a crime it is to attempt ... to force on our Party again, as dogmas, ideas which in a certain period had some meaning but have now become obsolete verbal rubbish ... ideological nonsense about right and other trash so common among the democrats and French Socialists.
>
> Quite apart from the analysis so far given, it was in general a mistake to make a fuss about so-called *distribution* and put the principal stress on it.[51]

True to form, clearer and more to the point, Engels blurts out:

> The idea of socialist society as the realm of *equality* ... should now be overcome, for it only produces confusion in people's heads.[52]

Take two 'dimensions' of comparison, like pay on the one hand,

---

51 K. Marx, 'Critique of the Gotha Programme', 1875, in K. Marx and F. Engels, *Selected Works in One Volume*, Moscow, 1968, pp. 320–1, italics in text.
52 F. Engels, 'Letter to A. Bebel', in Marx and Engels, *Selected Works*, p. 336, italics in text.

and the return on investment in education on the other. If pay in every job is equal, the return on the cost of getting educated for a particular job must be unequal (if educational requirements for various jobs differ, which they often do), and *vice versa*. These two equalities are mutually exclusive. Asked to choose the more egalitarian of the two alternative rules, many if not most people would name one-man–one-pay, rather than one-education–one-pay. There may be a multitude of good reasons for giving priority to the one or the other; but it seems impossible to claim that love of symmetry, order and reason can weigh in favour of either one. The symmetry between education and pay (the neuro-surgeon getting far more than the car-wash attendant) and the symmetry between the man and the pay (neuro-surgeon and car-wash attendant both getting a man's pay), cannot be ordered in terms of their greater or lesser symmetry, order or reasonableness.

When one equality, symmetry, proportionality, can only prevail at the cost of upsetting another, equality itself is patently useless as a criterion for giving precedence to one or the other. Love of equality is no better as a guide for choosing between alternative equalities than love of children is for adopting a particular child. The appeal of rationality merely calls for some order and not for one particular order to the exclusion of another. This has been put with great clarity by Sir Isaiah Berlin in his 1956 essay, 'Equality': 'unless there is some sufficient reason not to do so, it is . . . *rational* to treat every member of a given class . . . as you treat every other member of it.' However, 'since all entities are members of more than one class – indeed of a theoretically limitless number of classes – *any* kind of behaviour can be safely subsumed under the general rule enjoining equal treatment – since unequal treatment of various members of class A can always be represented as equal treatment of them viewed as members of some other class.'[53]

Symmetry requires that all workmen be paid the same living wage; among 'workmen' there are 'skilled men' and 'unskilled men', and among 'skilled men' there are hard workers and loafers, long-service men and newcomers, and so forth. Enough heterogeneity can be found within the 'workmen' category for reasonable men to hold that the initial rule of equality between workmen, or simply men, should be replaced by other rules of equality between skilled work-

53   Isaiah Berlin, 'Equality', *Concepts and Categories*, 1978, pp. 82–3.

men with equal length of service, equal industry, etc. each rule
establishing equality within the class to which it relates. While one
can break up any class into any number of other classes, the substantive reason for breaking up the class 'workmen' and replacing one
equality with several, is that the class is arguably too heterogeneous
and a more *nuancé* classification corresponds better to merit and
yields more rational equalities. *But this is just our say-so*; another
reasonable man might argue the opposite; we would both be display-
ing Berlin's 'love of order', the sense of symmetry which is the basis
of the presumption for equality. We say 'black' and he says 'red', and
no third person called in to adjudicate can refer us to some mutually
agreed criterion which will help decide which of the equalities we
champion is more rational, more symmetrical.

Berlin warns that since one can always find a reason for permitting
an inequality, the rational argument for equality is reduced to a
'trivial tautology' unless the argument comes complete with the
reason to be admitted as sufficient.[54] This is his typically courteous
way of saying that the rabbit has to be put in the hat first. What
reasons anyone finds sufficient for overruling one equality in favour
of another depends obviously on his value judgments, of which his
conception of justice will form a part; for it is now surely clear that the
application of preference-less, value-free principles of rationality,
order, symmetry, etc. can always be made to yield more than one,
mutually conflicting rule of equality.

There are rules, such as a person's right to his property, which are
plainly anti-egalitarian in one variable (property) while egalitarian in
another (the law). Most egalitarians would then hold that equality
before the law must be upheld, but the law must be changed as
regards property rights. This means that there must be no discrimi-
nation between rich and poor in the application of the law, and in
order for this rule not to clash with the rule that all men should have
the same property, the rich must be eliminated (without discriminat-
ing against them). While this promises a field day for pirouettes of
sophistry cither way, it is clear that for some unstated reason,
priority is being given to one equality over another.

Another aspect of symmetry, that having to do with the relation
between an activity and its inherent purpose or 'internal goal', has

54 Ibid.

also been proposed as an argument leading to egalitarian results.[55] If the rich buy medical care and the poor would but cannot, the purpose of medicine, which is to heal (rather than heal the rich) is deformed. It is irrational for medicine to heal rich people who are ill and not poor ones. Their needs with respect to medicine are the same and symmetry demands that they should receive the same treatment. To repair the irrationality, arrangements need be made to equalize rich and poor with regard to their access to the best medical care. If *only* access to medical treatment is equalized, *the remaining riches of the rich may continue to deform the purpose of some other essential activity,* which will create a need for equalizing with respect to *that* activity, and so on, *until no rich and no poor are left.*

But the rich's being rich, and the poor's being poor, may itself be found to correspond to the 'internal goal' of some other essential activity, such as lively competition in the economy for material riches. Equalizing the prizes between winners and losers would defeat *its* purpose and be irrational, etc. We now have one rationality entailing at least one irrationality, and while most egalitarians would have no trouble sorting this one out, their choice could not be based on the criterion of symmetry or reason. The 'love of symmetry' argument and its developments, which show that equality is preferred for its own sake, depend on the alternative to equality being inequality. This is, however, a special case obtaining in artificially simplified situations only.[56] If the alternative is generally *another equality,* the argument is intersting but unimportant.[57] Order in place of chaos may provide its own justification, but order as conformity to one rule in place of conformity to another does not entail the superiority of either rule; unless one rule can be proven to be 'better', more

---

55 Bernard Williams, 'The Idea of Equality', in P. Laslett and W.G. Runciman (eds), *Philosophy, Politics and Society,* 1962.

56 For example, the division of a God-given cake among people who are absolutely equal to each other; they are equally God-fearing, have equal deserts, equal needs, equal capacities for enjoyment, etc., to mention only those 'dimensions' of comparison which are usually thought to be relevant in the 'division of the cake', though there are obviously many others.

57 Cf. Douglas Rae et al., *Equalities,* 1981. Rae and his co-authors, very sensibly, want us to ask, not 'whether equality' but 'which equality?' (p. 19). They develop a 'grammar' for defining and classifying equalities, and to provide some light relief, by permutation find no less than 720 sorts of equality (p. 189, note 3). However, they adopt the position that one situation can often, if not always, be diagnosed as more equal than another, i.e. that at least a partial ordering of social situations is possible, according to *how equal* they are. My view is that ordering situations characterized by alternative equalities is inevitably done according to some other, often occult, criterion (e.g. justice or interest) and cannot be performed according to the criterion of equality itself.

conducive to an agreed value than the other, the choice between them is best regarded as a matter of taste.

A population whose members are unequal to each other in an indefinitely great number of respects can be ordered in conformity to indefinitely many alternative rules, ordering them by the colour of their hair generally excluding, except by coincidence, a ranking by any other characteristic; symmetry between treatment and colour of *hair* will imply asymmetry between treatment and *age* or treatment and *education*. However, there is usually quite wide agreement that for any given 'treatment', say the allocation of housing, only a handful of the indefinitely many dimensions in which applicants for housing may differ ought to be considered at all, e.g. rank on the waiting list, present accommodation, number of children and income. A rule of equality (proportionality, symmetry) can arbitrarily be laid down with respect to one of the four (generally entailing unequal treatment with respect to each of the remaining three), or a composite of all four may be formed with the aid of arbitrary weights, entailing unequal treatment with respect to any one but some rough-and-ready correspondence to the rational 'sum' of all.

The agreement on what dimensions of a population ought to be considered at all for choosing a rule of equality, is a matter of the political culture. Thus, in a certain culture there may be wide consensus that steelworkers' pay should not depend on how well they sing, yet students' stipends should depend on how well they play football.

When a certain equality becomes an uncontroversial, generally agreed rule, the surrounding political culture can be taken to have become, in a sense, monolithic, for it has obliterated as irrelevant all the other dimensions, with respect to which alternative rules might have been formulated. One-man–one-vote in the democratic culture is the perfect example. It may be argued that each voter is a single individual, the rule of proportionality requiring that each should have a single vote. It may, on the contrary, be held that political decisions concern different individuals to different degrees (the paterfamilias vs the bachelor being a possible example), so that the proper rule should be: equal-concern–equal-vote, implying greater-concern–multiple-vote.[58] On the other hand, one could maintain with the

---

58 Some of the same effect is achieved, in a totally unintended fashion, under one-man–one-vote by the phenomenon of electoral non-participation, providing it is correct to assume that those who abstain are less concerned in their legitimate interests by the result of the election

Representative Government of John Stuart Mill that some people are more competent to make political judgements, including judging candidates for office, than others, which calls for the rule: equal-competence–equal-vote, greater-competence–more-votes. Such arguments used to find some practical expression in most nineteenth-century electoral laws with provisions for property and educational qualifications (contested as they were most of the time, not least by the 'false consciousness' of the propertied and the educated). Obviously, the more the belief is eroded that some people legitimately have a greater stake in political decisions than others, or that everybody is not as good as everybody else at judging political issues and candidates, the less these inequalities can serve as relevant dimensions for ordering people's voting rights. In the limiting case only one-man–one-vote is left, beginning to look very much like the self-evident, the only *conceivable* symmetry of man and his vote.

By contrast, there is no consensus about the analogous role of one-man–one-pay, a rule calling for everybody getting the same pay either because they are all equal, one man being as good as another, or because their inequalities are not relevant to questions of pay. A great many rival rules continue to compete, suggesting variously that pay ought to be proportional to 'work' or to 'merit' (however defined), or to responsibility, seniority, need, educational accomplishment and so on, or possibly to hybrid composites of some of these or other variables.

It is anybody's guess whether some or most of these rival rules will

than those who do vote. The unintended effect could be transformed into an intended one by making it difficult to vote. The Australian law punishing abstention by a fine should, of course, have the obverse effect.

'Concern' is an unsatisfactory explanation of why people bother to vote, but I am unaware of any more satisfactory rival ones; cf. the highly contrived 'minimum regret' rule proposed by Ferejohn and Fiorina. For the basic statement that voting is irrational, see Anthony Downs, *An Economic Theory of Democracy*, 1957, p. 274.

Abstention is, however, only a rough-and-ready approximation to the rule of greater-concern–more-vote. In this respect, Professor Lipset's understandable mistrust of mass participation might find only very partial reassurance. For, although the extreme arbitrariness of one-man–one-vote is mitigated by the inclination to abstain of those who do not feel very concerned (and although their relative unconcern is a subjective feeling which need not coincide with the realities of their situation – perhaps they *should* be concerned) the fact that the unconcerned *could* vote if they felt like it, will still weigh in the political balance.

Suppose, for argument's sake, that it is the *lumpenproletariat* which habitually abstains. An electoral programme designed to attract the majority of the electorate *minus* the *lumpenproletariat* would always run the risk of being defeated by one designed to win over the majority of an electorate *including* the *lumpenproletariat*, in case the latter were so roused that it did bother to go to the polls, after all. Hence, all competing programmes might take greater account of it than would be indicted by the paucity of the votes it habitually casts, and indeed by its apparent unconcern.

be obliterated from the political culture with the passage of time, possibly leaving a single surviving one which will then look as self-evident as one-man–one-vote does today. Liberal ideology, at all events, does not yet seem to have made its choice. Unlike socialism, which would give to each according to his *effort,* pending the fullness of time when it can give to each according to his *needs* (but which, in actual fact, simply gives to each according to his *rank*), liberal thought is perfectly pluralistic in what sort of symmetries should prevail between people and their remunerations, finding much to be said for merit, responsibility, unpleasantness of the work and any number of other rules of proportionality, as long as it is *principles* which prevail rather than the blatant '*caprice of market contingencies*'.

Where does this leave equality? The answer, I think, is a fascinating lesson in how a dominant ideology, totally unconsciously and without anybody's directing design, adapts to the interests of the state. Liberalism only accords its respect to truly free contracts among equals, undistorted by 'concealed duress' and 'disguised oppression' (cf. pp. 111–12). Hence it would certainly not accept that people's pay should simply be what it *is*; it is deeply concerned by what it *ought* to be, and its concern revolves around notions of justice and equity. However, as it tolerates a large number of mutually contradictory rules of equality, condemning few as unjust and inequitable, it will also tolerate a structure of remunerations where not only is everybody's pay not equal to everybody else's, but where it is not proportional either to any single most-logical, most-just (or perhaps most-useful, most moral or most-anything) dimension of people's inequalities. Whatever it will be, it will not be a 'patterned' distribution.[59]

This is just as well, for *if it were,* what would be left for the state to *correct*? Its redistributive function, which it must keep exercising to earn consent, would be *violating order and symmetry, upsetting the approved pattern* in the act of levying taxes, giving subsidies and providing welfare in kind. On the other hand, if the pre-tax distri-

---

59   This is Nozick's term for a distribution characterized by dependence on a single variable (as well as for a set of distributions which is made up of a small number of such sub-distributions), cf. Nozick, *Anarchy, State and Utopia,* p. 156. If all income from employment depended on the variable 'work', under the rule of proportional equality 'equal pay for equal work, more pay for more work', and all other income on one other variable, the distribution of total income would be 'patterned'. If many contradictory rules are simultaneously at work and some incomes do not obey any obvious rule, the total distribution is 'patternless'; at least this is my reading of Nozick's use of this very suggestive and serviceable term.

bution is simply what it is without conforming to any one dominant norm of equality, the state has a great role to fulfil in imposing symmetry and order. This is why the pluralistic tolerance of a more or less patternless pre-tax distribution is such a precious feature of the liberal ideology. (By the same token, it is clear that the socialist ideology must not be pluralistic in this respect but must know right from wrong; for it is not serving a redistributive state which finds a pre-tax distribution determined by private contracts and *improves* upon it, but rather a state which directly decides factor incomes in the first place and can hardly propose to correct its own handiwork by redistribution.[60] 'To each according to his efforts on behalf of society', is the rule which must be claimed to characterize the whole distribution as decided by the socialist state, whatever other rules may shape it in reality. It is impolitic to invoke 'to each according to his needs'.)

At the same time, liberal ideology fosters the claim that certain rules of equality are still better (more just, or more conducive to other undisputed values) than others, its preference being for distributions which favour the many over the few. If this claim sticks (though as I have tried to show on pp. 138–69, there is no good reason why it should), it is the warrant for redistributive moves which meet the democratic criterion of attracting more self-interested votes than they repel. It bears repeating that redistribution meeting the Janus-faced purpose of favouring the many and getting its instigator elected, is not necessarily 'egalitarian' in the everyday sense of the word. Starting off with an initial distribution far removed from the equality of the one-man–one-pay kind, it will be a move *towards* it; starting off with a distribution where such a rule is already being obeyed, it would be a move *away* from it and towards some other kind of equality.

To conclude: analysis of the argument that love of symmetry, which is intrinsic in human nature, is tantamount to love of equality for its own sake, should have helped to focus attention on the multidimensional character of equality. Equality in one dimension typically entails inequalities in others. Love of symmetry leaves undetermined the preference for one sort of symmetry over another, one

---

60 'Modern capitalism relies on the profit principle for its daily bread yet refuses to allow it to prevail. No such conflict, consequently no such wastes, would exist in socialist society. . . . For as a matter of common sense, it would be clearly absurd for the central board to pay out incomes first and, after having done so, to run after the recipients in order to recover part of them' (Joseph A. Schumpeter, *Capitalism, Socialism and Democracy*, 5th edn, 1976, pp. 198–9).

equality over another. Thus, one-man–one-vote is one equality, equal-competence–equal-vote is another. It is only in the limiting case, where all men are taken to have one (i.e. the same) competence, that they are not mutually exclusive.

Similarly, the rules 'one-man–one-tax' or 'from each, equally' (i.e. poll tax), 'from each according to his income' (i.e. flat-rate tax) and 'from each according to his capacity to pay' (i.e. progressive income tax with some putative proportionality between tax and the tax-payer's residual means over and above his 'needs'), are generally alternatives. Only in the limit where everybody's incomes and needs are the same, are the three rules compatible.

There is no intelligible sense in which one of two alternative equalities is *more equal*, or *bigger*, than the other. As they are not commensurate (cannot be made to yield an algebraic sum), subtracting a lesser equality from a greater one so as to leave some residual equality is gobbledy-gook. Consequently, it cannot be affirmed that a policy change which enthrones one equality by violating another has, on balance, introduced more equality into the arrangements of society.

It makes perfect sense, however, to *prefer* one equality to another and to defend this preference on the ground that *de gustibus non est disputandum* (which is not the same as making an ethical judgement about their relative justice), as well as to allocate one's own preference to that of the majority on the ground that respect for democracy demands it. As a practical matter, people do speak of social and political arrangements being (yes or no, more or less) egalitarian, and though it is not always very evident what they have in mind, we might as well suppose that most often it is this democratic criterion they are implicitly employing. None of this, however, makes the slightest contribution to establishing the claim (to which the 'love of symmetry' argument is finally reduced) that what a majority will vote for also happens to be morally more valuable or corresponds more closely to the common good.

Envy

Few endowments are divisible and transferable and few can be levelled.

No effort to make society drabber will make it drab enough to relieve envy.

Hayek, invoking Mill, pleads that if we value a free society, it is imperative 'that we do not countenance envy, not sanction its demands by camouflaging it as social justice, but treat it . . . as "the most antisocial and evil of all passions"'.[61] Camouflaging it as social justice might not help it anyway. Looked at through a tougher radicalism than Hayek's, the justice of a demand does not imply that someone or other ought to see to its being granted.[62] On the contrary, there may even be an argument that it positively ought not to be granted: social justice, like pandering to other forms of political hedonism, may be held to be anti-social, likely to lead to the corruption of civil society by the state and to a dangerous deformation of both.

It is equally possible and far more usual, however, to regard envy as one regards pain, as something which should be relieved and whose cause should be removed if possible, without trying to be too clever about distant and hypothetical corrupting consequences of the remedy. If relief from pain is in the here and now, while the damaging effects of drugs are uncertain contingencies at the far end of a somewhat speculative process, it is tempting to go ahead with the treatment. It is, I think, in this manner that envy, despite its altogether un-virtuous connotations, comes to be considered by many if not most people a legitimate reason for altering certain arrangements of society. I propose, though only for argument's sake, to admit the analogy between envy and pain, as well as the closing of the horizon to the distant risk of damage that these alterations may do to the structure of civil society and of its being overwhelmed by the state. If we do this, we will be meeting on its own ground the liberal view of envy as a possibly minor but very straightforward and rugged reason – the last one if utility, justice and love of symmetry all fail – for holding that equality is valuable. The problem we shall then address is by and large this: if relieving envy is a worthy objective, are we committed to reducing inequality (unless a stronger one overrides this objective)?

As usual, the answer is determined by the manner of constructing the question. In an important article dealing with symmetry of

61   F.A. Hayek, *The Constitution of Liberty*, 1960, p. 93.
62   Commutative justice has an agreed procedure, issuing in judgments of courts of law, for deciding which 'demands of justice' should be granted. The demands of social justice, however, are not adjudicated in this way. Nobody's judgment in social justice entails a moral obligation for somebody else to have it executed.

treatment, unequal work and the conflict between non-envy and efficiency, Hal R. Varian defines envy as someone's preference for someone else's bundle (of goods – in one version including also the effort and ability to earn the income which it takes to buy them), and equity a situation where nobody feels any such preference.[63] A sacrifice of efficiency enables the bundles to be equalized, i.e. it can abolish envy. (Needless to say, this is a logical implication, not a policy recommendation.) If effort is a negative good, it may be possible for efficiency to be consistent with equity, for people may not envy a bigger bundle if it takes a bigger effort to earn it. The significant point for our purpose is that *all* inequalities are reduced to the *single* inequality of bundles. By equalizing bundles, we can eliminate inequality, hence envy, though there may be a more or less strong conflicting objective overriding the worth of non-envy.

Less sophisticated approaches *a fortiori* tend to subsume inequalities under the proxy of a sole inequality, generally that of money. Money is perfectly divisible and transferable. But it is manifestly impossible to make asymmetrical bundles symmetrical (e.g. proportional to an agreed attribute of their owners, or simply equal to each other) if they contain indivisible and non-transferable personal endowments like poise, or presence, or the ability to pass school examinations, or sex appeal. Those whose bundles are poorly endowed in any particular respect presumably resent this just as bitterly as they would different endowments of money. Moreover, the literally countless inequalities which simply cannot be made to conform to some symmetry or equality are closely relevant to the relatively few inequalities (money, or job opportunities, or military service) which can.

In defence of inequalities, Nozick offers the ingenious argument that envy is really hurt *amour propre,* and if someone feels hurt in one respect (low scoring at basketball, money-making) he will find other inequalities (linguistic ability, handsomeness) where he will be the higher scorer.[64] If the state, to reduce envy, eliminates a dimension of inequality (e.g. all incomes are equalized), self-esteem will seek comparisons along the remaining dimensions: 'The fewer the

63   Hal R. Varian, 'Equity, Envy and Efficiency', *Journal of Economic Theory,* 9, September 1974. For a development of this approach by a widening of the criterion of non-envy cf. E.A. Pazner and D. Schmeidler, 'Egalitarian Equivalent Allocations: a New Concept of Economic Equity', *Quarterly Journal of Economics,* 92, November 1978.
64   Nozick, *Anarchy, State and Utopia,* pp. 239–46.

dimensions, the less the opportunity for an individual successfully to use as a basis for self-esteem a non-uniform weighting strategy that gives a greater weight to a dimension he scores highly in.'[65]

This would be an excellent argument against a truly Utopian sweep of egalitarian measures which eliminated or greatly constrained possible inequalities. But such a contingency is really quite artificial and need not worry the convinced non-egalitarian. Even Chairman Mao's young cultural revolutionaries with their reputation for forthright methods, could not make much of a dent in the range of inequalities 'available' in Chinese society, drab as it may have been when they set out to make it drabber. The most successful egalitarian scorched-earth campaign could not reduce more than nominally the scope for getting one's self-esteem wounded by unflattering, and for getting it healed by flattering dimensions of inequality.

Nor would rejection of the 'wounded self-esteem' view of envy necessarily validate it as an argument for obliterating inequalities. For envy may be pain, dis-utility, resentment of an 'undeserved' asymmetry, a sense of deprivation relative to the superior endowment of a 'reference group', an external dis-economy of the riches of rich people, or whatever, without any of this telling us much about its causal dependence on inequality. There is no reason whatsoever for supposing that it is the Cartesian one of big-cause–big-effect, small-cause–small-effect (so that by *reducing* the extent of a given inequality or the number of inequalities or both, you could reduce envy, even if it were the case that by reducing the extent of *every* inequality to *nil*, you could eliminate it).

It is no more implausible to suppose other types of causation. An inequality may cause envy as a trigger causes a bang. A bigger trigger would not produce a bigger bang. If inequality is to envy as the size of the trigger is to the loudness of the bang, less inequality will not produce less envy – though absolute equality, if it were conceivable, would presumably produce absence of envy (not that one can ever tell, because the case cannot arise). This agnostic view, if adopted, makes the fight against inequalities in order to relieve envy look as misplaced as was the fight against windmills in order to affirm Don Quixote's chivalry.

The supposition of lesser-cause–lesser-effect which is the rational basis for expecting envy to be alleviated by levelling, gains credi-

65　Ibid., p. 245.

bility from the visible pleasure which always tended to greet acts of
pulling down, successful attacks against privilege throughout history.
It might, however, be a delusion to see 'the implication of a difference' in what is actually 'the consequence of a change'.[66] If patient
A lies in a crowded public ward and patient *B* in the luxurious
penthouse suite of the same hospital, *A* (and most other public ward
patients) may resent *B*'s privilege; when *B* is deprived of his suite and
is put in a private room, *A* may feel pleasure as a *consequence of the
change*. On the other hand, if *B* was in the private room right from
the outset, *A*'s resentment against *B*'s privilege, whatever its intensity, may well be no different than if *B* had been in a suite; the
implication of the difference between suite and room could well be
nil.

The essential point to grasp is that when chateaux burn and heads
roll, when the rich are expropriated and the privileged get their
come-uppance, the envious may feel elated that justice is being done,
that their 'relative deprivation' is being redressed. They may draw
satisfaction from a single *act* (expropriation), or possibly a pro-
tracted *process,* though the manifestation of change is less dramatic
than in the act (take the erosion of historic great fortunes through
taxation). The reverse should also be true. If *B* wins the lottery, or
marries his daughter to a desirable catch, *A*'s feelings (if any) of envy
would be provoked by the event, the stroke of luck, the undeserved
windfall accruing to *B*, even if after the windfall *B* is still the poorer
man of the two. On the other hand, a *state of affairs* (a given
unequality) may (or may not) engender envy independently of the
sensation engendered by the event, act or process which brought it
about.

The burning of the chateau, the breaking up of great fortunes, or
the taking of the rich man's money and its transfer to the poor man
will quite likely engender satisfaction in the envious, but only while
the drama of the *move* from one state of affairs to another lasts.
Once the chateaux have all been burned, they cannot be burnt again.
While the hovel-dweller may have been envious of the chatelain, he
now has cause to feel envious of the Jacobin lawyer, his airs and the
former Church property he managed to buy for funny money ('assig-
nats'), and nothing permits us to suppose that his envy has become

---

66 These were Alfred Marshall's highly suggestive terms for distinguishing between what our
current jargon calls 'comparative statics' and 'dynamics'.

less intense as its trigger has changed. But if the inequality is a mere trigger and envy's source lies in enviousness, what is the point in fighting inequalities which will yield to levelling, when there are always many more which will not?

Regardless of the breadth of levelling measures, any conceivable real-life situation must still contain a sufficiency of inequalities which are impervious to levelling, compensating and which resist any other practical remedy too. Envy is provoked by a person comparing his situation with the situation of certain others and perceiving inequalities. If one perceived inequality is eliminated, and the person is a comparing sort, his antennae are soon bound to make a half-turn and perceive another inequality (in terms of which he is 'relatively deprived'), out of the countless ones which might catch his eye, because *such scanning is inherent in his need to see his situation in relation to that of others* – or else he is immune to envy.

Demands for narrowing and, at the limit, removing certain inequalities, supported by the promise that envy will decrease as a result, do not seem to have a more compelling claim to being granted than demands which are supported by recourse to utility, justice, liberty, or demands which come uncluttered by any supporting moral argument. The promise of relief from envy is a redundant appeal to liberal credulity. The liberal does not need the promise. He is predisposed to approve such demands anyway. He has an 'existential' need to adhere to his own ideology and to recognize in the redistributive policies of the state the production of incontrovertible social value.

4

Redistribution

'Fixed' Constitutions

*Self-imposed limits on sovereign power can disarm mistrust, but
provide no guarantee of liberty and property beyond those
afforded by the balance between state and private force.*

With its key always within reach, a chastity belt will at best occasion
delay before nature takes its course.

In the state of nature, people use their life, liberty and property for
purposes adopted by themselves. A long tradition of political thought
holds that this sets them at cross-purposes, leading to loss of life,
insecurity of property and inability to produce the 'optimal' assort-
ment of public goods. The extreme form of this view, i.e. that in the
state of nature *no* public goods can be produced, is probably no
longer widely held. The state of nature is coming to be viewed as
capable and likely to produce *some* public goods, but not as many
and perhaps not as much as civil society endowed with a coercive
state.[1] The presumption is that endowed with a state, society is
enabled to make the sort of choices which lead to more resources
being devoted to public and less to private goods. The modern idea
that the state is a device whereby society can more nearly approximate the resource allocation which it *really* prefers, implies a much
older belief that the 'general will', or social preference, or collective
choice (or whichever species of the genus is invoked) has some
ascertainable meaning.

In coercing them to realize the general will or to give effect to

1 Cf. the Rawlsian view of the state of nature as a society which fails to produce the public
good 'distributive justice'.

187

collective choice, the state is competing with its subjects for the use of the scarce resource that is the liberty and property of each. It restrains them in what they may or may not do and forces them to devote part of their efforts and goods to the state's purposes rather than to their own. The same long tradition of political thought suggests that in doing this, the state is in fact forcing them to be happier (or better off) than they would otherwise be, for without at least latent coercion they could not resolve the notorious state-of-nature dilemmas of non-cooperation and free riding. At the same time, competition between the state (which successfully maintains the monopoly of force) and its subjects (whose one strong recourse is rebellion – usually risky, costly and hard to organize) is *prima facie* so lopsided, so grotesquely unequal, that if the state stops anywhere short of enslaving its subjects, cogent reasons are needed to explain why.

It is hard to formulate anything more crucial to political theory than this question, which has been implicitly answered each time historians have given a satisfying account of the fall of despotism, of stalemate and accord between a king and his barons, or of how a given state has ruled by custom and law, which constrained its choices, rather than by its own discretionary reason which did not.

This chapter is mainly devoted to the largely unintended consequences of securing political consent by redistribution. The pattern of redistribution develops as a result of both the state and its subjects pursuing, 'maximizing' their ends, interacting with each other to produce redistributive outcomes. These must be such that neither party can for the time being further improve his position within them. Broadly speaking, they have to reflect the balance of forces and interests concerned. Formal agreements between the state and its subjects, such as laws and constitutions under which the state is supposed to be restrained from maximizing its ends, either reflect this balance or they do not. If they do, the limits of state encroachment on the private rights of liberty and capital are naturally set by the power of the owners of these rights and a constitution or other formal agreement merely proclaims accomplished facts. If they do not, any such agreement is precarious. In abiding by it, the state is not in equilibrium. Its needs and ambitions will eventually lead it to circumvent, reinterpret, amend or simply disobey laws and constitutions. The better to clarify their role, or rather the reasons for their conspicuous absence from the subsequent argument, I start this chapter with what may seem a digression about the rule of law and constitutions, considered as binding agreements limiting the state's discretion to dispose of its subjects' liberty and property as and when its best interest dictates.

Montesquieu thought, oddly, that freedom could be defined as a state of affairs where man's actions were constrained by law only. Such a definition, besides other weaknesses, seems to rest on some implicit belief in the quality, the specific content of law. Unlike rules in general, characterized by their source and enforcement (By whom? Under what sanctions?), to be consistent with freedom law must also have some particular content – for instance it could be thought of as good, benign or perhaps just. Bad law either must not be called law, or it must be agreed to have the redeeming feature that at least it replaces arbitrariness and disorder by a rule. In the political domain, law – even bad law – has from time immemorial been prized as restraint on the sovereign, as the subject's shield from the despot's caprice. Impartial even when unjust, general and predictable, it provides some sense of security against the random use of state power. Significantly, the distinction republicans since Titus Livius have drawn between tyranny and freedom, runs not between good and bad law, but between government by men and the government of law. Hence the much too trusting definition of freedom in the *Spirit of Laws*. Subjection of the state to law, *even to law of its own devising*, has strangely enough been felt to be sufficient for disarming its tyrannical potential. Not till after the Jacobin experience did political theorists of the calibre of Humboldt, Guizot,[2] and J. S. Mill think of the possibility of the clever state creating self-serving laws which it could safely obey, while retaining its capacity to override the purposes of individuals in favour of its own.

If the rule of *mere law* is not a sufficient condition for an acceptable reconciliation of conflicting claims upon the subject's liberty and possessions and for protecting him from the powerful appetite inherent in the adversary nature of the state, one cannot aim at less than the rule of *good law*. Historically, two kinds of solutions have been pursued to the problem of how to get good law. One was not only to oblige the sovereign to obey his own laws, but to constrain

2 Looking back on his career as a statesman, Guizot (in the 1855 Preface to his re-edited *Histoire de la Civilisation en Europe*) sees his role in government as an attempt to render the struggle between authority and liberty 'avowed', 'overt', 'public', 'contained' and 'regulated in an arena of law'. In retrospect, he feels that this might have been wishful thinking.

his law-giving powers by getting him to agree to what republican Rome called *legum leges* – a super-law or constitution which can effectively make bad laws 'illegal'. The other, more direct solution was to secure adequate participation by all concerned in the design of laws. Either solution, 'constitutional monarchy' with the state alone making laws but only within the bounds fixed by the constitution,[3] and democracy with the state striking *ad hoc* bargains with its subjects over legislation, is designed to ensure 'fair and equal' competition between conflicting public and private ends. The latter *ad hoc* solution is roughly the one England stumbled into in 1688, liking it and pushing it to its logical fulfilment in 1767; since then, a majority in Parliament has been sovereign – it can make any law and govern any way it sees fit. Its sole constraint on law-making is a cultural one. This confluence of the constitutional and the democratic solution corresponds by and large to the American one, designed by the Founding Fathers with a rare combination of erudition and wordly wisdom, crowned by an astonishingly long run of success in which design must have played some part beside luck, and since copied in some of its features by many other states.

The point about having both belt and braces, i.e. a 'fixed' constitution in a democratic state, where laws are in any case the outcome of negotiated bargains between it and civil society, is the relatively subtle one that the threat to people's liberty and property can just as well come from the sovereign people as from the sovereign king. The danger, then, lies in sovereign power and not in the character of the tenant who holds it.

For obvious reasons, a sovereign assembly, a *demos* or its representatives, and a sovereign monarch or dictator tend to present rather different kinds of dangers. Which is worse is at root a matter of personal taste. The view that the assembly is liable to be more unjust than the king was quite prevalent at the Philadelphia Convention disgusted by Westminster, and in the secessionist South rebelling

---

3　An outrageous yet masterly historian of the eighteenth-century French absolute monarchy describes royal power as 'all-powerful in the spaces left by the liberties' of the estates and corporations (Pierre Gaxotte, *Apogée et chute de la royautée*, 1973, vol. IV, p. 78). These spaces – often mere *interstices* – seem analogous to the space allowed the state by constitutional bounds. The pre-revolutionary privileges and immunities in most of Europe west of Russia, and post-revolutionary constitutional guarantees, both limited the prerogatives of the state. However, the former were upheld by, and shifted backwards or forwards with, the balance of forces in society between state, the nobility, the clergy, the commercial interest, etc. The latter were 'fixed', and it is not at all clear what forces upheld them at any one time.

against a Northern majority. Ordinarily, however, it is easier to conjure up the image of a personal tyrant than Pitt's 'tyranny of the majority'. Liberal thought cannot readily reconcile its faith in the benignity of popular sovereignty with approval of constitutional devices which would shackle it, hamper it in doing good and in some cases in doing anything very much at all. No wonder that in the USA, for some decades now, there has been a tendency for the separation of powers to be overcome by reciprocal swaps of functions and attributions, if not by their unilateral usurpation. Thus the executive is making a great deal of administrative law, the legislative is making foreign policy in addition to running the economy, while the judiciary shapes social policy and direct the struggles of classes and races. If the three separate branches of the American federal government were finally all merged into the Harvard Law School, much of this might be performed in a less roundabout manner. (Paradoxically, that day might conceivably mark the beginning of the end of the ascendancy of lawyers over American society.)

There is something threatening and basically 'unfair' in the very notion of the sovereign state competing with its subjects for the use of their resources – 'unfair' in the simple, everyday sense of an almost obscene disproportion of size and force. No single person has much of a leg to stand on, while the idea of banding together to tame the state promptly raises one of the first questions in statecraft, Why ever should the state let them band together? With the odds looking so blatantly unfavourable to anyone the least bit mistrustful, it is as plausible to predict despair and pre-emptive rebellion by people likely to find themselves in the minority as to expect them peacefully to submit, under the democratic rules, to the appetite of the prospective majority.

Agreeing to constitutional guarantees, then, is an intelligent move, a gesture to reassure the minority that nothing really harsh is going to be done to them. As disarming the mistrust of the prospective minority is, so to speak, a condition for getting everybody's signature on the social contract, there may very well occur historical conjunctures where it is *rational for the state actually to suggest* limits to its own power if its purpose is to maximize it. It has long been known that it can be rational for the wolf to put on sheep's clothing and to refrain for a while from eating sheep. It is old wisdom that it can be rational to take one step back before taking two forward; it can also be rational to forestall an objection by stating it first, inoculate against a disease by infecting oneself with it, roll with the punches, spend to save, bend rather than be broken and take the long way round because it is quicker.

It is one thing to say that it is good for the state, or for the majority with whose consent it rules, to lull the minority into a false sense of security by offering constitutional safeguards. It is another to insinuate that states which do agree to constitutions typically have some such crafty motive in their conscious, calculating minds. The latter sort of allegation has its place only in conspiracy theories of history, and they are unlikely ever to be right. The recognition that constitutions limiting power can be positively useful for states seeking (to put it summarily) to maximize power may, however, still contribute to the proper historical appreciation of these matters. Those whose particular intellectual enterprise calls for seeing the state, not as the *locus* of a single will, but as the shifting and uncertain hierarchy of diffuse and sometimes partially conflicting wills, none of which can be said knowingly to make the state's decisions, might like to suggest that the hierarchy will tend, albeit perhaps clumsily, to grope for the choices most likely to promote its composite good made up of elements of survival, stability, security, growth, and so forth. The fact that in lurching and groping, states do not always reach worthwhile objects but occasionally fall flat on their faces, need not invalidate such a view. It may simply indicate that if there is an institutional instinct conditioning the state's conduct, it is not an unerring one, but nor would we expect it to be.

In his brilliant exploration of some paradoxes of rationality, Jon Elster suggests that a society binding itself by a constitution (in fact, it is the state that is bound, but the distinction between state and society is not pertinent to his purpose) follows the same logic as Ulysses having himself bound to the mast to resist the sirens' song.[4] If Ulysses were not tempted at all by the sirens, if he were sure of his strength to resist temptation, or else if he fully intended to yield to it, he would not want to be bound. Equipping himself with a 'constitution' which forbids him what he does not want to do, is rational in terms of his wish for an assurance against his own changing states of mind, his own weakness of will. Whether Ulysses stands for society, or for the state, or for a generation looking ahead and trying to commit future generations, it is *his own* concern that moves him. He

4   Jon Elster, *Ulysses and the Sirens,* 1979.

truly fears the sirens. Admittedly, he has shipmates but it is not to satisfy *their* concerns that he has himself bound.

My own view is different. It is that anything Ulysses-the-state volunteers to do to restrict his own freedom of choice is the result of his reading of the state of mind of his shipmates, *their* fear of the sirens and *their* mistrust of *his* character. It is not the calculus of one interest in the face of a given contingency, but the upshot of at least two, that of the governed and that of the governor. Ulysses asks to be bound lest his crew should want to get rid of so unsafe a captain.

The analogy with states and their constitutions is distorted by the bindings. Once bound, Ulysses cannot undo his shackles. Only his shipmates can release him. A state bound by a 'law of laws', being at the same time the monopolist of all law enforcement, can always *untie itself*. It would not be sovereign if it could not. The proper analogy is not with Ulysses and his shipmates approaching Scylla and Charybdis, but with the lady whose lord, reassured by her chastity belt, is safely off to the wars, while she, now mistress of herself, hangs the key of the padlock of the belt on her own bedpost.

The ultimate mastery of the state over the constitution is masked, in countries with a proper 'fixed' Franco-American type of constitution, by the provision of a special guardian – the Supreme Court in the USA, the Conseil Constitutionnel in France – watching over its observance. This guardian is either part of the state, or part of civil society. It cannot be in a third place outside, 'above' both. If it is part of civil society, it is subject to the state and can in the last analysis always be coerced not to denounce a breach of the constitution. Failing that, it can have its denunciation denounced by another guardian appointed to replace it. The question is obviously not whether this is feasible or whether a form of words can be found to explain that the constitution is thereby *really* being respected and on a 'higher plane' than hitherto but, rather, whether the stake is worth it. Nature will take its course, and the padlock of the chastity belt will be opened, no doubt in the name of *real* (as opposed to *artificial*) chastity, depending essentially on the balance of political support to be gained and to be lost by the move (i.e. Can the state politically afford to do it? and Can it afford *not* to do it?) *and* on the contribution, if any, which acting outside the constitution can make to its ends other than to sheer political survival.

On the other hand, if the guardian of the constitution is part of the state, there is a presumption that it will not have a separate, sharply divergent conception of the public good or, what is in practice indistinguishable from it, a separate and sharply divergent calculus of the balance of advantages to be reaped from interpreting the constitution one way or the other. The 'separation of powers' and the independence of the judiciary are, however, designed to undermine just this presumption. Their intended function is to make it altogether possible for such a divergence to emerge. The device, prior to the Crimean War, of making officers of the British Army independent by letting (and indeed obliging) them to own their commissions, was supposed to ensure that the Army's interest would not diverge from that of property and hence would not become a tool of royal absolutism. The device of selling French magistrates heritable and transferable title to their offices had the effect (though a totally unintended one) of ultimately allowing a divergence of interests to develop between the monarchy and the *parlements* to such an extent that in 1771, finding themselves confronted by a strong-willed adversary in Maupeou, they were expropriated and the loyal and the complaisant   among   them   became   salaried   officers   of   the state.

Evidently, when the guardian of the constitution is the creature of a previous tenant of state power, the emanation of a majority gone and past, there is quite likely to be a divergence. The American Supreme Court in the face of the New Deal, the French Conseil Constitutionnel in the face of the post-1981 socialist government of the Fifth Republic, are good cases in point. The Supreme Court obstructed or retarded some of Franklin Roosevelt's legislation affecting the rights of property till 1937, when it backed off, sensing that even if the Administration's bill to 'reform' it was running into the salutary buffers of bicameralism, it was yet inadvisable for the Court to be seen consistently to oppose the democratic majority. (Legitimacy is obeyed if it does not command much or often.) In time and with average mortality of lifetime appointees, the Court will come to think the way the Administration thinks, though a sharp change of regime can create short-term problems. Even these problems, however, will only deter the benign sort of state which it is not desperately important to deter anyway, for it is unlikely to have unconstitutional designs of major short-term impact on the rights of its subjects. Plainly, no possible conflict with the 1958 constitution would have deterred the overwhelming socialist majority in the French Assembly from nationalizing banking and most large industrial corporations in 1981.⁵ It was perfectly understood on all sides that the Constitutional Council might well not survive if it threw out the bill.

A really radical conflict between the conception of right embodied in the constitution and that of public good proposed by the state, particularly at the 'dawn of a new era' when there is a bad break in continuity, reflects a revolutionary situation, or a *coup d'état,* (or, as in Russia in October 1917, one on top of the other). Sweeping away an old constitution is in such moments but a minor effort in the spate of other, more portentous ones. In the face of less radical divergences, a fixed constitution can remain fixed till it is amended.

Amending the law of laws is an undertaking quite possibly different in degree, but hardly different in kind from amending a law or some other less formalized arrangement of society (and if there be a law laying down how the law of laws can be amended, *that* law can be amended, for it is ultimately always possible, by proposing a particular distribution of the resulting benefits and burdens, to assemble preponderant support for the amendment). At worst it may involve a good deal more fuss and legislative time and it may require a wider margin of consent over dissent. If so, a constitution intended to protect the freedom and property of the subject against certain kinds of encroachment by the state, does provide security against *lukewarm* attempts by an only marginally motivated state. This much, however, is true of *any status quo,* whether constitutional or just a fact of everyday life, for every status quo represents some frictional obstacle.

The task of every state, from the most repressive discretionary dictatorship to the purest legitimate commonwealth, is the reciprocal adjustment, to its best advantage, of its policies to the balance of support and opposition they engender. Though this degree of generality almost renders the statement trivial, at least it helps dissolve the notion of the 'law of laws' as some sort of ultimate rampart or 'side constraint' where the state pulls up hard, and behind which the individual subject can safely relax.

---

5 In response to opposition claims that the bill was unconstitutional, André Laignel, socialist deputy of the Indre, gave the reply which has since become celebrated, and might be preserved in future political science textbooks: 'You are wrong in [constitutional] law because you are politically in the minority.' Events proved him right.

Buying Consent

Majorities must be paid for out of minority money; this conditions leaves the state little choice about the redistributive pattern to impose.

In competitive electoral politics the winner's reward is profitless power.

A given state-of-nature society unmarked by a state, can be told apart from others by its given set of initial distributions of all the unequal attributes which distinguish its members. These are, as we have seen in another context, virtually countless in number. The various distributions, ceaselessly shifting in historical time, are 'initial' only in the sense that logically they precede the activities of the state. A relatively small number of them may yield to attempts at levelling. If a state is superimposed on this society, and if it relies on its subjects' consent to stay in power, it may, and under competitive conditions it will, find it advantageous to offer to change some 'initial' distribution in such a way that the redistribution will gain it more support (in terms of clout, or votes, or whatever 'mix' of the two it considers relevant to power).

Such a redistributive offer is obviously a function of the initial distribution. For instance, in a society where some people know a lot and others only a little, where knowledge is prized by both and (tall order!) absorbing knowledge is painless, the state might gain support by obliging the knowledgeable to spend their time, not in cultivating and enjoying their knowledge, but in teaching the ignorant. Likewise, if some people own a lot of land and others only a little, the former might advantageously be obliged to give land to the latter. A redistributive offer in the opposite direction, involving transfers of a good from the have-nots to the haves, would presumably prove to be inferior inasmuch as there would be much less to transfer. Poor-to-rich transfers would, in typical democratic circumstances, produce a less favourable, indeed a downright negative balance between support gained and lost.

If there are *any* number of inequalities (though only a few will really yield to levelling), the state can at least propose or pretend to level a number of them. If so, it is impossible to predict the most efficient redistributive offer from the initial distributions alone. Even the presumption that transfers from the haves to the have-nots (rather than the other way round) are politically superior, may not stand up if clout matters much more than votes and it is the haves who have the clout.[6]

In order to make a determinate solution possible, it would help to have a political culture where most inequalities were accepted as untouchable, so that neither the state nor its competitors would include them in a redistributive offer. In such a culture, for example, children would be allowed to be raised by their own (unequal) parents; non-income producing personal property would not have to be shared; people could wear distinctive dress; unpleasant work would be done by those who could not get any other, etc. Obviously, not all societies have this sort of culture, though those we call consent-based by and large do. Culture, then, would severely narrow down the possible variety of political offers. However, to rule out any freak programme and cultural revolution, it will be best to consider first a society where only one inequality is 'politically' perceived at all: the amount of money people have.

Money looks the natural object for redistribution because, unlike most other interpersonal differences, it is *par excellence* measurable, divisible and transferable.[7] But it has a subtler advantage, too. At least conceptually, there are political processes which run their course, achieve their objective and come to an end. The class struggle between capital and the proletariat is conceived in Marxist thought to be such a process. Once this terminal conflict is resolved and there is no exploited class left for state power to oppress, politics comes to a full stop and the state withers away. Likewise, if politics were about latifundia and landless peasants, or the privileges of the nobility and clergy, or other similar inequalities which, once levelled, *stayed level*, the state's purchase of consent by redistribution would be an episode, a once-for-all event. At best it could be history made up of a succession of such episodes. However, with money as the object, democratic politics can make sense as a self-perpetuating static equilibrium.

Why this is so is best appreciated by recalling the facile distinction that people so readily draw between equality of opportunity and of end-states. Moderate egalitarians sometimes suggest that it is oppor-

6   The latter need not be the case. In the winter of 1973–4, the British coal miners proved to have enough clout to break Edward Heath's government; yet with respect to the inequalities which would be liable to figure in a redistributive offer, they would clearly count as have-nots.

7   I prefer naively to talk of 'money' and leave it to others whether it is income or wealth or both that should be redistributed and what difference it makes.

tunity that ought to be equal while end-states arising out of *equalized* opportunities ought to be left alone (which could only be done with mirrors, but that is now beside the point). Peter and Paul should have the same chances of attaining any given level of income or wealth, but if in the end he were to make more, Peter should not be robbed to pay Paul. Inequality of income or wealth is in turn, however, the resultant of a large universe of prior inequalities, some of which can be equalized (but then at least some end-states must be permanently interfered with; compulsory free education must be paid for by somebody), while others cannot. If Peter has in fact made more money, some prior inequalities in his favour *must have* subsisted.

A little reflection shows that there is no other test of the equality of people's respective opportunities to make money, than the money they do make. For once inheritance of capital is abolished, everybody is made to go to the same school and every girl is given cosmetic surgery at eighteen, there are still ninety-nine well-known reasons why one person may be materially more successful than another. If these known reasons (notably one's parents) were all abolished and it were impossible to inherit more ability than the next fellow, we should be left with the unknown residuals habitually subsumed under 'luck'.

This need not stop anyone from choosing some stipulative definition of equal opportunity, making it an arbitrary subset (to include, say, equal attendance at school, 'careers open to talents' and provision of fixed-sum unsecured loans for starting a business, and to exclude everything else such as happening to be in the right place at the right time) of the set of reasons which make end-states unequal. One might stipulate that all who have danced with the most coveted girl at the ball are deemed to have had an equal opportunity to win her. If she gave her affections to one, rather than equally to all, that was luck.

The point is not only that equality of *opportunity* is conceptually dubious, nor that as a practical matter serious egalitarians must deal with *end-states* – for that is how you go about equalizing opportunities – though both points are valid enough. It is, rather, that each time end-states are equalized, sufficient underlying 'inequality of opportunity' will subsist *rapidly to reproduce unequal end-states*. They will not be identically the same ones. Redistribution must, intentionally or otherwise, have some influence on the *causes* of a distribution, if only through its much-invoked effects on incentives –

the idea being that if you keep taking away the golden eggs, the goose will stop laying them. Nevertheless, some new unequal distribution will almost instantaneously come about. It will require redistribution to be recurrent (an annual assessment?) or fully continuous (pay as you earn). In any case, there is no danger that the state, by vanquishing the inequality of money, would unwittingly depreciate its own role and 'work itself out of a job'.

In looking at the conduct of the state in competitive politics, we will for some of the above reasons make the large simplifying assumption that it rules over a society which is an amorphous collection of people lacking any pattern. It does not coagulate into groups, occupations, strata or classes on the basis of material and moral inequalities. It is the ideal democratic society in Rousseau's sense in that it does not break down into sub-societies, each with a general will of its own, in conflict with the general will proper. There are no intermediaries, historical or functional, personal or institutional, between the individual and the state. Though people are thus homogenous, I will nevertheless take it that they have significantly different amounts of money due to 'unequal opportunity' or, less controversially, to luck.

Quite unrealistically but expediently, I will also suppose that everybody's political choices are entirely determined by their material interest, and in a narrow sense at that: there is no altruism, no false consciousness, no envy and no idiosyncrasy. When given the chance, people go for the policy which gives them the most money or takes away the least, and that is all.

The other simplifying assumptions we need are less demanding. The basic democratic rules apply. Tenure of state power is awarded to a contender on the basis of a comparison of open competitive tenders describing redistributive policies. The actual tenant *is* the state. If another competitor were awarded tenure, *he* would become *it*. Tenure is for a specific period. There is some provision for premature termination – 'recall' – in case the conduct of the state is in gross breach of the terms of its tender offer. If there were no recall, and the period of assured tenure of power were long enough, the state might promise one thing and do another, inculcating in society the corresponding new tastes, habits and addictions and developing support for what it was doing rather than for what it had said it would do. Though this is obviously happening in real politics, for government would become quite impossible otherwise, our analysis would grow immensely complicated if we did not exclude it by postulating easy recall. Award of state power is to be decided by simple electoral majority, one-man–one-vote and secret ballot. Entry to politics is free, i.e. anyone may tender.

Under these assumptions, towards the expiration of each period of tenure there will be competitive bidding for votes by the state and its opposition. The highest tender will, at the appointed time, earn the award of fresh tenure. Which, however, is the highest tender? Neither the state nor its competitors have any money to offer which does not already belong to somebody in civil society. Neither can, therefore, offer to civil society a total net sum greater than zero. Yet each can offer to give some people some money by taking away at least that much from others. (It makes for ease of exposition if collecting taxes is, at this stage, taken to be a costless operation.) The redistributive policy such an offer represents can be regarded as a tender with discriminatory pricing, some votes being bid positive, and others negative, prices – with the crucial proviso that if the tender in question wins, the people whose votes have been bid negative prices will have to pay them no matter how they voted. (As is perhaps obvious, people offered a negative price for their votes may rationally vote either for or against the tender in question, depending on how much a competing tender, if it prevailed, would make them pay.)

Our argument will lose nothing if we simulate the two-party system and consider only two rival tenders, one submitted by the incumbent state and the other by the opposition (which may of course be a coalition), while assuming sufficient ease of entry of potential competitors to prevent the state and its opposition from reaching collusive agreements to share spoils and underpay votes. (The American political system, for one, has in recent years been showing symptoms of incipient *collusion,* in the form of the bipartisan commission taking over from the adversary-type legislature, where *competition* has led to stalemate over such questions as the budget deficit or the lack of control over social security expenditures. Despite the attractions of collusion, ease of entry and many other built-in elements of competitiveness make it in my view unlikely that government by bipartisan commission should get very far in superseding the basic rivalry of 'ins' and 'outs'.)

If society is differentiated by riches only, state and opposition have only two roles to divide between them, that of champion of the rich and champion of the poor. Who takes which role may be decided by historical accident; for our purposes, it may as well be decided by spinning a coin. The winning tender must attract 50.1 per cent of the votes. There are thus always 49.9 per cent of the people whose money can be used to buy the votes of the 50.1. Any greater percentage bought would be wasted. No rational tenderer should under these assumptions bid positive prices for more than 50.1 per cent. If he did that, he would by implication be taking money away from less than 49.9 per cent. He would be proposing to redistribute a lesser total sum among more people. In trying to get too many votes, he would be reduced to offering a lower price for each. He would be outbid by his competitor who (as future generals are taught to do) concentrated his fire to get the necessary and sufficient bare majority. In this streamlined political contest, any election result other than virtual dead heat would be proof that at least one competitor had not got his sums right and had handed victory to the other.

So far, so good; this simplified schema duly reproduces the complicated real world's tendency to make close-run things out of democratic elections in two-party systems where competent professionals on both sides strive to be all things to all men and fine-tune their electoral promises. What, however, seems left unpredicted is the winner. We know that the highest tender wins. But we do not know the terms of the competing tenders.

Let us arbitrarily suppose (the argument will gain no unfair advantage if we do) that you can get, say, ten times as much tax from the rich half of society as from its poor half, and that either competitor for state power can propose to tax the rich, or the poor, but not both at the same time. The latter condition makes redistribution conveniently transparent, though it is of course quite possible to redistribute without respecting it. Let us also suppose that both competitors have the same idea of taxable capacity, more than which they will not attempt to extract from either half of society. 'Taxable capacity' is an embarrassingly nebulous concept, to which I shall have to return later in dealing with the causes of 'churning'. It is usually employed in the sense of some economic capacity, having to do with the effects of varying degrees of taxation on taxable income, output, effort and enterprise,[8] the implicit assumption being that

---

8 If there were no such effects, taxable capacity would be equal to income, i.e. the very concept would be perfectly redundant. People could be taxed at 100 per cent of their income, for doing so would not adversely affect either their ability or their willingness to go on earning it.

everybody's willing performance of their tasks depends, *inter alia,* on how hard they are taxed. I am employing the concept in both this sense and also in a parallel one, as a relation between taxation and the subjects' willingness to abide by the rules of a political system under which a given share of their income or wealth is taken away from them, the implicit assumption being that the greater this share, the less the subject feels bound to respect rules under which he is made to surrender so much. 'Capacity' suggests that there is some limit beyond which the economic or political tolerance of taxation declines, perhaps quite abruptly. Both the economic and the political senses of the concept are shrouded in fog. No one has yet convicingly depicted the shape of the relation, nor did anyone measure its limits. Discussion of it is apt to degenerate into rhetoric. However, unless we are prepared to take it that for a society at any point in its historical career, there are such limits, and that it takes history, i.e. the long period or large events in the short period, to shift them by a lot, much in social affairs must fail to make sense. In the context of the problems we are pursuing there would, for instance, be no intelligible reason why, spurred on by democratic competition, the state should not subject large sections of society, possibly fully one-half of it, to marginal tax rates of 100 per cent.

(If there is no such thing as a 'taxable capacity' which taxation cannot exceed without bringing about a high likelihood of political or economic anomie, turbulence, disobedience and breakdown of some possibly obscure kind, unpredictable as to its specifics but unacceptable in any case, it must be feasible as of tomorrow to tax everybody at 100 per cent – 'from each according to his ability' – and to subsidize everybody at the state's discretion – 'to each according to his needs' – without first having to put society through the phase of the dictatorship of the proletariat. Despite its apparent convenience, this programme cannot really appeal to socialists who, if they had to choose, would probably rather agree that taxable capacity is limited than give up the requirement of fundamentally changing the 'relations of production', i.e. abolishing private capitalist ownership.)

Since the winning tender is one which is 'accepted' by not less than 50.1 per cent of the voters, the two competitors will seek to hit upon the winning combination of positive and negative 'prices' for the richest 49.9 per cent, the poorest 49.9 per cent and the middle 0.2 per cent of the electorate.

(1) The rich party might propose to tax the poor, redistributing the money so collected to its own constituency and (in order to form a majority coalition) to the middle. The poor party might symmetrically propose to tax the rich and transfer the proceeds to its own poor constituency and to the middle. Table 1 shows us what we would then have.

TABLE 1

	Rich party offers	Poor party offers
To the rich		−10
To the middle	} +1	} +10
To the poor	−1	
	0	0

(2) The rich party, however, would immediately realize that its offer under (1) is bound to be rejected, for there is always more money available for buying the votes of the middle out of the taxes of the richer half than out of those of the poorer half. It must, therefore, steal the poor party's clothes and turn upon its own constituency. (This is, of course, what rich parties do in real-life democracies.) Table 2 shows how the two tenders will then compare.

TABLE 2

	Rich party offers	Poor party offers
To the rich	−9	−10
To the middle	+9	} +10
To the poor	0	
	0	0

(3) Under (2) the rich party would win. It would get the acceptance of the rich who would prefer to be taxed 9 instead of 10, and of the middle who would prefer to get all the pay-off rather than having to share it with the poor. However, 'going for the middle ground' is a game two can play; to stay in the race, both must. So the outcome is as in table 3.

TABLE 3

	Rich party offers	Poor party offers
To the rich	−9	−10
To the middle	+9	+9
To the poor	0	+1
	0	0

Neither competitor can further improve its respective tender. Logically, both are equally apt to secure the consent of the majority. The rich party's tender is voted for by the rich, the poor party's by the poor. The middle is indifferent between the two offers. It is equally rational for it to join the top half or the bottom half of society or to toss a coin.[9]

The astute reader will have divined that the simple mechanism laid bare above, through which democracy produces redistribution,

9 With the same rules and the same players, Robert Nozick, in *Anarchy, State and Utopia*, 1974, pp. 274–5) reaches the contrary conclusion; he sees the rich party as the sure winner. Nozick's argument is that 'a voting coalition from the bottom won't form because it will be less expensive to the top group to buy off the swing middle group than to let it form;' 'the top 49 per cent can always save by offering the middle 2 per cent slightly more than the bottom group would.' 'The top group will be able always to buy the support of the swing middle 2 per cent to combat measures which would more seriously violate its rights.'

I cannot find the reason why this should be the case. An identical pay-off is potentially available to either the top or the bottom coalition. It is what the bottom coalition *gets*, or the top coalition *keeps*, if it succeeds in forming. (In my example, the pay-off is 10.) Rather than become the minority, both the top 49 per cent and the bottom 49 per cent would gain by offering some of the pay-off to the middle 2 per cent to make it join a coalition. The middle group would agree to the higher offer. The potential maximum offer is, of course, the entire pay-off (10 for both parties). But if either half did offer to give the whole pay-off to the middle for the sake of becoming part of the majority coalition, it would end up no better off than by resigning to become the minority. The game would not be worth the candle. The highest offer to the middle which it would be rational for either the top or the bottom half to make, therefore, would be the whole pay-off *less* the sum needed to make it just worth either half's while to coalesce with the middle rather than passively accept defeat.

This sum may be, for all we know, large or small (in my example, I used 1). Whatever it is, if it is the same for both halves of society, the top and the bottom coalitions are equiprobable and the result is indeterminate. For the contrary conclusion to hold, the poor must require a greater inducement to coalesce with the middle than do the rich. There seems to be no particular reason for supposing that this is more likely to be the case than not – at least, I cannot see one.

Let us note, before passing on, that in Nozick's scheme the top group and the bottom group would have to take the trouble of negotiating a coalition with the middle. In our scheme, the state and its opposition relieve them of this trouble by each presenting a ready-made deal, an electoral platform which they can simply vote for or against.

would continue to operate, *mutatis mutandis,* in a setting where a constitution forbade redistribution. (The Fifth and Fourteenth Amendments of the American constitution were, for a time, held to do so.)[10] If there is no way round it, perhaps by taming the guardian of the constitution, it must be amended, brought up to date, adjusted to changing circumstances. Instead of 50 per cent, it is then the qualified majority which the constitution requires for its own amendment, that becomes the dividing line in society between top and bottom, rich and poor. The pay-off out of which to fashion a redistributive offer which will, at least under the assumption of consent being solely a function of alternative offers of public money, secure support for amending the constitution, is the money that can be taken from the blocking minority if it is amended.[11]

The artificial mechanics of competitive political tendering, which produce the equally artificial result of finely balanced electoral indeterminacy, must of course be taken with a pinch of salt. Neither the state nor its opposition, no matter how coldly professional and competent at engineering electoral platforms, could possibly formulate patterns of seduction with anything like the precision required for our result. Nor would all voters correctly understand and evaluate the prices that were being bid for their support, i.e. the incidence on their income of complex redistributive policies. Many of these might be presented to look more lucrative to the gainers or less costly to the losers than the probable reality. Ignorance, the unpredictability of true incidence and the opacity of social and economic matter, would handicap not only the electorate but also those seeking to gain its support. Even if both competitors used the same data, the same surveys sold by the same pollsters, they could not risk sailing this close to each other. In reality, the coveted middle ground, too, must be much broader than in our illustration, and its benefits from redistribution more diluted.

Nevertheless, for all their artificiality, observing the workings of our schema of electoral democracy is more useful than looking at the mere spinning of wheels. It confirms in the simplest possible manner an intuitively plausible presumption: that material interest alone is insufficient to determine the award of power to one contender rather

10   Cf. F.A. Hayek on the 'Curious Story of Due Process', in *The Constitution of Liberty,* 1960, pp. 188–90.
11   If 25 per cent can block the amendment, the pay-off is whatever 24.9 per cent can be made to hand over to 75.1 per cent.

than another, for the contenders, even if they carry different flags, end up by appealing to substantially the same interests, which they attract by holding out much the same pay-off. The more familiar corollary of this is the 'convergence of programmes', the tendency (which some consider a strength of democracy) to narrow down the range within which policies (as well as the images candidates for high office must project) remain electorally viable. The obverse of this coin, of course, is the complaint of the non-conformists that electoral democracy precludes genuine, distinctive alternatives; the very principle of popular choice leads to there being little to choose from.

Our account of the 'pure', rich-to-middle tax-and-transfer kind of redistribution which the state, confronted by rivals in electoral democracy, would adopt under certain simplifying assumptions, is to a general theory of redistribution as, in economics, perfect competition is to a full theory of producers' behaviour. It is a stepping stone or heuristic device without whose help more general propositions might not emerge clearly enough. Though I neither claim, nor require for my arguments, to propose a general theory of redistribution, I do sketch some likely looking components of such a theory in the rest of this chapter. Their intent is to explain some of the dynamics of how civil society, once it grows addicted to redistribution, changes its character and comes to require the state to 'feed its habit'. From *benefactor* and *seducer,* the role of the state changes to that of *drudge,* clinging to an illusory power and only just able to cope with an inherently thankless task.

We have learnt that consent is, by and large, not bought with acts of once-for-all state help to the majority at the expense of the minority. Help and hindrance must be processes, to maintain a stipulated state of affairs which, without such maintenance, would revert to something rather (though never exactly) like what it was before. The beast must be fed *continually.* If this must be performed under conditions of open democratic competition, whatever of its subjects' liberty and property the state manages to appropriate, must be redistributed to others. If it does not do so, the redistributive offer of its competitor would beat its own and power would change hands. Tenure of power, then, is contingent upon its not being used at the state's discretion. The resources over which it gives command must be totally devoted to the purchase of power itself. Thus, receipts equal costs, output equals input. The analogy with the firm which, in equilibrium, can by maximizing profit do no more than earn its factor costs (including the entrepreneur's wages), is compelling.

We are nearing the heart of the matter, bumping as we do at this juncture into the theory of the state. If the *point in being the state* were to have power (that is, if that were the state's *maximand*, its end), it would mean very little to say that the state *has* maximized it in the situation whose equilibrium conditions we have deduced above. Social power, as we know from Max Weber, is its holder's capacity to make, by recourse to combinations of physical force and legitimacy, another do what he would not have otherwise done. The quintessential democratic state has the capacity to make given subjects in civil society surrender to it given parts of their good. They would not have done it without its 'power'. But it has no capacity to make them surrender any more nor any less. It would lose 'power' if it tried. It must tax the subset S of society an amount T, and it must distribute T' to another subset U. It cannot alter either S or U, it cannot vary T nor have T' fall short of it. *It must not* indulge its sympathies, follow its tastes, pursue its hobbies, '*make* policy' and generally promote the good as it conceives it, on pain of being booted out.[12] Though it can make another do *something* the latter would not have done, it cannot *choose what* it will make him do. It lacks the other essential attribute of power: *discretion*.

If power as an end in itself meant 'being in power', it would not matter to the power-holder that he must use it in one unique way, only for this and not for that, as long as he held it. But it would make for shallow theory to put *this* in the role of *maximand*. By the same token, we would get only a theory of snobbery if we were to put holding a title of nobility as the purpose of the noble's existence, stripping out estates, privileges, ethos and social and economic functions. The state could not *use* this residual sort of power, nor seek more of it. It could only have or not have it. If it were satisfied with it, *pure electoral democracy would be a sort of terminal stage of political development,* and our argument would be substantially at an end.

But while relief from further labours might be a pleasant by-product for the writer and his reader, allowing the state to be motivated by such a shallow, near-empty concept of power would grossly misrepresent historical experience. It would contradict, or at least leave unexplained, the state's evident striving over most of

12 Cf. the essay of J.G. March, 'The Power of Power', in D. Easton, *Varieties of Political Theory*, 1966.

modern history for more *autonomy,* for discretion in deciding *what* it will make people do. Only the will to have power *as a means* can properly explain that. The logic of competition, however, is such that democratic power in the limit becomes the antithesis of power as a means to freely chosen ends.

That the wheel thus comes round full circle is yet another illustration of the distant consequences of actions in and upon society being mostly unintended, unforeseen or both. A state seeking to govern mainly by consent instead of by repression *cum* legitimacy, may have fallen victim to lack of foresight, weakness of will or inconsistency. But it might equally well have been rational, when seeking greater freedom of manoeuvre, readier obedience, lesser reliance on narrow class support – in short, when seeking more discretionary power – to look for it in democratic reforms, in increasing reliance on consent. At the outset, it positively provoked its subjects to make demands upon it, as a vendor might drum up custom for his wares by passing out samples and testimonials, in order to create a political market in which consent could be earned in exchange for state provision of utility and equality. At the end of the day (most such days lasting about a century), such states found themselves, in a special but quite precise sense, virtually powerless, having their policies decided for them by the need of competitive electoral equilibrium and generally running hard to stay in the same place. It is academic to ask whether they could have foreseen this sort of result. Plainly, they have not. In exoneration, they had less warning than Adam before *he* ate from the tree of knowledge.

Addictive Redistribution

Help and need feed upon one another; their interaction can give rise to uncontrolled cumulative processes.

By helping to create entitlements and to form interest groups, the state changes society in its image and at its peril.

Redistribution is potentially addictive in two distinct though related respects. One concerns the behaviour of persons and families – society's fine-grained basic stuff. The other acts upon groups, affecting in so doing the coarser, more visibly 'structural' features of society. Fusing the two into a single group theory (since we could always say that families are small groups and isolated individuals are incomplete groups) might have had the elegance of greater generality, but the split treatment seems to me clearer.

The root ideas concerning the habit-forming effects of redistribution on persons and families are old and well worn. Their public acceptance reached its zenith with Cobden and Herbert Spencer (to whom one might add the peculiarly American phenomenon of W. G. Sumner). For no better reason than the boringness of virtue, they have since lost much of their currency.[13] Victorian homilies about self-reliance, about God helping those who help themselves and about the corrupting effect of charity, have practically disappeared from public discourse. On the other hand, the fully fledged welfare state has now been functioning long enough, and it has permeated the life of broad enough strata in society, to make it possible for theorizing to take the place of moralizing about these matters. A general sort of hypothesis would suppose that a person's behaviour over some period is affected, in a number of unspecified ways, by the receipt of unrequited help in the past or present period. Filling the empty box, it would be reasonable to assume, for instance, that receipt of help makes people consider future help more probable. Some of the self-reinforcing cumulative features of the provision of social welfare would inspire the more specific hypothesis that the more a person is helped in his need, and the higher he rates the probability of the help forthcoming (until, in the limiting case of certainty, he ends up by having *entitlements*), the more his conduct will be reliant on it.

In line with the normal relation between practice and capacity, therefore, the more he is helped, the lesser will become his capacity to help himself. Help over time forms a habit of reliance on, and hence the likelihood of a need for, help. Habit, moreover, is not simply temporary adjustment to passing conditions. It implies more than changes in momentary, short-term behaviour. It involves a longer-term, quasi-permanent adaptation of the parameters of behaviour: it changes character. These changes may to some extent be irreversible. Withdrawal of the help in question becomes progressively harder to bear and adjust to; at some stage, it attains the proportions

---

13 Herbert Marcuse may be credited with reviving a somewhat elliptical version of the old-time belief in redistribution degrading the beneficiary's character. He saw the individual *injuring himself* in acquiescing in his own dependence on the welfare state. (*An Essay on Liberation*, 1969, p. 4.)

of personal catastrophe, social crisis and political impracticability. The noise and turmoil provoked by contemporary Dutch, British, German, Swedish and American attempts (I am listing them in what seems to me their order of seriousness) marginally to rein in welfare expenditures as a proportion of national product, lend themselves well to being interpreted as 'withdrawal symptoms' in a condition where the addict requires a progressively larger dose of the addictive substance to 'feed his habit'.[14]

There are straightforward ways in which the adaptation of behaviour and character to the public aids that are forthcoming, is capable of setting off the self-feeding processes which can be discerned in heavily redistributive societies. For instance, a degree of public care for the welfare of mothers and children relieves, if it does not remove altogether, the most pressing material need for family cohesion. Reassurance about the minimum needs of mother and child will induce *some* (not necessarily substantial) proportion of fathers to desert them who might not have done so otherwise. (As connoisseurs of the American Great Society era will recall, publicly diagnosing this phenomenon has brought much undeserved abuse and charges of racist arrogance on Daniel P. Moynihan's head, though his facts stood up very well to the attacks.) Their desertion, in turn, disables the truncated residual family unit, greatly reducing its capacity to look after itself. Hence a need arises for more attention and more comprehensive assistance to one-parent families. Once reliably provided, such aid in turn encourages *some* (initially perhaps small) proportion of unmarried young women to have children (or to have them early). In this way, additional incomplete families are formed. They have little capacity for fending for themselves. Hence the need for public assistance further expands, even as reliance on it becomes widespread enough to cease to offend class or community standards of respectable conduct.

Much the same kind of reaction may be set off by public care for

14   The OECD reported in 1983 that over the period 1960–81, public expenditure on health, education, old-age pensions and unemployment benefits rose from an average of 14 per cent to 24 per cent of GNP in its seven largest member countries. This rise was not primarily due to greater unemployment, nor to demographic bad luck (the effect of the latter is still mostly in the future). The OECD state that 'populations which have become increasingly dependent on the welfare state will continue to expect support' and in order for continuing support to absorb no more than the actual proportion of GNP, i.e. for its relative weight to be stabilized, some quite ambitious assumptions about the future growth of the cost of existing entitlements and of the economy would have to hold true. The OECD refrains from pronouncing on the likelihood of actual performance measuring up to these assumptions.

old people, relieving their children of a responsibility and contributing both to the self-sufficiency and the loneliness of grandparents who, but for state care, would be living with their descendants as a matter of course. By the same token, some of the people who would have produced and reared children as the most basic form of old-age insurance, now rely on the state insuring them instead. Whether the consequent reduction in the birth rate is a good thing or not, it sets off demographic shock waves which can unpleasantly rock society for a couple of generations, among other things by endangering the finances of the Ponzi-letter scheme of unfunded public old-age 'insurance'.

Analogous processes, where effects become causes of further effects of the same Janus-faced kind, may be at work in (or at least are consistent with) many other areas of redistributive action. Their common feature is the adaptation of long-run personal and family behaviour to the availability of unrequited aids, which are first passively *accepted,* then *claimed* and ultimately, in the course of time come to be regarded as enforceable *rights* (e.g. the *right* not to be hungry, the *right* to health care, the *right* to a formal education, the *right* to a secure old age).

Such adaptations are obviously liable to leave some people happier and others, perhaps even some among the beneficiaries of state help, unhappier, though it looks very problematical to say anything more than this. Something, however, can be said about some wider political implications, notably in terms of the environment in which the state operates and seeks to attain its ends. Functions which used to be performed by a person for himself (e.g. saving for retirement) or by the family for its members (e.g. looking after the sick, the very young and the very old) in a decentralized fashion, autonomously, more or less spontaneously if not always lovingly, neither will nor can any longer be so performed. They will be performed instead by the state, more regularly, more comprehensively, perhaps more fully and by recourse to coercion.

The assumption of these functions by the state carries with it side-effects of some momentum. They affect the balance of power between the individual and civil society on one side, the state on the other. Moreover, the addictive nature of social welfare and the fact that its beneficiaries can generally 'consume' it at nil or negligible marginal cost to themselves, powerfully influence the scale on which it will be produced. It seems plausible to argue that as the disabling, dependence-creating effects of aid are unintended, so is in the last analysis the scale of redistribution to produce social welfare. It is yet another example of the disconcerting habit of social phenomena to get out of control and assume shapes and sizes their initiators might never have envisaged. In the face of the habit-forming feedbacks at work, it is doubly unsatisfactory to apply to this particular form of redistribution the fiction of some deliberate social choice.[16]

Partial loss of control over the scale of production of social welfare, and over the corresponding expenditure, is an important aspect of the predicament of the adversary state. I will revert to it when considering the phenomenon of 'churning'. However, I have only just begun to look at addictive redistribution and have yet to consider the workings of the sort of redistribution which fosters the proliferation of distinct, cohesive groups in society that, in turn, exact more redistribution.

Let us now put behind us the simplifying assumptions of an amorphous, structureless society which gave us the neat equilibrium solution of the preceding section on 'buying consent'. Society is now more like it is in reality, with its members being differentiated from each other by countless unequal attributes, among which the source of their livelihood (farming, lending money, working for IBM), their domicile (town or country, capital or province), their status (worker, capitalist, lumpen-intellectual, etc.)are but a few of the more obvious ones. People who differ from others in a number of respects can be sorted into groups according to any and each of these respects. Each member of society can be simultaneously a member of as many

---

16   There is, in all circumstances, a *general* reason for regarding social choice as a fictitious concept, namely that while majorities, leaders, caucuses, governments etc. can make choices *for* society, (except in unanimous plebiscites about simple proximate alternatives) choices cannot be made *by* society. No operative meaning can be credited to such statements as 'society has chosen a certain allocation of resources.' There is no method for ascertaining whether 'society' preferred the allocation in question, and no mechanism by which it could have chosen what it supposedly preferred. It is always possible to agree to some question-begging convention whereby certain actual choices made for society shall be called 'social choices', for instance if they are reached by the mechanism of a state mandated by majority vote. The convention will create a fictitious concept, whose use cannot fail to bias further discourse.

There may, in addition, be other reasons for objecting to the concept in *particular circumstances*. If a certain pattern of redistribution is addictive like drug-taking, it is a euphemism to say that society 'chooses' to maintain or accentuate that pattern. At bottom, this is the general problem of today's wants substantially depending on their satisfaction yesterday and through all previous history (cf. also p. 19). We should, however, recall that addiction is not the only conceivable relation between what we get and what we want. There is a range of possibilities between the extremes of addiction and allergy. The proper field of choice theories is the middle region of the range. But even in the middle, it is not 'society' that chooses.

groups as he has attributes in common with somebody else. All members of a given group resemble each other in at least one respect, though differing in many or all others.

There is, thus, a very large number of potential groups, each partially homogenous, into which the heterogenous population of a given society could, under propitious circumstances, coagulate. Some of these groups, though never more than a tiny fraction of the potential total, will actually be formed in the sense of having a degree of consciousness of belonging together and a degree of willingness to act together. Happily, there is no need here to define groups more rigorously than that. They may be loose or tightly cohesive, ephemeral or permanent, have a corporate personality or remain informal; they may be composed of persons (e.g. a labour union) or be coalitions of smaller groups (e.g. a cartel of firms, a federation of unions). Finally, they may be formed in response to a variety of stimuli, economic, cultural or other. We will be interested in those groups which form in the expectation of a reward (including the reduction of a burden), to be had by virtue of acting as a group, and which continue to act together at least as long as that is needed for the reward to continue accruing. Defined in such a way, all groups I wish to consider are *interest groups*. All need not, however, be egoists, for the concept I have chosen can accommodate altruistic pressure groups or groups of eccentrics, plain cranks who act together to obtain a putative benefit for others (e.g. the abolition of slavery, the promotion of temperance and literacy, or the putting of fluoride in everybody's drinking water).

In the state of nature, members of a group, acting cohesively, obtain a group reward, i.e. a benefit over and above the sum of what each would obtain if acting in isolation, in two ways. (1) They may jointly produce a good (including of course a service) which, by its nature, would not be equally well, or at all, produced otherwise. It is not certain that there are many such goods. Streets or fire brigades are likely examples. The group reward is secured for the members, so to speak, autarchically, without making anybody outside the group contribute, and without making him worse off. (2) They may jointly extract the group reward from outside the group, by changing the terms of trade which would prevail between non-members and the members when acting singly. Guilds, trade unions, cartels, professional bodies are the most prominent examples of proceeding in this way. In the state of nature, such tilting of the terms of trade, making the group better off and others presumably worse off, would not be based on *custom* (for how did 'tilted' terms come about before becoming customary?), nor on sovereign *command* (for there is no political authority). Their only possible source is *contract* (without this presupposing markets of any particular degree of perfection). Hence, they connect to notions of alternatives and of choice.

The freedom of others not to enter into a contract with the group, no matter how unpalatable it may be to exercise it, makes group reward a matter of bargaining. This is most explicit in negotiated, one-of-a-kind transactions but routine, repeated transactions in organized markets with large numbers of contracting parties and corresponding to various configurations of monopoly, monopsony or competition of greater or lesser imperfection, all represent at least implicit bargains where the element of negotiation is latent.

At least for our immediate purpose, which is to understand the difference between the group structure of the state of nature and the group structure of civil society, the critical determinant of group behaviour is the 'free rider' phenomenon. Free riding manifests itself both within a group and in its relations with others. Its basic form is well known from everyday life. The passengers in, say, a cooperative bus must over some period jointly bear the full cost of running it.[17] Otherwise the bus service will stop. However, *any* full allocation of the cost (defined with proper regard to the period) will do. The bus will go on running even if one passenger pays all and the others all ride free. There is no obvious, most-logical, most-efficient, most-egalitarian or most-fair rule for sharing out the total burden to be borne. If all passengers were cost accountants reared on the same accountancy textbooks, they might all grope towards a fare structure reflecting, for each trip taken by a passenger, the length of his trip, the number of stops offered along the route, the average frequency of the service and its peak vs off-peak pattern, the density of other traffic, physical wear and tear and a host of other variables entering into the long-period marginal cost of the trip in question. However, while all may regard it as technically correct (i.e. good cost accounting), there is no reason why they should all agree that the fare structure thus constructed is equitable, nor why they should wish to

17 I am choosing the example of the bus because it makes the free-rider problem more palpable, and not because I believe that buses can only be provided cooperatively. A universe where all buses are run by private operators for a profit is conceivable. A universe where this is true of streets may not be conceivable.

adopt it even if they did think it equitable. Altruism would make each want to pay for the others. A sense of equity might make them charge higher fares to those who profit most from the service, so as to capture and share out some of the 'consumers' surplus' accruing to the latter. A certain conception of social justice, as distinct from equity, might make them fix high fares for rich and low ones for poor people.

Sorting out in some manner a suitable fare structure to cover the cost of a *given* service, however, is only half the battle. If variations in the service are feasible, the cooperators must also reach agreement on the variant to be provided. If the bus stopped at every front door, nobody would have to walk but it would take ages to get downtown. If it is only to stop at some front doors, whose shall they be? Should the passengers favoured in this way pay more for the greater benefit they enjoy, compensating those who have to walk a way to the bus stop? No single 'right' way seems to emerge which the members of the group would all want to adopt for allocating the group burden and sharing out the group reward, either on grounds of ethics or of interest, let alone both. Vague rules like 'all pulling their weight', 'all paying their way' and 'all getting their fair share' can only be understood in relation to what they *have in practice* agreed, for there is no other common standard for one's proper 'weight' to be pulled, one's 'fair share' to be got. This is the more so as some members of the group may disagree with the others on what *ought to have been* agreed in fairness, good logic or justice without, however, opting out of the cooperative. Finally, whatever route and fares may have been fixed, each selfish passenger, on boarding the bus, might reasonably take the view that his hopping on it makes no difference to the cost of running it; the cooperative group as a whole is looking after the books and if there should be a shortfall, he would prefer not to be the one to make it up.

If all members of a state-of-nature group were selfish in the above sense, they would all want to minimize their burden and, in the borderline case, to ride free. For the group reward to accrue – for the bus to go on running, for a strike threat to be taken seriously in collective bargaining, for market-sharing quotas to be respected in defence of a cartel price, etc. – a given group burden must nevertheless be fully borne. It is widely believed that the free-rider problem, as an obstacle to cooperative solutions, is more acute for the large than for the small group *because* in the large group the free rider's anti-social behaviour has no perceptible impact on the group reward and *a fortiori* none on his own, hence it pays him to ride free, while in a small group he perceives the feedback of his anti-social conduct upon the group's reward and his share of it.[18] However, while it is probably true that people behave better in small than in large groups, the feedback effect is unlikely to be an important reason. A member of the small group may perfectly well perceive the reduction in group reward due to his misbehaviour. It is nevertheless rational for him to continue to misbehave as long as the *incidence* of the consequent reduction of group reward upon *his* share of it *just falls short* of the share of group burden he escapes by free riding.[19] This condition may easily be satisfied by any group regardless of size, up to the point where free riding causes the group to fail altogether. Most of the reasons why small groups are easier to form and to maintain than large ones, have to do with the greater visibility of each member's behaviour. Moral opprobium, solidarity, shame have less chance to sway people lost in a mass.

Consequently, if state-of-nature interest groups do get formed and the whole group burden is being carried by somebody or other, despite the incentive selfish group members have to ride free, at least one of three conditions need to hold (though they may not suffice without other circumstances being propitious too).

(a) Some members of the group are *altruistic* and actually prefer to bear the 'others' share' of the burden or let the others have 'their share' of the reward. The others can accordingly ride free to some extent, though not necessarily scot-free.

(b) Though all members are selfish, some are *non-envious*. If they must, they will carry more than their share of the burden of group action rather than allow the group to fail altogether, because the burden they assume does not, at the margin, exceed the reward accruing to them, and they do not grudge the free riders' getting a better deal still.

(c) All group members are both *selfish and envious*. Free riding must

18   This thesis is put in Mancur Olson, *The Logic of Collective Action*, 1965, p. 36. Cf. also the same author's *The Rise and Decline of Nations*, 1982, for the argument that 'encompassing organizations', e.g. the association of all labour unions, all manufacturers or all shopkeepers in a corporative state, 'own so much of the society that they have an important incentive to be actively concerned in how productive it is' (p. 48), i.e. to behave responsibly. The encompassing organization is to society as a person is to a small group.
19   For a review of various authors' contrasting conclusions about the effect of group size on free riding within the group, cf. Russell Hardin, *Collective Action*, 1982, p. 44.

somehow have been kept below the critical level at which the grudge felt by the envious 'paying passengers' against the free riders would have outweighed the net benefit they derived from carrying on with and for the group.

Case (a) corresponds to volunteer civic action, self-sacrificing pioneer effort, 'leading your troops from the front', and, perhaps, also to political activism and busybodyness; other satisfactions than the good of the group may also not be totally absent.

Case (b) underlies, for example, the creation of external economies, which would not come about if those whose (costly) action calls them forth would greatly resent their inability to keep others, who bear no cost, from also benefiting.

Case (c) is the most demanding; here the free-rider problem becomes critical to the formation and survival of the group. A cooperative solution must here repose upon two supports. To start with the second, there must be in the cooperative solution reached by selfish and envious members of an interest group, enforcement involving an effective threat of punishment, retaliation.[20] Where access to the group reward is technically easy to control, enforcement is passive. It resembles a coin-operated turnstile. If you pay your coin, you are in; if not, not. More awkward situations call for the invention of active, possibly complex methods of enforcement. Social ostracism of the blackleg, harassment of the employer, 'blacking' of his goods and his supplies may be necessary before a new (or old but

---

20 It is perhaps tempting, in this light, to regard interest groups as miniature states and the theory of the state as a case in some general theory of interest groups. If we did this, the traditional dividing line in political theory between state of nature and civil society would get washed away. There are major objections to such an approach: (1) The state has a unique attribute – sovereignty, (2) The approach is question-begging. It treats as axiomatic that for the potential members of the 'group' (i.e. all members of society), 'group reward' exceeds 'group burden', i.e. there *is* a pay-off from tackling the free-rider problem. But how does the pay-off manifest itself? It is usually accepted that the pay-off from forming a trade union is higher wages or shorter hours, and the pay-off from forming a cartel is excess profits. The pay-off from the social contract is the realization of the general will, obviously a different category of pay-off; even its algebraic sign depends entirely on the values of the interpreter of the general will – the Sympathetic Observer of the 'social welfare function'. (3)The theory of interest group formation may have room for the state which only imposes cooperative solutions that make some better off and none worse off. It has not enough room for the state that imposes solutions that make some better and others worse off, i.e. that is a group redistributing benefits within itself. Nor is it suited to accommodate the state that has its *own* maximand, pursues its *own* ends in opposition to its subjects.

The very enumeration of what could or could not be adequately handled by assimilating the state to interest groups with coercive features shows what a strait-jacket the contractarian approach is for the theory of the state.

not very strong) union can impose the closed shop. Retaliation against a price-cutter and cartel-breaker may take the most cunning forms. Even so, it is not invariably effective. John D. Rockefeller, who was a great practitioner of these cunning methods, had so little confidence in their reliability that he eventually resorted to amalgamation of *ownership* instead – hence the creation of Standard Oil. Summary justice in the American West against violators of vital group understandings (e.g. that range cattle and horses are not stolen, mining claims are not jumped and lonely women are not molested), was an attempt to shore up a precarious way of life whose viability greatly depended on no 'free riding', on everybody playing the game.

Before enforcement, there must be understandings, agreed terms to be enforced. What will be the share of each in the group burden, and how will the common reward be shared out (unless, of course, it is totally indivisible)? The immediate reflex for most of us would be to say 'equitably', 'justly' or 'fairly'. As these are not *descriptive* but evaluative terms, however, there is no assurance that most group members will judge any given allocation as equitable, just, etc. Still less is it certain that if they did, the equitable, etc. set of terms would also be the most likely to secure adoption in the 'cooperative solution', i.e. to ensure group cohesion. Strategically placed members, 'hold-outs' or bargaining sub-groups may have to be conceded very much better terms than members who 'have nowhere else to go'. Manifestly, the better the terms a member or sub-group can extort from the rest of the group, the more nearly will it have approached free-rider status and, hence, also the limits within which the group can carry free riders without breaking down.

It may be thought that once it was up against such limits, threatened with breakdown, the group would seek to preserve itself by recourse to new, more effective methods of enforcement of group understandings, cost and reward allocations or codes of conduct and would retaliate more vigorously against its free riders. Some such tightening up may in fact be feasible. But the group is not the state; it lacks most or all of the state's repressive powers; its ascendancy over its members is different in kind, as is *their faculty to opt out* if pressed.[21] A group's capacity to develop enforcement is heavily

---

21 For the fundamental difference between 'groups' (including political communities) where people can 'vote with their feet' and others where they cannot, see Albert Hirschman, *Exit, Voice and Loyalty*, 1970.

conditioned by the nature of the reward it is designed to produce, and of the sort of burden that must be carried to make the reward accrue. There is no presumption that it will be always, or very often, adequate for controlling the free-rider problem and enabling the group to survive or, indeed, to form in the first place.

If so, it is reasonable to impute to the state of nature – as to an ecological system containing prey, predator and parasite – some equilibrium in the group structure of society. Equilibrium hinges on the *destructive potential* of the free-rider phenomenon. The latter limits the number and size of interest groups which manage to form. The resulting universe of groups, in turn, determines the tolerated number of free riders, and the *actual* volume of their 'parasitical' gains consistent with group survival.

Interest groups extracting rewards not available to single individuals from transactions with others, are benign or malign depending principally on the observer's values. If their transactions are wholly or mainly with other interest groups, the extra rewards secured by one group may be seen by the disinterested observer as being at the end of the day broadly compensated by the extra benefits the other groups manage to secure at *its* expense. This is roughly the 'pluralistic', 'end-of-ideology' view of how modern society works. Instead of classes struggling for dominance and surplus value, interest groups bargain each other to a standstill. Though modern society does not actually work like this, there is perhaps some presumption that state-of-nature society might. If it is comprehensively organized, net gains and losses due to cohesive group action can be hoped to be small (though 'on paper' everybody gains as an organized producer at the expense of his own alter-ego, the unorganized consumer). Moreover, 'excessively' hard bargaining by a group *vis à vis* other groups in poorer bargaining positions, is liable to set up some of the same sort of self-regulating, self-balancing effects as 'excessive' free riding does *within* a group, so that as group formation remains within limits, so does the inordinate exploitation of group strength bordering on free riding.

Our framework is now ready for inserting the state. We want to answer the question, What difference does the functioning of the state make to the equilibrium group structure of society? Clearly, where a state exists, sovereign *command* is added to *contract* as the means for extracting group reward from others. In addition to market-oriented groups, rational incentives arise for state-oriented ones to be formed, or for groups to start facing both ways, towards their market and towards the state. The greater the reach of the state, the greater is the scope for profiting from its commands, and as Marx has not failed to notice, the state was 'growing in the same measure as the division of labour within bourgeois society created new groups of interests, and, therefore, new material for state administration'.[22]

When society consists only of persons, families and at worst perhaps very small groups, they give or withhold their consent in democracy to the state's rule in response to the available incentives. They are, so to speak, perfectly competitive 'sellers' of their consent – in George J. Stigler's clever term, 'price-takers'. The 'price' they accept or decline is contained in the global redistributive offer the state designs to buy a majority in the face of rival offer(s). A state-oriented interest group, however, instead of merely reacting to the going offer, actively bargains, and trades the votes and clout it represents against a better redistributive deal than its individual members would get without coalescing. The group reward, then, is the excess redistribution it manages to extract by virtue of its cohesion. Like any other 'price-maker', it can to a certain extent influence, in its own favour, the price it gets. In the politial context, the price it sets is for its allegiance, support.

The reward – a subsidy, tax exemption, tariff, quota, public works project, research grant, army procurement contract, a measure of 'industrial policy', regional development (not to speak of Kultur-politik!) – is only in a proximate sense 'given' by the state. This is plainly visible in the pure, taxing-Peter-to-help-Paul type of redistri-bution, but becomes more masked in its more impure (and more usual) forms, particularly when the redistributive effect is produced jointly with other effects (e.g. industrialization). The ultimate 'donors' – taxpayers, consumers of this or that article, competitors, rival classes and strata, groups or regions which might have been, but were not, favoured by some policy – are hidden from the bene-ficiaries both by the insoluble mysteries of true incidence (Who 'really' ends up by paying, say, for price control? Who bears the burden of a tax concession? Who is deprived of what when the nation's athletes get a new stadium?), and by the very size and thickness of the buffer that public sector finances constitute between the perceptions of the gainers and losers.

22   K. Marx, 'The Eighteenth Brumaire of Louis Bonaparte', in K. Marx and F. Engels, *Selected Works in One Volume*, 1968, p. 169.

A given group which, by lobbying and bargaining, succeeds in extracting some advantage from the state, would typically and not unreasonably, consider that its cost is infinitesimal by any sensible yardstick that men used to public affairs might apply:[23] the aggregate of all such special advantages already conceded to others, or the great good it will do, or the total state budget, etc. Like the cartoon tramp holding out his hat – 'Could you spare 1 per cent of gross national product, lady?' – the group will feel induced to formulate demands by the perfectly sensible recognition that granting them is a matter of small change to the state. It might never put a demand for unrequited aid, even of a much lesser order of magnitude, to persons or other groups, for it would not care to ask for charity. At the same time, if it did bring itself to do so, how far would it get with 1 per cent of the income of Peter and Paul? And how would it go about successfully begging from enough people to make it worth while? Given the choice, it is an inferior tactic for a group to address its claims to another group rather than to the state. The reasons have to do with the nature of the 'quid pro quo', as well as with the fact that the state alone disposes of the panoply of 'policy tools' for diffusing and smoothing out the incidence of the cost. There is only one instrument, the state, whose position of universal intermediary enables the successful postulant to get, not at some suitably modest fraction of some people's income, but at that of a whole nation.

There are yet more potent ways in which the chance of obtaining rewards 'from' the state rather than through the market, directly from persons or groups in civil society, transforms the environment in which interest groups get organized and survive. A given pay-off may be significant enough to a potential group to incite it to form and engage in the joint action required to get it. Its corresponding cost, by virtue of the intermediary role of the state, is apt to be so widely diluted across society and so difficult to trace as to its incidence, that 'nobody really feels it,' 'everybody can afford it.' The state-oriented group, by extracting a benefit whose cost is borne by the rest of society, is acting out the role of the free rider *vis à vis* society in precisely the same way as the member of a group *vis àvis* the rest of his group.

Unlike the individual free rider who beyond a certain point either

---

23 Like the American senator, referring to the deliberations of the Senate Finance Committee: 'A billion here, a billion there and before long you are talking real money.' My source is hearsay, but '*se non e vero, e ben trovato.*'

meets some resistance, or destroys his group, however, and unlike the market-oriented 'free-riding' group which is resisted by those who are expected to concede its excessive contract terms, the state-oriented group meets *not resistance, but complicity.* It is dealing with the state, for which condoning its free-rider behaviour is part and parcel of building the base of consent on which it has (whether wisely or foolishly) chosen to rest its power. Consent-building by redistribution is closely moulded by the pressure of political competition. The state, competing with its opposition, will have only limited discretionary choice about whose demands it will grant and to what extent. It will rapidly find itself presiding over a redistributive pattern of increasing complexity and lack of transparency. When another 'free rider' is allowed to come on board, the 'paying passengers' have every chance of remaining oblivious of the fact, as well as of its incidence on the 'fares' they have to pay. Though they will hardly fail to gain some general awareness of free riding going on and may even have an exaggerated idea of its extent, in the nature of the case they will fail to perceive specific marginal additions to it. Nor can they, therefore, be expected to react defensively to the incremental free rider.

While the dilution of costs *via* the vastness and complexity of the state's redistributive machinery attenuates resistance to free riding by groups, free riding *within* state-oriented interest groups is rendered relatively innocuous by the special nature of the burden group members must carry in order to reap the group reward. A market-oriented group must fully (though not necessarily 'equitably' nor 'justly') allocate among its members the burden of group action – the cost of running the group bus, the discipline and loss of pay involved in obeying a strike call, the lost profit of restricted sales, the self-denial needed to respect a code of conduct. Unless one of the conditions sketched above in this section (altruism, non-envy and ample surplus of group reward over group cost, and successful restraint of free riding) is met, the free-rider problem will abort that caused by the interest group before it can arise: the group will decay, fall apart or fail to reach its cooperative understanding in the first place.

A state-oriented group, however, typically carries a featherweight burden. It need ask little of its members. It suffices for dairy farmers to exist *as such* for the state, with the opposition at its heels, to devise a *policy for milk* (and butter and cheese) which will provide them with better returns than the market, unassisted by a milk policy, could do. In return, the group need not even prove performance of the implicit political contract by 'delivering the vote'. Dairy farmers have wide latitude to 'ride free' in two senses: they can vote for the opposition (which, if known, might simply cause the state to re-double its efforts to devise a more effective butter policy), and they can fail to pay membership dues to help finance dairy industry lobbying.

Neither type of free riding is likely greatly, if at all, to reduce its effectiveness in extracting a redistributive reward. Even when an interest group has politically 'nowhere else to go', so that the implicit threat of its throwing its support behind the opposition is ineffective because not credible, or when its bargaining strength is for some other reason less unbeatable than that of dairy farmers, so that it does need an effort to get its way, the money it can usefully spend on lobbying, political contributions and the like is generally very small beer compared to the potential pay-off. If all group members do not chip in, a few can (and a few sometimes do) effortlessly cover the necessary costs for the whole group. Much the same is likely to happen when group interest requires its members to wave banners, to march, to link arms or to throw stones. Many free riders might stay at home but the normal group will usually contain enough willing members for the conditions of case (b) (p. 216) to be fulfilled and a nice and loud demonstration to have the required impact. In sum, as political action is on the whole extraordinarily *cheap*, state-oriented interest groups are very nearly *immune to their own free-rider problem*.

With the state as a source of reward for interest groups, free riding loses most of its destructive potential as a check on group formation and group survival. In terms of the 'ecological' parallel used above, prey, predator and parasite no longer balance each other out. The defensive reactions of the prey are blunted: there is no market mechanism to signal society that a given interest group is raising its claims upon it; its exactions are screened from it by the size and complexity of the state's fiscal and other redistributive apparatus. Moreover, while the mechanism of bilateral contracts between con-senting parties works symmetrically, in that it is as efficient in concluding acceptable as in rejecting unacceptable terms, the demo-cratic political process is constructed to work asymmetrically, i.e. to concede a large variety of group claims rather than to deny them. Hence, even if the 'prey' were specifically aware of the 'predator', it would have no well-adapted defence mechanism for coping with it.

Moreover, 'predator' groups, in terms of my argument about the relative cheapness of cohesive political action, can survive and feed upon society almost no matter how infested they may be with their own free-rider 'parasites'. As a corollary of this, the parasite can prosper without adverse effect on the predator's capacity to carry and nourish it. More of one thing does not bring in its train less of another. Any large or small number of free riders can be accommodated in a population of interest groups which, in turn, can all behave as at least partial free riders *vis à vis* the large group that is society.

The above might suggest the sort of unstable, weightless indeterminacy where interest groups can, at the drop of a hat, just as soon shrink as multiply. Having no built-in dynamics of their own, it takes stochastic chance to make them do the one rather than the other. Any such suggestion which would, of course, run counter to the bulk of historical evidence (to the effect that more often than not, interest groups increase in number and influence over time), is as good as barred by two further features implicit in the interaction of group and state. First, whether or not the granting of a group reward is successful in winning the support of the group and reinforcing the state's tenure of power, it will generally increase the state's apparatus, the intensity and elaborateness of its activity, for the granting of each group reward requires some matching addition to its supervisory, regulatory and enforcing agencies. By and large, however, the more the state governs, the greater tend to be the potential rewards that can arise from successfully soliciting its assistance and hence the greater the pay-off to group formation. Second, each grant of a group reward shows up the 'soft touch' character of the state caught in the competitive predicament. Each grant, then, is a signal to potential groups which consider themselves similarly placed in some respect, improving in their eyes the likelihood of actually managing to obtain a given potential reward if they organize to demand it.

On both these scores, therefore, the bias of the system is to cause interest groups to proliferate. Whether the process is first set off by the state's offer of a favour or by a group's demand, is a chicken-and-egg question of very limited interest. Regardless of the initial impulse, the incentives and resistances appear to be arranged in such ways as to cause redistributive policies and interest group formation *mutually to sustain and intensify* each other.

Interactions between group pressure and redistributive measures need not be confined to matters of narrow self-interest. Groups may form and act to promote the cause of a third party, e.g. slaves, mental patients, the 'Third World', etc. Such 'persuasive lobbies' may not possess enough clout to let them trade their political support directly against policies favouring their cause. However, they may succeed in influencing public opinion to the point where state, opposition or both will consider it good politics to include in their platforms the measure demanded. Once adopted, such a disinterested measure both widens the accepted scope of state action and the apparatus for executing it, and serves as a precedent inciting other persuasive lobbies to organize and promote the next cause.[24]

Behind every worthy cause there stretches a queue of *other causes of comparable worthiness*. If cancer research deserves state support, should not the fight against poliomyelitis also be assisted, as well as other vital areas of medical research? And don't the claims of medical research help to establish a case for supporting other valuable sciences, as well as the arts, and physical culture, and so on in ever-widening ripples? It is easy to visualize the rise of successive pressure groups for research, culture, sport, while an avowedly anti-culture or anti-sport pressure group seems simply unthinkable. Once again, the bias of the situation is such that its development will be onward and outward, to embrace more causes, to press home more claims, to redistribute more resources, hence stimulating more new demands – rather than the other way round, backward and inward, to a less pronounced group structure and a less redistributive, more 'minimal' state.

Anchored in the subconscious of educated liberal public opinion, there has for long been a sense of distinction between good and bad redistribution, between the honouring of just deserts and the currying of favours. In a recent, thoroughly sensible book, Samuel Brittan has done much to make the distinction explicit.[25] It is on the whole good to redistribute income so as to produce social justice and

24 Cf. W. Wallace, 'The Pressure Group Phenomenon', in Brian Frost (ed.), *The Tactics of Pressure*, 1975, pp. 93–4. Wallace also makes the point that causes feed on the mass media and the mass media feed on causes, from which it may be possible to infer further that some kind of cumulative process might get going even in the absence of the state. Would, however, people in the state of nature watch so much television? That is, isn't the habit of prolonged television-watching a product, in part, of people being less interested in doing state-of-nature things, either because it is no fun any more or because the state is doing them instead?
25 Samuel Brittan, *The Role and Limits of Government: Essays in Political Economy*, 1983.

security, health and education. It is bad to redistribute to favour special interest groups. Farm subsidies, 'industrial policy', rent control, accelerated depreciation, tax relief on home-mortgage interest or on retirement saving are on the whole bad, because they distort the allocation of resources – in the sense of making national income lower than it would otherwise be.

Two observations should briefly but urgently be made. One is that (unless we first define 'distortion' in the way required to produce the answer we want), nothing really allows us to suppose that taxation to raise revenue for a worthy objective or to dispense distributive justice, does not 'distort' the pre-tax allocation of resources. *A priori*, all taxes (even the one-time Holy Grail of welfare economics, the 'neutral' lump-sum tax), all transfers, subsidies, tariffs, price ceilings and floors, etc. must generally change the supplies and demands of interrelated products and factors. When we say that they distort them, all we are really saying is that we do not approve of the change. It is mildly self-delusive to assure ourselves that our approval is much more than the reflection of our prejudices, that it is an informed diagnosis, a function of some 'objective' criterion such as allocative efficiency reflected, somehow or other, in national income (rather than in the more controversial 'total utility' or 'welfare'). Whether the after-tax, after-welfare subsidy, after-tariff, etc. allocation of resources has given rise to a higher or lower national income than the pre-tax, pre-tariff, etc. one would have done, is an index number problem which has no *wertfrei* 'objective solution'. It is not a matter of knowledge, but of opinion, which may of course be 'sound opinion'. Most reasonable men might share the judgment that if all state revenue were raised by, say, a heavy excise tax on a commodity like salt which people simply must have, and all of it were spent to gratify the whims of Madame de Pompadour (an engagingly simple view of the bad old days to which few would own up though many still half-believe in), national income (let alone utility) would be less than under most other redistributive configurations known to history.[26] Less fanciful revenue–expenditure patterns, however, might

26 Madame de Pompadour would spend all her income on Sèvres china, and the rest of the people all their income on salt if the salt tax was set high enough to leave them no money for anything else. Note that since the demand for salt does not vary with its price, taxing it (rather than articles in more elastic demand) should not cause much distortion! Nevertheless, as all the national income is spent on salt and china, we may judge that it would be reduced by the salt tax.

give rise to genuine perplexity as to their incidence on the national product. Even those least inclined to agnosticism might honestly question the 'non-distortive' nature of some revenue-raising tax, however virtuous the cause in which it was levied.

The other observation is plainer and more important. It is simply that it really makes no practical difference whether we are able 'objectively' to tell good from bad redistribution. If we have one, we will have the other, too. A political system which, by virtue of competitive bidding for consent, produces redistribution we regard as conducive to equality or justice, will also produce redistribution we will regard as pandering to interest groups. By no means is it clear that there are 'objective' criteria for telling which is which. Still less evident are the means which could possibly constrain or stop the one while letting through the other.

To sum up. While in a political system requiring consent and allowing competition the state seems logically bound to engender redistribution, it does not in the everyday sense 'determine' its scope and scale. Once begun, the addictive nature of redistribution sets in motion unintended changes in individual character and the family and group structure of society. Though some may be regarded good and others bad, no selective control over them appears practicable. These changes react back upon the kind and extent of redistribution the state is obliged to undertake. Probabilities increase that a variety of cumulative processes may be set in motion. In each such process, redistribution and some social change mutually drive each other. The internal dynamics of these processes point ever onward; they do not seem to contain limiting, equilibrating mechanisms. Attempts by the state to limit them provoke withdrawal symptoms and may be incompatible with political survival in democratic settings.

Rising Prices

Inflation is either a cure or an endemic condition. Which it is depends on whether it can inflict the losses required to accommodate gains elsewhere.

Governing them helps to make the governed ungovernable.

No phenomenon has more than one complete explanation. A complete explanation, however, can be encoded in more than one system of expressions. Yet in English, Japanese or Spanish, it must remain much the same explanation. Alternative theories explaining a properly identified social or economic phenomenon are often fiercely competitive and insist on mutual exclusiveness. Yet they are either incomplete and wrong, or complete and identical in content to each other. If the latter, they must lend themselves to translation into each other's system of terms.

Alternative theories of inflation are a case in point. They are notoriously competitive. One conducts its argument in terms of excess demands for goods, summing it up as a shortfall of intended saving relative to intended investment. This is in turn linked to an excess of the expected return on capital over the interest rate, or words to that effect. Another posits some relation between present and expected future prices and interest rates on the one hand, and attempts by people to reduce (or increase) their cash balances on the other, the attempts driving up present prices. For those who like a dose of physics in their economics, the 'velocity' of some suitable variant of the 'quantity' of money will rise, or perhaps a broader variant of money will prove to be more suitable to which to apply a constant velocity. Whichever way it is put, the idea of people adjusting the real value of the money they hold to what they think they had better hold, expresses in terms of the excess supply of money what other theories put in the form of the excess demand for goods. Yet another theory would make the distribution of real income between high-saving capitalists (or the corporations they own) and low-saving workers, conform to whatever distribution is needed to provide just the amount of saving that will match investment. Inflation is to reduce consumption and boost profits by devaluing wages while, if cost-of-living indexation or agile wage bargaining prevents it from doing so, inflation will just go on running round in circles and accomplish nothing. The translation of this theory into the language of either of the others is perhaps a little less straightforward, but well within the capacity of the economically literate. (He may need some nudging. He is likely to have his favourite 'language', and may detest translating.)

One object of these musings is to underpin my contention that putting two theories of price levels (and embarrassingly calling one of them 'monetarism') in the centre of exited controversies of a near-religious kind, is beneath the intellectual quality of certain of the protagonists. The controversy is either spurious, or it is implicitly about other things and the debate would gain by making them explicit.

My other object in insisting on the essential equivalence of the reputable theories is, however, to make sure that no pretence of innovation shall be read into the nutshell explanatory scheme I am about to put forward. It is merely another brutally abridged 'translation' of received theory, largely running in the terminology used in the previous section of this chapter. Why it may be just worth making, and how it has its proper slot in the entire argument of this book, should become clear as we go on.

Take a society composed, for simplicity, only of organized interest groups. Each sells its particular contribution to the well-being of the others and buys theirs. The number of such groups is finite, hence each can influence its selling price, and we shall assume that all have done so in such a way that none can better its position. Let the advent of the millennium transform the membership of each group into like-minded altruists, who now engage in collective action to make the members of the other groups better off (without minding that this may impoverish their own fellow group members). They lower the price of the good or service they contribute, trying to improve the terms of trade for the others. However, as the others have become similarly inclined, they 'retaliate' by lowering their prices, not just to restore the original position, but to overshoot it since they want the first group to become better off than it was to begin with. The first group then retaliates, and so on. There is no built-in reason why the leap-frogging process should stop at any particular place, after any particular number of inconclusive rounds. The several 'price-makers', competing to make their contracting parties better off, will generate a rush of falling prices.

The near-perfect obverse of this millennium is, of course, some approximation to modern society as it has been taking shape in the last half-century. Over this period, while prices of assets have been known to move both up and down, the price 'level' of current goods and services has never fallen. Much of the time it has risen, and the tone of current discourse would suggest that this is now quite widely accepted as an endemic condition, to be lived with and kept within bounds by one means or another (without serious hope of eradication). *Endemic* inflation *would,* of course, be generated by a society of self-seeking interest groups where vain attempts to gain distributive shares produced interaction in an upside-down mirror image of the imaginary interaction of the altruists described in the preceding paragraph.

Progressively better articulated versions of an explanation running in terms of attempted gains and refusal of the matching losses, can be easily conceived. We could take a state-of-nature society where interest groups, having bargained and reached stalemate, are merely seeking to protect (rather than actually enlarge) their absolute and relative shares. Though they would accept windfall gains, they refuse to take windfall losses. (Perhaps unfairly, this would be my concise reading of the idea found in much of modern Panglossian macro-sociology, of pluralistic equilibrium resulting from the reciprocal adjustment of all major adversary interests, with no one ending up very angry). Any exogenous shock (unless it is a windfall gain, by a fluke enriching everybody in the same proportion) must consequently set off an inflationary spiral. The theory provides no reason why, once started, the spiral should ever stop, and no element governing its speed (or its acceleration). However, it accommodates reasonably well the classic war-and-harvest-failure type of causation, while ascribing to the structural features of society the reasons why price stability, once lost, cannot be regained (i.e. why inflation fails to do its job).

Making the customary one-way passage from state of nature to political society, such a theory can spread its wings and fly. Instead of being an exogenous shock, here the tug-of-war about distributive shares is not set off by a shock from outside, but is generated by the system itself, endogenously. It is what the interaction of the state and interest groups (including single business corporations at one end of the scale, entire social classes at the other), is mostly about. From here, it is a natural step to go on to some heavily politicized variant of the theory, with redistributive gains, due to state-oriented group action, setting off either market-oriented or state-oriented counter-action or both by the losers, including such lusty hybrids where a losing group acts against some section of the neutral public (e.g. truckers blocking highways and streets) to force the state to make good its loss.

A properly articulated theory might further incorporate such elements as inertia, money illusion or the differential power of various groups over their own terms of trade. It should allow for the stealthy nature of much redistribution due to the vastness and sheer complexity of modern fiscal and economic policy 'toolboxes', the frequently uncertain incidence of policies, as well as the seductive optical trick whereby incremental budgetary expenditure effects 'real' redistribution in the present while the incremental budget deficit ostensibly shifts the 'financial' burden to the future. The stealth inherent in the mechanics of many forms of redistribution – *overt to the gainers, covert to the losers* – for all that it is largely fortuitous and unplanned, may be supposed to lead to delayed or only partial counter-moves on the part of the losers; so that inflation may not nullify all redistribution. Once no one who can help it will give any more way, however, further redistribution at their expense is *ex hypothesi* bound to fail. As long as the attempt to do so continues, inflation to frustrate it must continue, too. If the nature of democratic politics is such that the attempt is endemic, so must be inflation.

A less abstract scenario would have a role written in for some unorganized section, stratum or function of society, captive bond-holders, small savers, widows and orphans (and all sufferers from 'liquidity preference'), which would have to end up losing if the gainers agreed to by the state were to gain, yet the *designated* losers manage to recapture the loss they were supposed to undergo. Inflation will, so to speak, 'search out' and wrest from weak hands, if there are any such, the resources the gainers were intended to gain. It will have acted as a cure of the resource imbalance. Having dealt with its own cause, it could then abate. The corollary is that once everybody is equally wordly-wise, organized, alert and absolutely determined to defend, in the market, in the picket line, in the party caucus or under banners out in the street, whatever he holds, inflation becomes powerless to change distributive shares. It becomes instead one of the more powerful means by which such shares are defended against pressures originating either in the political process or in nature.

A theory of inflation couched mainly in terms of the bulwarks the democratic state helps build around the very distributive shares whose manipulation is perhaps its principal method of staying in power, need not offer an explanation of why these shares are what they are to start with, nor why interest groups have a particular degree of price-making power. It can, of course, be plugged into the main corpus of economic theory which does contain such explanations. The plugging-in would in fact be the natural sequel to the 'translation' of this sort of vaguely sociological and political discourse into more rigorous economics of one kind or another. The exercise, however, would only serve to lay bare the relative lack of novelty of the present approach, whose real claim to a *raison d'être* is not that it helps understand inflation but that, through looking at the use or uselessness of inflation, it helps understand the mounting contradiction between redistribution building consent for state power and promoting the very conditions where *society becomes refractory* to its exercise.

In the section on addictive redistribution, I proposed the thesis that as democratic values are produced, ever more people get, use and come to require public aid, whose availability teaches them to organize for getting more of it in various forms. A consideration of inflation readily furnishes the antithesis. Redistribution changes personal, family and group character in such a way as to 'freeze' any given distribution. In breeding 'entitlements' and stimulating the rise of corporatist defences of acquired positions, it makes redistributive adjustments ever more difficult to achieve. Ringing the changes, 'making policy', erecting any novel pattern of gainers and losers overtaxes statecraft. If some overriding fact of life makes it imperative that there be losers, withdrawal symptoms start to show, tantrums are thrown, latter-day Luddites yield to the death wish and wreck their own livelihood rather than see it diminish, while misinvested capital moves heaven and earth to be rescued. If the state finds society 'ungovernable', there is at least a presumption that it is its own government that has made it so.

Churning

A cascade of gains whose costs must be borne by the gainers themselves, ultimately breeds more frustration and morose turbulence than consent.

Democracy's last dilemma is that the state must, but cannot, roll itself back.

Whether by simple-minded tax-and-transfer, or by the provision of public goods mostly paid for by some and mostly enjoyed by others, or by more roundabout and less transparently redistributive trade, industrial etc. policies, some of the state's subjects are on balance being hindered so that others may be helped. This holds true regardless of the aim of the exercise, i.e. even if the redistributive effect is an incidental, indifferent, unintended and maybe unnoticed by-product. The general common feature of these transactions is that *on balance* the state is robbing Peter to pay Paul. They are not 'Pareto-optimal'; they would not get unanimous assent from a self-interested Peter *and* Paul. In this sense they rank below 'social contracts' of the type where sovereign coercion is called in only in order to assure everybody of everybody else's adherence to a cooperative solution, so that Paul can gain without Peter losing (in Rousseau's infelicitous phrase, so that both can be 'forced to be free', i.e. better off than either could be without being forced to cooperate).

They rank below the some-gain-and-none-loses type of arrangements, *not* because we always prefer an arrangement where Paul gains without Peter losing, to one where Paul gains a lot and Peter loses a little. Some would regard it as positively good to take Peter down a peg or two. There may also be some other ground for favouring one over the other even if we do not believe that deducting one's loss from the other's gain to find the true balance of good makes sense. The some-gain-and-some-lose type of arrangements are inferior to the some-gain-and-none-loses sort only because the latter are *ipso facto* good (at least if envy is ruled out of the calculus), while the former require a ground on which to base the claim of their goodness. Gainers-only arrangements *requiring coercion* are interesting intellectual constructs. It is a moot point whether they really exist in reality, or that, if they do, they play an important part in the relations between state and society.[27] Some-gain-and-others-lose arrangements, on the other hand, are what consent and the adversary relations between state and subjects mainly revolve around.

Before having one last look at the dead end the state seems fated to manoeuvre itself into in the course of dealing out gains and losses, it seems to me necessary, and more than just pedantry, to protest against a spreading misconception of the very mechanics of robbing one to pay the other. For some time now it has been the custom to consider the fiscal functions of the state under the headings of

---

27 It is anyway difficult to think of a *pure* public good which could not at all be produced in the state of nature, though it is arguable that goods with a high degree of 'publicness' would be produced on a 'sub-optimal' scale. However, the very notion of an optimal scale is more fragile than it looks, if only because tastes for public goods may well depend on *how they are produced*, e.g. *politics may breed a taste for political solutions*, and make people forget how to solve their problems by cooperating spontaneously.

allocation and *distribution*.[28] Under allocation are subsumed the *who does what* decisions about providing public goods, 'steering the economy' and making sure that markets perform their work. Distribution as a fiscal function deals with *who gets what*, with undoing the markets' work. The conceptual separation has led to treating these functions as a sequence, inducing social engineers to roll up their sleeves and set to work: 'First we allocate, then we distribute what the allocation has produced.' The supposition that, in a system of strong inter-dependences, distribution depends on allocation but allocation does not depend on distribution, is remarkable.[29] Those who so blithely make it, would in fact get quite cross if it turned out to be valid. If robbing Peter did *not* result in his consuming less champagne and fewer dancing girls, and paying Paul did not lead to his getting more health care and to his deserving children staying longer at school, why did the social engineers bother at all? What did the redistribution accomplish? The decision to let Paul get more and Peter less, is implicitly also a decision to allocate ex-dancing girls to teaching and nursing. This fails to be true only in the freak case of an impoverished Peter and an enriched Paul jointly requiring the services of the *same* total 'mix' of dancing girls, hospital nurses and schoolteachers as before.

Carrying on from the allocation–distribution dichotomy, liberals consider that politics is about two different sorts of domains. One is the basically non-conflictual one of allocation, giving rise to 'positive-sum games'. The other is the grimmer, conflictual who-gets-what domain of 'zero-sum games'. (Note again, as in chapter 3, pp. 162, 165, that as these are not games, the invocation of game theory language is a little trendy, but let that pass.) I have insisted, perhaps more than sufficiently, that these alleged games cannot be played separately, and that allocative decisions are at the same time distributive decisions and *vice versa*. A who-gets-what decision conditions what shall be provided and hence who does what. Emancipating one decision from the other recalls the Marxist ambition to distinguish the 'government of men' from the 'administration of things'.

While it may be legitimate to view changes in allocation as capable, if all goes well, of yielding positive sums so that math-

28 Explicitly, I think, since 1959, and the publication of R.A. Musgrave's basic textbook *The Theory of Public Finance*.
29 I have noted (p. 158), dealing with Rawls's distributive justice and the 'background institutions' that go with it, a particularly stark form of this supposition.

ematically nobody *need* lose as a result of the change, what do we say if somebody *did* lose? It is no use saying that the loss is really attributable to an attendant zero-sum distributional decision, and that if only the distribution had been different, the loser need not have lost; since a different distribution would have entailed a different allocation. The statement about the two decisions would be incoherent even if it ran in terms of sums of money, or apples, for we could not just suppose that the allocative gain would have been preserved if we had tried to distribute it differently. It would be doubly incoherent if it ran in terms of mixed bundles of goods, let alone utilities, for this would strike many people as an attempt to seek the residual balance between more apples for Paul and fewer pears for Peter.

The burden of this argument, if there is one, is that redistribution is *a priori* not a zero-sum game (for it has effects on allocation) and that it seems very difficult to tell *empirically* what it is. Calling it 'zero-sum' evokes a false image of the state's redistributive function as something neutral, harmless, leaving intact the interests of parties other than Peter and Paul. The evocation is false for two reasons. First, even if (abstracting from the cost of administering and policing these arrangements) the resource cost of Paul's gain in some accounting sense exactly offset the resource cost of Peter's loss, the two could still be held to be unequal from a 'welfare' or class war angle. Second and more important, resource allocation must correspond to the new distribution. Contracts, property relations, investment, jobs, etc. all have to be adjusted.

Greater or lesser repercussions must impinge on everybody's interest, though some interests may be affected only imperceptibly. These repercussions are themselves redistributive – perhaps unintentionally and perversely so.[30] The total effect is to extend and magnify, well beyond the interests of the parties ostensibly concerned, the

---

30 Contrast the position taken by Nozick, *Anarchy, State and Utopia*, p. 27: 'We might elliptically call an arrangement "redistributive" if its major ... supporting reasons are themselves redistributive. ... Whether we say an institution that takes money from some and gives it to others is redistributive depends upon *why* we think it does so.' This view would not recognize unintentional, incidental, perverse redistributions, and may or may not regard our 'direct churning' as redistribution. Its interest is not in whether certain arrangements do redistribute resources, but in whether they were meant to.

The distinction may be interesting for some purposes. It recalls the one the courts make between premeditated murder and manslaughter, a distinction which is more significant to the accused than to the victim.

secondary turbulence of allocation-*cum*-distribution induced by a given act of primary redistribution.

At least conceptually, we must keep track of three separate elements of turbulence. The first is *direct redistribution*, where the state imposes an arrangement making some interests better off at the expense of others (whether intentionally or not). The second is the unintended reallocation-*cum*-redistribution induced by the first. Let us label this secondary turbulence, which absorbs some energy and involves some trouble of adjustment (and not only to dancing girls), '*indirect churning*'. '*Direct churning*' describes fairly fully the third element. It is, from the accounting point of view, gross redistribution leaving either no or only some incidental net balance. This occurs when the state grants some aid, immunity, differential treatment or other gain to a person or an interest, and (quite possibly willy-nilly, only because no other way is more practicable) meets the resource cost by inflicting a more or less equivalent loss, normally in a different form, upon the *same* person or interest. Superficially, this may look absurd though I hope it does not. The state has a quite compelling *rationale* to churn this way. The argument for sheer churning has a good many strands. Following but a few should suffice for seeing its force.

It is not absurd to suppose, for a start, that there is some lack of symmetry (somewhat akin to critical mass or to the justly despised 'change of quantity into quality') between people's perception of their large and small interests. Many of them just do not notice, or shrug off, gains or losses beneath some threshold. Having arrived at this diagnosis, the state must rationally apply the calculus of political support-building in its light. In certain situations, its rational course will be to create a few large gainers (whose support it can thus buy) matched by many small losers (who just shrug if off). This is why it may be good politics to put a heavy duty on foreign wheat to oblige the growers, and let the price of a loaf rise just that little bit,[31] and more generally to favour the producer interest over the more diffuse consumer interest, independently of the fact that the producer is organized to extract a price for his support while the consumer is not, or is so less effectively. It is needless to remind ourselves that if the

31   The calculus seems to work out the other way round in states, notably in Africa, where the rural population is physically too cut off from politics and it is best to sacrifice agricultural interests to the urban proletariat, the state employees, the soldiers, etc. by a policy of low farm prices.

state, in making the running or just by keeping one step ahead of the opposition, goes round every producer group to exploit this benign asymmetry, every one of its subjects playing a double role as producer and consumer will make one noticeable gain 'financed' by a large number of quite small losses. The net balance of redistribution, if any and if it can be ascertained, will be submerged under large flows of gross gains and gross losses impinging on much the same people; 'direct' churning will be going on. The quantities of resources churned through indirect taxes, subsidies and by price-fixing, may well dwarf any net transfer associated with the churning.

An equally commonplace argument leads from 'industrial policies' to churning. Whether to promote its growth or to save it from decline and extinction, the political benefit from helping a business firm or an industry (especially as it 'provides jobs') is likely to exceed the political damage caused by a small and diffuse increase in the costs faced by other firms and industries. The upshot, then, is that it is good for the democratic state to make every industry support every other in various, more or less opaque ways.[32] There results a broad overlap of self-cancelling gains and losses, leaving perhaps only narrow slivers of some net gain here, some net loss there. Quite *where* any such slivers are located must itself be in some doubt. Given the intricate nature of the social and economic stuff that is being churned, it is altogether on the cards *both* that the industry which was meant to be helped was actually harmed, *and* that nobody can tell for sure which way any net effect went, if there was any at all.

Another strand of the argument about churning is the apparent asymmetry between the capacities of democratic states to say yes and to say no. Resisting pressure, rejecting the demands of an interest or simply refraining from doing some good for which there is much disinterested support, more often than not has an immediate, indisputable and perhaps menacing political *cost*. The political *benefit* of saying no, on the other hand, is usually long-term, speculative and slow to mature. It is devalued by the discount that insecurity of

---

32   P. Mathias, *The First Industrial Nation*, 1969, pp. 87–8, lists British policies to help the textile industry; the Corn Laws; the ban on the export of sheep and wool; the bounty on the export of beer and of malt; the ban on the import of the latter; the Navigation Acts, etc. as examples of measures where one industry was helped at the expense of another *and vice versa*. Professor Mathias remarks that this would look inconsistent and irrational if the economic policy of the era were to be regarded as a logically organized system.
   A crazy quilt of cross-subsidization, etc. may, however, have a perfectly adequate political logic of its own, for all that it is self-contradictory as an 'economic' policy.

tenure places on distant pay-offs, as well as by the trivial 'drop in the bucket' nature of most individual yes-or-no choices.

In a richly differentiated society with a large variety of concerns and interests, the state is constantly making numbers of small decisions in favour or against some such interest, each merely involving 'a million here and a million there'. Admittedly, their sum soon runs to billions and, with 'a billion here and a billion there, soon you are talking real money'. Yet none of the individual decisions takes the state in one leap from the realm of millions to the realm of real money. The day of reckoning is in any case more than a week away ('a long time in politics'), and as compromises and the fudging of issues have a *sui generis* advantage over 'polar' solutions, the state usually ends up by at least partially satisfying any given demand. However, both Peter and Paul have frequent occasions for making various demands upon the state; the more times they have successfully demanded in the past, the more often are they likely to present demands now. As the bias of the system is such that the state tends to say at least a partial 'yes' to the bulk of them, the major result is bound to be churning. *Both* Peter *and* Paul will be paid on several counts by robbing *both* of them in a variety of more or less transparent ways, with a possibly quite minor net redistribution in favour of Paul emerging as the residual by-product.

A corollary of the above is that some people or groups will gain from some direct or unintended redistributive arrangements while losing much the same sums from others. Not all can, let alone will, see through this and recognize their *net* position, if indeed a *net* position has objective meaning. Since economic policy causes prices and factor incomes to be other than what they would be in a *policyless* capitalist state, and since it may in any case be inherently impossible to 'know' the ultimate incidence of the total set of directives, incentives, prohibitions, taxes, tariffs, etc. in force, a subject need not be stupid to be mistaken about where the churning around him really leaves him.[33]

---

33 Even the most basic, direct 'net' redistributive arrangement can mislead, causing mischief all round, as Tocqueville has noted. The landowning nobility of continental Europe attached great value to their tax exemption, and commoners resented it. True to form, Tocqueville recognized that in reality the tax came out of the rent of the noble's land, whether it was technically he or his serfs or farmers who paid it. Yet both the nobles and the commoners were led and misled, in their political attitudes, by the *apparent* inequality of treatment rather than by its *real* incidence. (*L'ancien régime et la révolution*, 1967, pp. 165–6).

It is in the state's interest to foster systematic error.[34] The more people think they are gainers and the fewer who resent this, the cheaper it is – crudely speaking – to split society into two moderately unequal halves and secure the support of the preponderant half. With free entry into the competition for state power and hence the extreme unlikelihood of collusion among the rivals, however, the opposition must seek to dissipate systematic error as fast as the state succeeds in inducing it, in fact to induce systematic error of the opposite sign by telling the gainers that they are losers. Whoever is in power in democratic states, it is the steady endeavour of the opposition to persuade the broad middle class that it is paying more in taxes than it is getting back, and to tell the working class (if such an old-fashioned category is still admitted to exist) that the burden of the welfare state really rests on *its* back. (When in opposition, 'right' and 'left' both arrive at some such conclusion from opposite premises, roughly as follows: living standards of working people are too low because profits are too low/too high.) Whatever the real influence of these debates, there is no good reason to assume that they simply cancel each other out. It seems *a priori* probable that the more highly developed and piecemeal is the redistributive system and the more difficult it is to trace its ramifications, the more scope there must be for false consciousness, for illusions and for downright mistakes by both the state and its subjects.

Contrary to the sharp-edged outcome of a pure rich-to-middle redistributive auction in a homogenous single-interest society (see pp. 199–204), complex, addictive, heterogenous interest-group

---

34 Randall Bartlett, *Economic Foundations of Political Power*, 1973, makes the related point that governments seek to mislead voters by producing biased information about public expenditures, taxes, etc. It seems fair to add that the cost-of-living indices and unemployment statistics of some modern states are not above suspicion either. One might reflect further on the conditions under which a rational state would choose selectively to publish truthful statistics, lies and no statistics, allowing for the effort needed to keep secrets (especially selectively), the inconvenience of the right hand not knowing what the left is doing, and the risks involved in coming to believe one's own lies. The right mix of truth, falsehood and silence looks very difficult to achieve – even the Soviet Union, which chooses its preferred 'mix' more freely than most other states, seems to have mixed itself a poisonous brew.

The fostering of systematic error by mendacious statistics, however, is kid's stuff compared to some of its other forms. In the development and propagation of a *dominant* ideology, defined as one favourable to the *state's* purposes, systematic error is generally being fostered without conscious design, i.e. far more effectively and durably than by mere lying. For instance, the powerful notion that the state is an *instrument in the hands of its citizens* (whether of all citizens, of the majority or of the propertied class) has certainly not originated in any Ministry of Propaganda. Educators inculcating doctrines of the state producing public good, and the requisite norms of good citizenship, are doing so in all sincerity.

churning seems to produce a much fuzzier pattern. Very probably it can produce several such patterns and we cannot really predict which one it will be. Since there is a large number of alternative ways in which a highly differentiated, disparate society's multiplicity of interests can be lined up on two nearly equal sides, there is no longer a presumption (such as I have established for a homogenous society) of *one best, unbeatable* pattern of redistribution which a political competitor can match but not outbid. Hence, there need be no strong tendency either for the convergence of programmes or the disappearance of genuine political alternatives. A somewhat rightist and a recognizably leftist policy can be serious rivals of each other.

Any rivalry, however, still entails competing offers of *some* net transfer of money, services, favours or liberties from some people to others, for with other things equal, he who makes *some* such offer can, under simple everyday assumptions about why people support a policy, generate more support than he who makes *none*. This is the case even if there is much fuzziness about the shape of the winning offer (note that a deterministic reliance on 'natural constituencies' and on the programmes which either constituency imposes on its champion, will not do; many interests no longer fit into any natural constituency, left, right, conservative or socialist, but swell the 'swing middle' which must be bought). Our theory becomes blurred, as it probably should in its descent to a progressively less abstract level.

The central thrust of the theory, however, does not get altogether lost. With tenure heavily dependent on the consent of its own subjects, competititon still drives the state into some redistributive auction. The comparability of rival offers is more limited than in the abstract rich-to-middle tax-and-transfer version. There is no longer one simultaneous tender offer of a coherent set of positive and negative payments for support, addressed to particular segments of society. Instead, there is a prolonged cascade (perhaps ebbing and flowing with the electoral calendar), of quite diverse aids and fines, bounties and bans, tariffs and refunds, privileges and hindrances, some of which may be difficult to quantify. The opposition cascade is promise, the state cascade is, at least in part, performance. Comparison of the two is evidently not a light undertaking for a person with manifold concerns ranging from civil rights to the mortgage on his house, fair trade in his business and poor teaching at his children's school, to name but a few in random order.

Rival offers need not be closely similar, nor need they completely exhaust the whole potential 'pay-off' available for redistribution. The concept of the potential pay-off itself must be reinterpreted in a less precise manner. It can no longer be treated as co-extensive with taxable capacity, the less so as a good deal of redistribution is an indirect result of various state policies and totally bypasses taxes. When all this is duly said, however, political competition still means that neither rival can afford to content itself with offering much lower net redistributive gains than its tentative estimate of the net loss it can safely impose on the losers.

The interdependence, within any differentiated social system, between who gets what and who does what, and the few common-place assumptions about psychology and the working of consent-dependent political regimes, introduced in this section, steer the issue from competitive equilibrium to what I propose to call the last democratic dilemma.

Over and above any direct redistribution, a great deal of indirect churning will be generated. The state will also engage, off its own bat and responding to piecemeal political incentives, in additional direct churning. The addictive effect of (gross) gains under churning, no-tably the stimulus provided to interest group proliferation, is likely to cause churning to grow over time despite the absence and quasi-impossibility of further net gains. False consciousness, systematic error, a degree of producer-consumer schizophrenia and some free-riding bias in group action in favour of extorting gains (and never mind that after every *other* group has extorted *its* gain, the first group's share in the resulting total of costs will have wiped out its gain) – all these deviations may suffice to offset, up to some point, the inconveniences and costs of churning and still produce political benefits on balance. The more churning there is, however, the more the balance is liable to tip over, *both* because more churning takes more government, more overriding of mutually acceptable private contracts, more state influence over the disposal of incomes and the rights of property (which may *upset one half* of society), *and* because of some perhaps dim, inarticulated frustration, anger and disappoint-ment that so much redistributive ado is at the end of the day mainly about nothing (which may *upset the other half*).

Rather like the individual political hedonist who finds that as the state increases the pleasure it bestows, after some point (which he may or may not have actually reached yet) the accompanying pain increases faster and it would be best if one could just stop before quite getting there, society is also likely to reach some point of marginal pleasure–pain equivalence where 'it would like to stop.' However, there is no operative meaning in this 'would like to'. Society cannot call a stop, nor can it make any other decision (though majorities can make a limited range of decisions in its name and the representatives of the majority can decide additional matters in *its* name, and the state may carry them out in *their* name, none of which is in dispute here). Should it find too much of its arrangements churned more than it feels is congenial or indeed tolerable, society has no obvious recourse against the democratic political process which yielded this result. It may respond with uncomprehending rage, with what former French President Valery Giscard d'Estaing aptly called 'morose turbulence' and sullen cynicism. Its frustration will obviously threaten the political survival of the state which, by inadvertence, line of least resistance and the pressures of the social structure called forth by its own consent-seeking, has pushed churning too far.

On the other hand, net goes with gross, genuine redistribution is accompanied by churning. If continued tenure of power dictates a certain genuine redistribution, a growing volume of churning on top of it is nearly certain to be induced for one good reason and another. Yet if the former is consistent with political survival, the latter may be excessive for it. There may consequently no longer be *any* possible political equilibrium position, not even one of unrewarding state drudgery. A genuine existential impasse may be reached: the state both must and must not redistribute.

It is this contradiction which conditions the mixed-up, disoriented split personality of many present-day democratic states.[35] Ideology must go hand in hand with interest. In recent years, the dominant ideology of Western democracy has been cautiously co-opting a sprinkling of previously rejected elements of theoretical anarchism, libertarianism and traditional individualism; before we know where we are, Herbert Spencer will be radical chic. On a less cerebral plane, deeply felt claims mount for 'rolling back the state'. As the quarter-turn of ideological fashion unfailingly signals, it has in a sense become clever policy for the state to roll itself back.

---

35 As I write (1984), the jury is still out on the Reagan administration and Mrs Thatcher's government. Both seem at the same time to be rolling *and* not rolling back the state. Comparing their strong commitment on the one hand and the slightness of the result on the other, one is reminded of the irresistible force meeting the immovable object.

Torn between a rational interest to go on producing the 'democratic values' that the beneficiaries have taught themselves to depend on (and at least to continue upholding if not furthering the group interests whose support it cannot afford to forgo), and an equally rational interest to respond to the mounting *poujadisme,* frustration and ungovernability of much the same people and much the same interests by doing virtually the opposite, the state twists and turns and explains away its own incoherent evolutions with incoherent rhetoric. In two minds, by fits and starts fighting its own nature, it resists its own attempts to make itself shrink.

Towards a Theory of the State

It would be rational for a state pursuing its own ends to escape from the treadmill where its power is used up in its own reproduction.

Did Plato's Republic 'degenerate' on the way from democracy to despotism?

This is the place for drawing some of our threads closer together. Depending on the scale and perspective of the analysis, it is possible to regard the state in several ways. One is to take it as an inanimate tool, a machine. It has no ends and no will; only persons have ends. Explanation and prediction of its movements must, therefore, deal at one remove with the persons who wield the tool and shift the levers of the machine. Another is to merge the machine and the people who run it, and consider the state as a live institution which behaves as it would if it had a will of its own and a single hierarchy of ends; as if it could choose between alternatives and in doing so seemed to conform to the rudiments of rationality. We have throughout adopted the latter view, not because it is more realistic (neither is), but because it looks the most fertile in plausible deductive consequences.

Once we think of the state as having ends and a will of its own, theories and doctrines which have the state serve the interests of Hobbes's seekers after eminence, Rousseau's myopic deer-hunters or Engels's oppressor class, take on a strongly question-begging quality: for however convincing the accounts they give of how the state *could* or *does* serve such interests, they furnish no reason why it *should* serve them. Yet while the supposition that a will seeks the fulfilment of its ends can be taken as read (it is implicit in rationality; besides, it is hard to think of a will floating freely, not associated with *any* end), a supposition that it seeks to serve the ends of *others* needs justification, explicit support of some sort. There is, in my view, no such support for it in either the contractarian or the Marxist theory of the state. It may, in fact, be a misnomer to call either one a theory of the *state*, though they are both theories of the individual (or class) subject's *interest* in the state. Moreover, as I have contended in chapter 1, even if it had good reasons to, the state could not pursue the interests of its subjects unless they were homogenous. Its adversary relation to them is inherent in its having to take one side or the other between conflicting interests if it is to have any 'policies' at all.

A successful theory of the state should not have to rely on the gratuitous assumption that the state is subservient to some interest other than its own. It should lend itself to the explanation of the state's role in political history in terms of *its* interest interacting, competing, conflicting with and duly adjusted to the interests of others.[36]

What, however, is the proper view of the interests of the state? When do we say that it is using its power to fulfil its ends? I have from the outset reconciled the possibility of 'minimalness' and rationality by laying down the 'marker' that a state will choose to be minimal ('capitalist', 'policyless' – alternative terms I consider to have substantially the same effect as 'minimal'), if its ends lie beyond politics and cannot be attained by the use of power – if they are not the satisfactions of governing. On the other hand, all the policies a non-minimal state does adopt are, tautologically, in its interest, in the fulfilment of its ends, except when it is being foolish. Some of these policies, however, can yet be told apart from the others. Into this split, the thin end of a theory of the state might be wedged.

Certain policies, and the specific measures they call for, can at least conceptually be singled out as having a common negative feature: they appear to contribute to no *plausible end,* satisfy no manifest *taste,* augment no conceivable *enjoyment* of the state other than the

---

36 Historiography tends to deal more satisfactorily with states appearing in the shape of kings and emperors than with states which are faceless institutions. All too often, the latter are confused with the country, the nation; the historical driving force springing from the *conflict between state and civil society* is left at the edge of the field of vision. When the game is Emperor vs Senate, the king and his burghers vs the nobility, or the king vs established privileges and 'ancient freedoms', historians are less apt to make us lose sight of which interests make the state do what it does.

maintenance of its tenure. They just help keep it *in power*. They use power in order to *reproduce* it. If it is right to say that Roman senators felt no altruistic love for the *plebs,* yet gave them bread and circuses, they 'must have' done so because it seemed to them necessary for the maintenance of the existing order. If one can take it that Richelieu did not actually prefer townsmen to nobles, yet favoured the former and sought to weaken the latter, he 'must have' done so in order to consolidate royal power. (The 'must have' is in inverted commas to invite the reader's complicity and indulgence. So much of historical explanation is, inevitably and I think properly, no more than the elevation of the least unreasonable hypothesis to the rank of the true cause.)

Some measures, in addition to reproducing the state's power, *may* contribute to its other ends as well. Their nature is such that no presumption stands to the contrary. When a President Peron or a contemporary African government pampers the urban masses, we can say that it 'must' be doing so because it has staked its political survival on their support (or acquiescence), but it is not absurd to allow that it likes them, too. Hence, it may be actually pleased to make workers, clerks and soldiers better off at the expense of haughty cattle barons or obtuse tribal villagers. The shape of these measures *reveals* their support-buying, power-maintaining function, yet it *permits* the supposition that some other end is being fulfilled, too. Much of the redistribution undertaken by the modern democratic state has this shape.

There is sufficient historical evidence, however, of a clear-cut class of other policies and acts of state which use state power *without* intelligibly, plausibly visibly contributing to its maintenance. The religious policies of James II, Charles XII of Sweden's campaigns or the profligacy of the Naples Bourbons have, if anything, weakened their hold on power. Gladstone's failed attempts to give Home Rule to Ireland, the *Kulturkampf* fought by the Second Reich, or American near-belligerence on Britain's side in 1940 *used up* some of the support enjoyed by the respective governments. Though they may have been the right thing to do, it is hard to argue that they were good politics. If such policies are nevertheless pursued, they 'must' fulfil an end other than the prolongation of the tenure of power. When Peter the Great brought in Germans to run Russia, made himself odious and ruthlessly upset the old ways, he was *using up* power in the short run (he had a margin to spare) even if the longer-run effects strengthened the throne (which is arguable).

A parallel should make the distinction clearer still. Conceptually, we are used to the idea of 'subsistence wages'. Marx has built his whole unfortunate theory of value and capital on the idea of the labour-time 'socially necessary' for the reproduction of labour. Only a part of the labourer's time is used up to produce the subsistence he needs to go on labouring, and subsistence is all he gets.[37] No matter that subsistence turns out to be impossible to pin down. As an idea, it is simple and powerful and it leads straight to surplus value and the class struggle. In our framework, the use of the power necessary for its own maintenance takes the place of the subsistence wage spent on the maintenance of the labourer. The surplus value that his labour time has produced in addition, accrues to capital as the pay-off to domination. In our scheme, 'surplus value' would correspond to whatever satisfactions the state can afford to procure for itself over and above the maintenance of its tenure of power. Another, less 'analytical' parallel is that between income and discretionary income, power and discretionary power.

Discretionary power is what the state can use to make its subjects listen to Bach and not listen to rock; to change the course of mighty rivers and transform nature; to build presidential palaces and government offices in keeping with its taste and sense of proportion; to deal out rewards and privileges to those who deserve it and to keep down those who deserve that, regardles of political expediency; to do good and aid causes its subjects care little about; to pursue national greatness, to invest in the well-being of a distant posterity and to make others adopt its values.

Our theory would not be a social theory if it had no sting in its tail, no indirect, roundabout secondary effects and no 'feedback loops'. Thus, it is entirely likely that once the state has made people observe the cult of Bach, *and* they have in due course taught themselves to like it, they will 'identify' better with the state which gave them their tastes. Likewise, the splendour of the presidential palace, the achievement of national greatness and 'being first on the moon' may in the end implant in the public consciousness a certain sense of the state's

37   In modern parlance, the labourer has 'maximized' when accepting to work for subsistence wages. No better alternative was offered to him. A different, more 'strategic' sense of maximization, however, would have him attempt to influence the available alternatives. He could try to organize a union and bargain collectively, or strike. He could seek redress in 'distributive justice' thorugh the democratic political process. He could also fall in behind the 'vanguard of the working class' and join the struggle to modify the 'relations of production'.

legitimacy, a perhaps growing willingness to obey it regardless of hope of gain and fear of loss. Hence, they may serve as a cunning and slow-acting substitute for buying consent. Like Peter the Great's administrative reform, however, they require a discretionary margin of power *now* even if they are certain to yield greater legitimacy or a stronger repressive apparatus or both *later*.

Instead of saying, tautologically, that the rational state pursues its interests and maximizes its ends, whatever they are, I propose to adopt, as a criterion of its rationality, that it seeks to maximize its discretionary power.[38, 39]

Discretionary power permits the state to make its subjects do what it wants, rather than what they want. It is exercised by taking their property and liberty. The state can appropriate people's money and buy things (including their services) with it. It can also override their spontaneous intentions and order them to serve its purposes. When the state is defending its tenure in open competition, however, all the property and liberty it *can* take is, by the definition of competitive equilibrium, absorbed in the 'reproduction' of power, i.e. in the maintenance of its tenure by redistribution. The existence of a discretionary surplus would contradict the assumption of competition, under which it is impossible so to rearrange or enrich the redistributive pattern as to obtain more support for it (cf. the earlier section of this chapter on the 'profitless', break-even character of equilibrium). This condition loses some of its precision and rigidity as we move to lower levels of abstraction; we introduce fuzziness, a margin of error, but no novel set of reasons to render likely the emergence of an appreciable discretionary surplus.

At this point, the state has completed its unwitting transformation,

38　If it takes the application of a fixed 'amount' of power to stay in power, with the surplus (if any) available for exercise at discretion, anything which maximizes power must also maximize the discretionary surplus. The fastidious may therefore wince at 'discretionary power' as the *maximand*; why not just plain power?

However, the convenience of a built-in separation between 'being in power' and 'using power to freely chosen ends' seems to me to outweigh the inelegance of the solution. If the *maximand* is discretionary power, we can describe competitive equilibrium in politics as the position where discretionary power is nil. This has the didactic merit of rhyming with the position of the perfectly competitive firm whose profit is nil after it has paid for all its factors of production.

39　Political theory, as we have seen, asks questions of a teleological nature and treats the state as an instument: What can states do for their citizens? What ought they to do? What are the obligations and limits of civil obedience?, etc. I know of only two serious precedents of attributing a *maximand* to the state itself. Both do so in the context of theorizing about the production of public goods. One is Albert Breton, *The Economic Theory of Representative Government*, 1974. He postulates that the majority party will behave so as to maximize a from being the seducer freely offering utilitarian improvement, one-man—one-vote and distributive justice, to being the drudge only just coping with its self-imposed redistributive obligations. Moreover, it has entrapped itself in several predicaments at once. One is competition, being on the treadmill. Another is the changing character of society in response to its own redistributory activity, notably addiction to aid, free-rider behaviour by each interest group towards all others and progressive loss of control over redistribution. An extreme form of this predicament is to be up against an 'ungovernable' society. Finally, as direct redistribution is overlaid by ever thicker layers of churning, in the ultimate democratic predicament there is no possible equilibrium: society both demands and refuses the state's redistributive role. The latter, in maintaining consent, ought both to go on expanding and to 'roll itself back'.

Were we to dismiss this terminal self-contradiction as mere dialectic word-play and allow equilibrium to persist, however, the latter would still not represent a proper maximum for the state, except in the tenuous sense in which the earning of the subsistence wage is a 'maximum' for the labourer. With no, or negligible, discretionary power, the state is better off than in any other available posture, in each of which it would lose power altogether and be replaced by its opposition.[40] It is rational for it to cling to this position. It may well content itself with it and just soldier on. Nevertheless, if it could deliberately change some of the available alternatives, i.e. modify in its favour the social and political environment to which it adjusts when 'maximizing', it could make itself better off. *Recognition* of

---

function increasing in some way with the chance of re-election, power, personal gain, image in history and its view of the common good. The other is Richard Auster and Morris Silver, *The State as a Firm*, 1979. Here the *maximand* is the difference between tax revenue and the cost of the public goods produced by the state. Auster and Silver hold that unlike monarchy or oligarchy, democracy amounts to 'diffuse ownership' among politicians and bureaucrats, and hence there is no residual income-recipient to profit from a surplus of taxes over the cost of public goods (leading to their over-production). I would interpret this to mean that in democracy there is no 'maximizer'.

Note also, as examples of an approach which proceeds, so to speak, from the 'producer's' motives rather than those of the 'consumer', W.A. Niskanen Jr, *Bureaucracy and Representative Government*, 1971, where 'bureaux' seek to maximize their budgets, and B.S. Frey and F. Schneider, 'A Politico-Economic Model of the United Kingdom', *Economic Journal*, 88, June 1978, who find that when the government is unpopular, it pursues popular policies and when it is popular, it indulges its own ideology.

40 Formally, discretionary power would have become negative in such postures, hence (total) power would be inadequate to ensure its own maintenance; the tenancy of the state would change hands.

some such possibility (though not necessarily any *action* to realize it) may in fact be regarded as a criterion of another, higher order of rationality. Making itself *less dependent on its subjects' consent,* and making it *harder for rivals to compete,* would amount to improving the environment instead of adjusting to it.

It is not, of course, actually irrational for the state not to do this. I am not arguing some historical necessity, some inexorable dynamics which must cause any state, if sound of mind, to become totalitarian. On the other hand, I would not accept that, like Plato's Republic on its way from democracy to despotism, the state 'degenerates' in the process. If it has improved its ability to fulfil *its* ends, it has not degenerated, though it may well have become less apt to serve the ends of the observer, who would then have every reason to be alarmed by the change. I am arguing, though, that it is rational in a higher, 'strategic' sense of rationality different from the 'tactical' sense of optimal adjustment, for the state generally to become more rather than less totalitarian to the extent that it can get away with it, i.e. maintain majority support at the stage where it still needs it. It is also rational for a rival for power to propose, under democracy, a more totalitarian alternative if this is more attractive to the majority though more unattractive to the minority.[41] Hence, there is in competitive, democratic politics, always a latent propensity for totalitarian transformation. It manifests itself in the frequent appearance of socialist policies within non-socialist government and opposition programmes, and in socialist streaks in the liberal ideology.

Whether or to what extent this potential is realized is a matter almost of hazard, of the fundamentally unpredictable historical setting. By neat contrast, no potential *the other way round,* for the democratic transformation of a totalitarian state, can be logically derived from any maximization assumption that would admit of the state having the kind of ends, whatever they are specifically, whose attainment calls for the discretionary use of power.

---

41 Such proposals reach beyond the bounds of the simple sort of electoral competition set out earlier in this chapter. In addition to promising the majority the minority's money (equalizing incomes), they might, for instance, include the equalizing of schools (*Gleichschaltung* of education) or the equalizing of 'economic power' (nationalization of the 'means of production'), or some other property, privilege, immunity of the minority, including its creed (Huguenots, Mormons) or race (Jews).

5

State Capitalism

What is to be Done?

State capitalism is the fusion of political and economic power. It ends the anomaly of armed force being centred in the state, while the ownership of capital is dispersed throughout civil society.

People will finally be stopped from claiming through politics what is denied them by economics.

When he laid down the agenda for the out-of-power elite in 'What Is To Be Done?', Lenin wanted his party to conquer by professionalism, secrecy, centralization, specialization and exclusivity. Harsh and chilling, his programme was not the sort the seeker after power can openly lay out before a public he needs to seduce. Laying it out would have spoilt his chances, had they ever depended on broad public support or any manner of capturing supreme power, other than by the previous tenant's default, that is to say by the collapse, in the chaos of a lost war and the February 1917 revolution, of the defences of the regime he sought to replace. He was for taking society unawares, securing the essential instruments of repression and using them without much regard for popular consent. As he put it almost on the eve of the Bolshevik assumption of power in October 1917, 'people as they are now' rather than as they are supposed to become in 'anarchist utopias', 'cannot dispense with subordination', which 'must be to the armed vanguard of all the exploited and working people, i.e. to the proletariat',[1] undiluted by petty-bourgeois cant about 'the peaceful submission of the minority to the majority'.[2] He

1 V.I. Lenin, 'The State and Revolution', in *Selected Works*, 1968, p. 296.
2 Ibid., p. 279.

thought it 'splendid' of Engels to declare that 'the proletariat needs the state, not in the interests of freedom but in order to hold down its adversaries.'[3] Once in power, he scolded that 'our government is excessively mild, very often it resembles jelly more than iron';[4] he called for the fiction of an impartial judiciary to be forgotten, stating ominously that as organs of proletarian power, 'the courts are an instrument for inculcating discipline,'[5] and explaining that there is 'absolutely *no* contradiction in principle between Soviet (*that is* socialist) democracy and the exercise of dictatorial powers by individuals.'[6] (This truth must be treated as a powerful one, derived as it is from the 'material base' of society, for 'unquestioning subordination to a single will is absolutely necessary for the success of processes organised on the pattern of large-scale machine industry.'[7] In effect, in its first six months, Lenin's government largely liquidated the Menshevik or just plain grass-roots nonsense about the decentralized authority of factory soviets, share and share alike, worker self-management and the proliferation of pretexts for endless discussions and 'meetingism' at all levels in the name of direct democracy.)

This was all quite strong stuff, unpalatable and unashamed, fit for the victors' ears and not designed to reconcile the victims. The agenda for an *incumbent state* depending on the consent of *more* than a minute 'vanguard', seems to me diametrically different. Excepting the case of taking over a state laid flat by defeat in a major war, a cynical minority is as likely as not to spoil its own chances by its very cleverness, so uncongenial to the rest of society. Instead of professionalism, the incumbent state at the start of the road to discretionary power needs amateurism; instead of secrecy and exclusivity, openness and broad co-option.[8]

A consent-dependent incumbent state must not talk or act too knowingly and professionally about power, how to get and how to use it. It must not for a moment appear, nor even see itself, as (an albeit benign) conspiracy, about to take in society while pretending to stay subjected to its mandate. It must, indeed, sincerely feel that it is

3 Ibid., pp. 306, 325. The quotation is from Engels's 1875 'Letter to August Bebel'.
4 V.I. Lenin, 'The Immediate Tasks of the Soviet Government', in *Selected Works*, p. 419.
5 Ibid.
6 Ibid., p. 421, italics in text.
7 Ibid.
8 Even Lenin's own creature has come a long way towards affecting this sort of consciousness: in the 1977 Soviet Constitution, it calls itself 'the state of the entire people', serenely unworried by the absurdity, at least for Marxists, of a state being everybody's state!

obeying the popular mandate in its own way (the only way in which it can be 'really', 'wholly' obeyed).

If the effect of its policies is to entrap its subjects and to deprive them of the independence of livelihood they need for withholding their consent, this must take place as a slowly emerging by-product of constructive state actions, each of which they find easy to approve. Entrapment, subjugation should no more be the consciously set aims of the state than monopoly profit the aim of the innovating entrepreneur.

The state's tenure is precarious to the extent that its power remains one-dimensional, *merely political* power. This is largely the case in historical settings where economic power is dispersed throughout civil society, conforming to the inherently dispersed nature of the institution of private property. Such settings may look natural to us, but they are by no means the historical norm. From an analytical point of view, too, they are a freak, an anomaly.

In the face of the state's monopoly of organized armed force, it is an illogical oddity to find economic power lodged, as it were, in other places. Is it not an oversight, a strange lack of appetite on somebody's part for the duality of these two sources of power to persist for any length of time? For the emphasis, by modern historians of various persuasions, on the possible causal relations running both ways between capital ownership and state power, merely deepens the mystery of why money has not yet bought the gun or the gun has not yet confiscated the money.

One type of political theory, not without twisting and turning, defines away this anomaly by flatly denying the separateness and autonomy of political power (except for 'relative autonomy', which is too conveniently elastic a concept to merit serious attention). Political and economic power both cohabit in the metaphysical category 'capital' and jointly serve the 'objective' need of its 'expanded reproduction'. However, if we deny ourselves the facility of such a handy solution, we are left with what looks like a remarkably unstable system.

A tilt of the system toward anarchy or at least a measure of ascendancy of civil society *vis à vis* the state, would correspond to the dispersal of hitherto centralized political power. Once it got going, such dispersal could easily gain momentum. In a full-blown process to disperse political power, private armies, by keeping the tax collector away from their territory, would bankrupt the state, contributing to the atrophy of the state army and presumably to the further spread of private armies.[9] There is not the least trace at present of a tendency for social change to take any such turn. The eventuality of a dispersal of political power to match dispersed economic power looks a purely symbolic 'empty box'.

A tilt the other way, towards state capitalism with the ascendancy of the state over civil society, corresponds to the centralization of hitherto diffuse economic power and its *unification,* in one locus of decision, with political power. The summary answer to the incumbent's rhetorical 'what is to be done?' is *'fuse political and economic power* into a single state power' and *'integrate citizenship and livelihood'* so that the subject's whole existence shall be ruled by *one and the same command–obedience relation, with no separate public and private spheres, no divided loyalties, no countervailing centres of power, no sanctuaries* and *nowhere to go.*

In the consciousness of state and public alike, this apocalyptic agenda must take on a prosaic, quiet, down-to-earth and anodyne aspect. It should, and quite easily does, translate itself into some formula which the ruling ideology has rendered largely inoffensive, such as 'the strengthening of democratic control over the economy' so that 'it should function in harmony with society's priorities'.

When I say that contrary to the ruthless cleverness stipulated by Lenin, the state can best maximize its power over civil society by being at the outset somewhat amateurish and candid, the benefit of transparent confidence in the painless and benign character of economic and social engineering is foremost in my mind. It is positively good for the state to believe that the measures found necessary to establish 'democratic control' over the economy will in due course have, as their principal effect, an enhanced say by the people in the proper use of the country's producitve apparatus (or consequences of a similar description). It is good for it sincerely to consider voices which assert the exact opposite as obscurantist or in bad faith.

It is conducive to the state's ultimate purposes to substitute conscious direction of the social system for automatism, for every such 'voluntarist' step is likely, by cumulative systemic changes, to induce

9 Weak medieval kings and strong territorial lords both exercised near-sovereign political power only over the land they 'owned' (though this was but a quasi-ownership), the patterns of *dispersed* political and *dispersed* economic power coinciding as they have never done since. On the other hand, centralized political *and* economic power have often coincided. They still tend to go hand in hand in 'second' and 'third world' countries.

a need for *more* guidance in some of the most unexpected places. The less efficient (at least in the sense of 'the less self-sustaining', 'the less spontaneous' and 'the less self-regulating') the workings of the economic and social system become, the more direct control the state will have over people's livelihoods. It is one of the numerous paradoxes of rational action that a degree of well-intentioned bungling in economic and social management and the usual failure to foresee the effects of its own policies, are peculiarly appropriate means to the state's ends. It is government *incompetence* which, by creating a need for putting right its consequences, steadily enlarges the scope for the state to concentrate economic power in its own hands and best contributes to the merging of economic with political power. It is very doubtful whether government *competence* could ever get the process going from a democratic starting position.

Stressing the paradox, we might go a little further and argue that the spirit which best helps the state emancipate itself from its ungrateful role of democratic drudge is one of confident innocence and uncomprehending sincerity. In my choice of adjectives, I am inspired by the example of a tract by a socialist theorist on the programme of the united French Left prior to its 1981 electoral victory. In this work, it is explained in manifest good faith that nationalization of large-scale industry and banking would *reduce* statism and bureaucracy, provide an additional *safeguard* for pluralistic democracy and create a *really free* market.[10]

Schematically, the state would find itself advancing, by small and steady degrees, towards discretionary power by first merely following the standard liberal prescription. It should at the outset 'rely on prices and markets' for the allocation of resources 'and then' proceed to redistribute the resulting social product 'as justice required'.[11] The inconsistency between an allocation and a distribution arrived at in this way, should alone suffice to bring about partial imbalances, false signals and symptoms of waste. In the face of the emerging evidence that 'markets do not work', industries fail to adapt to

10   Jean Elleinstein, *Lettre ouverte aux Français de la République du Programme Commun*, 1977, pp. 140–51. Like the gentleman in the Park who mistook the strolling Duke of Wellington for a certain Mr Smith ('Mr Smith, I believe?' – 'If you believe that, Sir, you will believe anything'), Elleinstein manifestly believed that nationalization would do these things rather than their opposites. It is this trusting simplicity that best suits the state (and of course its leaders) in the difficult transition from democracy to socialism.
11   To readers of J. Rawls's *Theory of Justice*, 1972, and of chapter 3 of this book, these phrases will have a familiar ring.

changes in time, unemployment persists and prices misbehave, support should built up for the state to launch more ambitious policies. Their intended effect would be the correction of malfunctions induced by the initial policy. One of their unintended effects may be to make the malfunctions worse or cause them to crop up somewhere else. Another is almost inevitably to make some existences, jobs, businesses if not whole industries, wholly dependent on 'economic policy', while making many others feel some partial dependence.

This stage – often approvingly called the 'mixed economy', suggesting a civilized compromise between the complementary interests of private initiative and social control – has, however, merely pierced, without razing to the ground, the maze of obstacles, ramparts and bunkers where private enterprise can in the last resort, and at a cost, shelter the livelihood of those, owners and non-owners alike, who have occasion to oppose the state. Only the abolition of private capital ownership ensures the disappearance of these shelters. A 'mixed economy' needs to go to extreme lengths in terms of state controls in order for private enterprise to cease being a potential base of political obstruction or defiance. Planning, industrial policy and distributive justice are promising yet imperfect substitutes for state ownership; the essential, almost irreplaceable attribute of the latter is not the power it *lends to the state,* but the power it *takes out of civil society,* like the stuffing you take out of a rag doll.

The transition to socialism, in the sense of an almost subconscious, sleep-walking sort of 'maximax' strategy by the state, *both* to augment its potential discretionary power *and* actually to realize the greatest possible part of the potential thus created, is likely to be peaceful, dull and unobtrusive. This is its low-risk high-reward approach. Far from being any noisy 'battle of democracy ... to centralise all instruments of production in the hands of the state'; far from involving some heroic revolutionary break with continuity; far from calling for the violent putting down of the propertied minority, the transition to socialism would probably be the more certain the more it relied on the slow atrophy of initially independent, self-regulating subsystems of society. As their free functioning was constrained, the declining vitality of successive chunks of the 'mixed economy' would eventually lead to a passive acceptance of a step-by-step extension of public ownership, if not to a clamour for it.

In a section of his *Capitalism, Socialism, Democracy* devoted to 'The Sociology of the Intellectual', Schumpeter makes the point that intellectuals (whom he defines, a shade severely, as people 'who talk and write about subjects outside of their professional competence' and 'have no direct responsibility for practical affairs'), 'cannot help nibbling at the foundations of capitalist society'. They help along the ideology that corrodes the capitalist order which is notoriously impotent at controlling its intellectuals. 'Only a government of non-bourgeois nature ... under modern circumstances only a socialist or fascist one – is strong enough to discipline them.' With private ownership of capital and the autonomy of particular interests (which they are busy ideologically to undermine), the intellectuals can to some extent hold out against a hostile state, protected as they are by 'the private fortresses of bourgeois business which, or some of which, will shelter the quarry'.[12] State capitalism offers greater (and in terms of such intangibles as social status, being listened to at the top and having a captive audience at the bottom of society, incomparably greater) rewards to compliant, non-nibbling intellectuals than does private capitalism. Such rewards may or may not compensate them for the latent risk, in a world of no 'private fortresses', of having nowhere to shelter should they find themselves nibbling at the system after all. Why intellectuals, of all groups, strata, castes or whatever, should have a privileged relationship with the socialist state, why they are solicited and rewarded, is a puzzling question;[13] that it is 'strong enough to discipline them' seems to me, if anything, a reason for *not* soliciting and rewarding them. That the socialist state attracts the intellectual is understandable enough, given the role of reason in the formulation and legitimation of activist policy. (I have argued the natural leftward bias of the brainy in chapter 2, p. 94). What is less obvious is why this love does not remain unrequited, why the socialist state accepts the intellectuals at their own valuation – a strange position to take on the part of a monopsonist, the sole buyer of their services.

Even if there were some hard-to-fathom yet rational reason for pampering *them, nobody else need be pampered*. The above and regrettably inconclusive digression about intellectuals was to provide

---

12   Schumpeter, *Capitalism, Socialism, Democracy*, 5th edn, 1977, pp. 146–51.
13   If only it bore more lightly the burden of the influence of György Lukács, whose hermetic and foggy style its authors tend to follow, *The Road of the Intellectuals to Class Power*, 1979, by the Hungarian sociologists G. Konrád and I. Szelényi, would be a very worthwhile contribution to an eventual answer to this question. Their original ideas can only be approximately discerned through the swirling Lukácsist obscurity.

sharper relief to this thesis. Trotsky's deduction in the *Revolution Betrayed,* that once the state owns all capital, opposition is death by slow starvation, perhaps overstates the case. It is nonetheless right in sensing the potent constraining force that comes down on bread-winners when the political and the economic, instead of broadly cancelling each other out, are amalgamated and encircle a person. The subsistence wage needed to reproduce labour may or may not have an ascertainable sense. (I would certainly argue that at least in Marx's theory of value, it is a tautology. Whatever wage happens to be paid, no matter how low or high, it is identically equal to the subsistence wage.) But if the subsistence wage did have objective meaning, only state capitalism would have the assured ability to keep everybody's actual wage down to subsistence level.

Recourse by the dissatisfied wage-earner to the political process and *appeals to the state* for distributive justice are, of course, absurd *in a world where the state is both party and judge,* i.e. where it has successfully merged economic and political power. The point for the state in achieving such a merger is not primarily that opposition to it becomes slow starvation, though that is a valuable enough result. It is rather that it can obtain non-opposition in return for *mere 'subsistence',* or if that term is too fluid to serve, in return for less than it would have to pay for consent in a competitive political setting.

In what is for some reason regarded as a substantial contribution to the modern theory of the state, the American socialist James O'Connor considers that if its surplus were not spent on social investment, or dissipated in the interest of such privately owned 'monopolies' as may survive, state-owned industry could lead to the 'fiscal liberation' of the state.[14] By implication, if there are no, or only few, 'private monopolies' left to dissipate the surplus on, and the state is under no competitive pressure to undertake more 'social investment' than it sees fit, it will have achieved its rational purpose, for which 'fiscal liberation' is a perhaps narrow but evocative label. Not only is it maximizing its discretionary power by making the most of a given social and economic environment (for instance, the environment defined by democratic politics and a 'mixed economy'), but it has improved the environment itself by cleansing civil society of the economic power that was diffused within it. In such an environment, far more discretionary power is potentially available

14   James O'Connor, *The Fiscal Crisis of the State,* 1973, ch. 7.

for the state to maximize, so that in creating it *and* making the most of it, it has, so to speak, maximized the maximum.

Is, however, its success complete? A crucial link seems to be missing for state capitalism to be a workable system. For if the state is the sole employer, it can liberate resources for its own discretionary use by telling people what to do, without overpaying them for their obedience. But what is to prevent a rival from spoiling all and bidding for political power by promising higher wages – as he would bid for political power under private capitalism by promising more distributive justice? What is to stop *politics from undoing economics*? Can we, to be more specific, take it for granted that once economic power is fully concentrated in the state, democratic political forms *ipso facto* lose their content and, even if piously preserved, become empty rites?

For all his pragmatism, J. S. Mill was, for one, quite categoric on this point: 'if the employees of all these different enterprises were appointed and paid by the government, and looked to the government for every rise in life; not all the freedom of the Press and the popular constitution of the legislature would make this or any other country free otherwise than in name.'[15] What he describes is, substantially, the socialist position (though presented with the seamy side up). For fully fledged socialists the idea of the owner of capital voluntarily surrendering his dominance by bowing to the caprice of the ballot box is, at best, comic. For them, the replacement of bourgeois by socialist democracy entails safeguards of one sort or another against the ballot box producing retrograde results. Electoral outcomes must respect the realities of the new 'relations of production' and the question of the state losing tenure to some demagogic rival must not arise.

All states, however, do not *first* acquire a socialist consciousness and *then* set about nationalizing capital. Doing things in that order is a distinctly third-worldly scenario. Elsewhere, it is not necessarily the most feasible. The state of an advanced society may both want and have to embark on its self-emancipating, 'maximizing' course while still committed to the 'bourgeois' democratic rules. Though their competitive aspect may have reduced it to drudgery, it will submit to

15   J.S. Mill, *On Liberty* (ed. by A.D. Lindsay), 1910, p. 165. It is edifying to reflect that it was none other than the Levellers who, in their democratic fervour, proposed to withhold the franchise from *servants* who, 'depending on the will of other men', could not be trusted with the vote. Cf. C.B. Macpherson, *The Political Theory of Possessive Individualism*, 1962, pp. 107–36.

these rules both because it has, at least as yet, no power to do otherwise, and because it has at the outset no convincing reason for taking the risk of bending them. It can advance – or should we say sleep-walk? – some way towards the goal of 'maximax', and perhaps pass the point of no return, without first transforming 'bourgeois' into 'people's' democracy. Electoral politics is in fact a natural promoter of state ownership, once the 'mixed economy' has lost enough of its capacity (and willingness) to adapt to change for nationalization to become the obvious saviour of industries and jobs in jeopardy. The state can with advantage let itself be carried some way down this social democratic road, where the continuing operation of the competitive politics of consent serves as a spur to the growing concentration of economic power in its own hands.

Popular sovereignty and competitive politics with free entry, however, are ultimately inconsistent with the *raison d'être* of state capitalism and would in fact break it up as a working system. Under democracy, people are encouraged to *try and get, by the political process, what the economic one denies them*. The whole thrust of chapter 4 was to isolate and present the awkward consequences, for state and civil society, of this contradiction. Though awkward and in their cumulative effect malignant, however, they are not lethal for a system where political and economic power and responsibility are reasonably separate. On the other hand, when these are united, the contradiction becomes much too powerful. Multi-party competititon for tenure of the role of sole owner of the economy and employer of the entire electorate, would be combining mutually destructive features in one system. It would be tantamount to asking the wage-earners to fix, by voting, their own wages and workloads. An effort of imagination is needed to visualize the result.[16] Social democrat or

16 Free entry, secret ballot and majority rule, combined with preponderant state ownership of capital, means that tenure of state power and hence the role of universal employer, is awarded to the party offering higher wages and shorter hours than its rival. Productivity, discipline on the job, consumption, investment are all determined on the hustings. Political competititon ensures their greatest possible incompatibility, resulting in a total shambles.

The 'Yugoslav road to socialism' can be interpreted as an attempt to get round the contradiction between state capitalism and bourgeois democracy, not by the obvious method of suppressing all political competition, but by taking it out at the level of the state and putting some of it back at the level of the individual state enterprise. Employees cannot elect the government, but they elect a workers' council and have some indirect say in the choice of the enterprise manager, the level of wages and profit-sharing bonuses and, hence, more indirectly still, in output and prices.

To the extent that this is so, the enterprise tends to maximize value added *per employee*, i.e. it will generally try to use more machines and materials and fewer people, than are collectively available. The resulting tendencies to chronic inflation accompanied by unemployment, are

democratic socialist, the state cannot for long live with rules which inexorably produce a self-devouring social system.

Owner and employer, it now has sufficient power to start bending the democratic rules to escape demagogic and incompatible outcomes, adapting the old political process to the functional requirements of the new social system with its new 'relations of production'. Possible solutions available to it are of two basic types. One is to retain bourgeois democracy with multi-party competition, but progressively to restrict the *scope* of popular sovereignty, so that the winning party is not awarded tenure of all state power, but only power over areas where decisions cannot produce incompatibilities with the planned functioning of the economy. (Whether such areas can be found at all depends, of course, in part on how hard you look for them.) The hiring and firing of people, command over the army and the police and matters of income and expenditure, must be reserved to a permanent executive not subject to election and recall, for (as responsible citizens can readily see) otherwise demagogic overbidding would rapidly lead to breakdown. The non-elected permanent executive would in time find that to ensure consistency of the sources and uses of all resources, it is obliged to assert its *leading role* over all areas of social life including the educational and the cultural, although it may (at some risk to public calm) admit the consultative role, in non-critical matters, of some elected multi-party assembly.

The other type of solution is to restrain and reform political competititon itself, notably by *regulating entry,* to the effect that while an elected assembly continues technically to dispose of state power as a whole, it becomes difficult and eventually impossible to elect people who would dispose of it inappropriately. For instance,

---

fought with complex administrative means. Politically, the system breeds insider cliques, caucuses and deals. Economically, it is prevented from being a total shambles by individual enterprises having, at least in principle, to compete for a living with each other and with imports on a spontaneously operating market; there is 'commodity production for exchange'.

Capital is said to be in *social* rather than in *state* ownership. It is impossible to find out what this means. It does not mean syndicalism, cooperative ownership or municipal socialism. It seems to me that it is intended to mean 'good state ownership' in opposition to 'bad state ownership' (in much the same way as 'social' planning means good and 'bureaucratic' planning means bad planning). Most of the owner's prerogatives are in practice exercised by state bureaux calling themselves 'banks' rather than, as in orthodox socialist countries, 'ministries' or 'planning offices'.

If this hybrid system is less suffocatingly totalitarian than the thoroughbred state capitalist world to the northeast of it, this is perhaps due as much to history, character and accident as to 'systemic' differences.

the state executive in place could screen prospective candidates adhering to several parties from such a point of view. Since all are state employees (as are their parents and children, spouses, relatives and friends), it could discourage the candidature of those who might not respect its necessary *leading role*. Such screening would permit the free democratic election of responsible, non-demagogic representatives. Caring as much for the well-being of their families as for that of the country, they could be relied upon to support (in informal consensus, formal coalition or 'national front' and purged of petty party rivalry) the responsible, non-demagogic government of the state – affording it the security and continuity of tenure which it needs for the steady, unhurried realization of its ends.

There may well be other, more insidious and unobtrusive ways for competitive democratic rules to bend, lose their content and become empty rites so that compertiton for state power ceases to be a genuine threat to the incumbent. In no way a 'historical necessity', nor something which happens of itself 'untouched by human hand', this result is yet the logical corollary of preponderant state ownership and a necessary condition for the functioning of the social system of which such ownership is a part.

Recall, then, is abolished in practice. One way or another, people are stopped from using the political process *for dismissing their own employer.* Failing such prevention, the employer–employee relation would assume farcical shapes: would-be employers would have to ask the employees to employ *them,* work would become round-the-clock consultation and pay would be self-assessed (to each according to what he says he deserves).

With the abolition of recall, revolution moves up on the scale of political alternatives. From last resort, it is transformed into the first and in fact the *sole recourse* of the disappointed political hedonist, the non-conformist, the man hating to be lied to, as well as the man hating his job. For the really deep, all-pervading change brought about by the *Gleichschaltung* of economic with political power is that as dispersed, autonomous structures of power are flattened, all strain becomes a strain between state and subject.

Little or nothing can henceforth be settled in bilateral negotiations *between* subjects, owners and non-owners, employers and employees, buyers and sellers, landlords and tenants, publishers and writers, bankers and debtors. Except clandestinely and criminally, there is little give and take where, at least by rights, only the state can give.

Bargaining and contract are largely displaced by command–obedience relations. Independent hierarchies disappear. Groups between man and state become, at best, 'transmission belts' and at worst false fronts with emptiness behind.

This may well be a great facility for the state. However, it is also a source of danger. Everything now is the state's fault; all decisions that hurt are its decisions; and tempted as it may be to blame 'bureaucracy' and 'loss of contact with the masses' for smelly drains, boring television programmes, uncaring doctors, overbearing supervisors, shoddy goods and apathetic shop-girls, it is in a cleft stick. As a state it must not admit to being at fault, yet it can disavow its servants and proxyholders only so often.

Thus, totalitarianism is not a matter of fanatical minds and bullying wills 'at the top', nor of the terrifying naivety of their ideologists. It is a matter of self-defence for any state which has played for high stakes *and won*, exchanging one predicament for another. Having gathered all power to itself, it has become the sole focus of all conflict, and it must construct totalitarian defences to match its total exposure.

What is to be done to protect state capitalism from revolution? It may be that the danger is largely academic, an empty box, a mere matter of logical completeness, for revolutions have been made obsolete by technical progress. Quick-firing weapons, armoured vehicles, water-cannon, 'truth drugs' and, perhaps above all, central control of telecommunications, may have made the position of the incumbent state much easier to defend than to attack. Not for nothing is the successor state of *Kathedersozialismus* called that of *Panzersozialismus*. Lately it is being said that the computer has reversed the technical trend in favour of the incumbent state. Though it is hard for the layman to grasp why this should be so (the contrary looks *prima facie* more likely), we must leave the question for more qualified minds to resolve. In any event, if modern revolutions are at all conceivable, there is a presumption that for the very reasons that oblige it to be totalitarian, state capitalism runs greater risks and needs stronger defences against revolt than states that do not own, but merely redistribute what *others* own.[17]

17 One of the weakest of several weak reasons advanced by Trotsky why there is not and 'there never will be' such a thing as state capitalism, was that 'in its quality of universal repository of capitalist property, the state would be too tempting an object for social revolution' (Leon Trotsky, *The Revolution Betrayed: What is the Soviet Union and Where is it*

Terror and state television sum up the commonplace conception of what is needed for state security. No doubt they both have their roles in obviating recourse to actual repression, rather in the manner of preventive medicine reducing hospital and medical costs. However, the best defences start at a deeper level, in the moulding of character and behaviour, in inculcating the belief that certain basic features of social life, the 'leading role', the non-recall and continuity of the state, its monopoly of capital and its primacy over individual right, are immutable. The state's determination to use its subjects should never waver, never wax and wane. Their lot must be preordained, stable; it should not worsen significantly yet should improve only with deliberate slowness; rapid change either way is bad, but of the two, rapid change for the better is more dangerous. As in economics 'it is all in Marshall,' so in sociology 'everything has been said by Tocqueville.' Three chapters in his *Ancien régime et la révolution* tell it all: how rising prosperity and the advance toward equality brought on revolution (Book III, ch. IV); how bringing solace to the people made them rise up (Book III, ch. V); and how the royal government prepared the ground and educated the people for its own overthrow (Book III, ch. VI).

Prospects of change for the better make people excitedly unhappy, fearful of missing out, aggressive and impatient.[18] 'Safety-valve' type

---

Going?, 5th edn, 1972, p. 246). He has, however, a more compelling reason: in his order of ideas, *state* capitalism must be *privately* owned; the state, like some giant corporation, must belong to shareholders able to sell and bequeath their shares. If they cannot sell and their sons cannot inherit, the system is not state capitalism. (While being sure of what it was *not* Trotsky had some changes of mind about what it *was*. See also A. Ruehl-Gerstel, 'Trotsky in Mexico', *Encounter*, April 1982.)

It is sad to see a Marxist reduced to such a position. For Trotsky it ought to be 'commodity production', the alienation of labour, its domination by capital and the mode of appropriation of surplus value which define the 'relations of production', not whether shares are sold or inherited.

It must be added that Lenin's use of 'state capitalism' to designate a system of private enterprise under close state control, was no worthier of socialist respect. In particular, it is hard to see how the state, which (despite some 'relative autonomy') must, by virtue of the relations of production, be controlled and dominated by private enterprise, nevertheless controls it.

18   Some of these and related ideas are formalized in the powerful essay 'La logique de la frustration relative' by Raymond Boudon in his *Effets pervers et ordre social*, 2nd edn, 1979. Prof. Boudon seeks to establish that the good observed correlation of discontent and frustration with *improved* chances, need not depend on some particular psychological assumption, but can be deduced from rationality alone, along the lines of utility-maximization in the face of risk.

At the other, non-rational end of the spectrum of human motives, Norman Cohn's classic work on medieval revolutionary mystics finds the same correlation between better conditions and prospects and revolutionary action. See his account of the German Peasant War of 1525: 'The well-being of the German peasantry was greater than it had ever been ... [the peasants] concessions and reforms, whether great or little, early or late, nearly always turn out to be too little too late, for as a matter of historical experience they raise expectations of change more than in proportion to the actual change. If this possible feature of social psychology has a high probability of being the case in any given conflict of interest between state and society, it must always be wrong for the state to yield. Even if it was a mistake to start off with the reins too short, it is yet better to hold them steady than to loosen them too perceptibly.

Except for the paroxysm of indiscriminate terror in 1937–8 and the few years of haphazard experimentation after 1955, both of which came close to endangering the tenure of the regime and were ended none too soon, Soviet practice since about 1926 seems to me a successful application of these prescriptions. The stability of the modern Soviet state, despite the many good reasons why it should have collapsed on its clay feet before now, is at least consistent with the hypothesis that reform, relaxation, social mobility, dynamic striving for innovation and decentralized initiative, whatever they may do to a society's efficiency and material well-being, are not the ingredients needed to keep it calm, docile, enduring and submissive in the face of totalitarian demands upon it.

The State as Class

*The right bureaucracy may help make capitalism 'responsible'
and lend socialism 'a human face'. Its control, however, is too
precarious to shift the constants of either system.*

If there must be class conflict in a world of scarcity, who but the universal capitalist can act out the role of dominant class?

It is hardly extravagant to claim that a pattern of ownership is well enough described by simply answering the question, 'who owns what?' It is by a plain answer to this plain question that we can make

---

far from being driven on by sheer misery and desperation, belonged to a rising and self-confident class. They were people whose position was improving both socially and economically' (Norman Cohn, *Pursuit of the Millennium*, 1970, p. 245).

   There is by now a sizeable body of literature in support of the thesis that revolutions typically follow the relaxation of pressures, the brightening of outlook, reforms. It seems to me important to stress that there may well be *other* good reasons for this than the supposition that reform is a symptom of the state being 'on the run', getting *weaker*, hence becoming *fair game* for *prudent revolutionaries* who calculate risk-reward ratios.

the doctrinally least pretentious distinction between *private* and *state* capitalism, and most easily understand alternative configurations of power in society.[19] The hopeful assurance that when it is nationalized, capital is 'socially owned', for all that it is meaningless, can be a useful euphemism for policy purposes. The more ambitious claim, that there is some ascertainable difference between 'state' and 'social' or 'socialist' ownership, so that the suspected despotic potential of *state* ownership is not present in *social* ownership, need not be taken seriously until it is shown how the operation of 'society' exercising its property rights, differs from that of the state exercising them.

In the *Anti-Duehring*, Engels protests that mere state ownership is spurious socialism unless the means of production have 'actually outgrown management by joint-stock companies', for otherwise even state-owned brothels could be regarded as 'socialistic institutions'.[20] Just how large would brothels have to grow, then, to qualify as *socialist* instead of merely *state-owned* establishments? Seeking in size the magic quality which transforms state property into socialist property clearly will not do. The scientific socialist notion of the means of production 'outgrowing' joint-stock company management has long since succumbed to the test of a century of industrial growth.

In fairness to Engels, it is his *Anti-Duehring* again which provides the plainest formulation of a more durable Marxist alternative for identifying kinds of property and social systems. He explains that in a world of scarcity (*alias* 'in the realm of necessity'), the division of society into antagonistic classes must continue. Class conflict, of

19 It is interesting to find expressly non-Marxist reasons for defining state capitalism in the Leninist spirit as 'the symbiosis of state and corporations' (in P.J.D. Wiles, *Economic Institutions Compared*, 1979, p. 51). What, then, is *private* capitalism, and how do we tell it apart from state capitalism? Wiles considers that the latter term is 'abusively applied' to the Soviet Union because it 'certainly has an ideology which sets it quite apart from real state capitalism'. *Real* state capitalism, being *'more or less indifferent about property'* is devoid of a proper ideology.

This is true only in terms of a convention to define real state capitalism as one which is indifferent about property. Which actually existing systems, which countries would such a definition cover? Take the testimony of a prominent state capitalist, a member of one of the Grands Corps at the summit of the French civil service, later to become Minister of Industry: 'no amount of *dirigisme* is worth a powerful public sector.' (J-P. Chevènement, *Le vieux, la crise, le neuf*, 1977, p. 180, my translation.) *His* state capitalism is certainly not indifferent about property. If there are *state* capitalisms that *are*, they are not conspicuous. Are they, perhaps, too easy to mistake for *private* capitalisms?

20 F. Engels, 'Socialism: Utopian and Scientific', in K. Marx and F. Engels, *Selected Works in One Volume*, 1968, pp. 421–2, note.

course, entails the existence of a state to ensure the dominance of one class. Thus the 'socialist state' is not a contradiction in terms. The state which owns all the means of production is a repressive socialist state. As there are still classes, it could not yet have withered away, it must continue to repress the exploited on behalf of the exploiter. It can only wither away once abundance has replaced scarcity, i.e. when class conflict has ceased. (If socialism *never* overcomes scarcity, a contingency Engels does not explicitly treat, the state will never wither away and it will, in perpetuity, own the means of production. As long, therefore, as the state does not succeed *too well* in 'setting free the forces of production' and hence does not *inadvertently bring on a world of abundance,* it is safe.)

Pending abundance and the withering away of the state, 'socialism in a world of scarcity' and 'state capitalism' are, for practical purposes, synonymous. The division of labour is still a necessity; production is for exchange rather than for need; there are two functionally distinct classes, with the oppressor class appropriating the surplus value produced by the oppressed class. Unlike in private capitalism, the surplus is appropriated, albeit in spite of the oppressed class but in its long-term interest (or in that of the whole society). Who, however, *is* the oppressor class?

Putting it in less moth-eaten language, the drama is ready to be played but an actor and a role do not match. The state owns, the oppressed do not, but nor do the presumable oppressors. There is no ruling class with a power base cemented in ownership. In its place, usurping its prerogatives, is supposed to stand a peculiar social category, a hermaphrodite body which has a class interest without being a class, which dominates without owning: the bureaucracy.[21]

Before the bureaucracy can *rule,* ownership must lose its significance. Hence schemes of social explanation built on the threesome of citizenry, bureaucracy and state always contain some variant of the familiar case about the 'growing separation of ownership and control'. For this thesis, ownership has come to be reduced to a right to any (private or social) dividends the managing bureaucracy chooses to distribute. Control is, among other things, the *discretion* to allocate people to capital and vice versa in decisions to invest, hire

---

21   The word is used here in a very general and non-pejorative sense, to include the category of hired managers and administrators who man the bureaux. It refers to a role in society and is not meant to express any like or dislike for it.

and fire, and to judge the deserts of those concerned when allocating and distributing.

Each society will have bred its distinctive bureaucracy. England is credited with having an Establishment, France indisputably has her *grands corps* (just as, the other way round, the *grands corps* possess their France), Russia used to have the higher grades of the *tchin* and now it has the *nomenklatura,* remotely echoed in the USA by the top half-million lawyers and corporate officers. Without any risk of contradiction, all societies can be said to be governed by their 'power elites'; much of modern industry is undoubtedly run by professional managers; while the intellectual demi-monde keeps unveiling such ruling entities as 'the media', 'the bearers of authority' or the 'technostructure'.[22]

Granted the tacit assumption that *separation* of ownership and control entails *loss* of control by the owner, rather than the much less drastic *delegation* of control with possibility of recall (an assumption I shall look at presently), rule by the bureaucracy can be deduced from a stripped-down version of Michels's 'iron law'. Every organization needs but a few organizers for many organized. It is the former who man the bureau. Once they are in, the bureaucrats rule because those outside are ill placed and insufficiently motivated to dislodge them.

In a very uncharacteristic utopian mood, Lenin assured us that one day administration will be so simple as to be 'within everybody's scope', 'easily performed by every literate person',[23] allowing 'the complete abolition of bureaucracy',[24] where 'all will govern in turn'.[25] (His practice, of course, was to discourage with the utmost firmness any attempt at 'governing in turn'.) For the time being, however, administration is said to be getting, if anything, more

---

22 Cogitation and field research have, as I understand it, jointly established that the technostructure is composed of people who make the decisions which require knowledge. (Obviously, few decisions are left for the rest of us to make.) The technostructure removes from ownership all reality of power. The 'liturgical aspect' of economic life induces the technostructure to affirm the sanctity of private ownership. It is, however, equally adept at keeping in its place the private and the public shareholder. (Why, in that case, does it prefer to be faced by private shareholders, if only 'liturgically'?) In any case, it would be 'supreme foolishness' to fear one's shareholders. The technostructure is more interested in growth than in profit. And so on. These revelations are drawn from J. Kenneth Galbraith and N. Salinger, *Almost Everyone's Guide to Economics*, 1979, pp. 58–60.
23 Lenin, 'The State and Revolution', p. 292.
24 Ibid., p. 340.
25 Ibid., p. 345.

complex. Though many of us are already bureaucrats, the prospect of the rest of us taking *turns* at it is both impractical and unattractive. This supports the notion that the bureaucracy is a category apart.

The more literally one takes the assumption that ownership does not entail control over property, the larger loom the implications. Ownership of capital becomes irrelevant to power, both in the usual sense of power to make people do things and in the sense of power over the 'appropriation of surplus value', including the capitalist's dividend. There is only a *grace-and-favour dividend* to the putative owners, to 'the people' in socialism, to 'shareholders' in private capitalism. Why fight about property, then? Nationalization, the wrecking of the 'private fortresses of bourgeois business' becomes a pointless and misguided endeavour. A bureaucracy controlling the instrument of the state and safely usurping some of the most import-ant prerogatives of ownership, could with impunity steer society one way or another, enthrone private property or abolish it, or split the social system down the middle, without its interests being visibly better served by one course than by the other. Whether it took the 'capitalist road' or the 'socialist' one, or just chased its own tail, would be a toss-up.

In reality, however, bureaucracies usually have manifest reasons for coming down on the side of the status quo. They do not normally seek to change it. Indeed, Trotsky's suspicion of Stalin preparing a new Thermidor 'to restore capitalism', would look less grotesque if he had found reasonable grounds for supposing that Stalin and the 'bureaucracy' he directed would at least not lose the power, control or whatever they possessed and prized, if 'capitalism were restored'. Yet almost in the same breath in which he uttered his bizarre accusation, Trotsky removed its possible ground by pointing out that the Soviet bureaucracy is 'compelled' willy-nilly to protect the system of state ownership as the source of its power, implying logically that a system of private ownership would not have yielded as much power to it *even if the new private owners were to have come from its own ranks,* with each deserving apparatchik becoming a top-hatted cigar-smoking capitalist.

The most interesting implication of the 'ownership is not control' thesis, however, is the support it gives to the belief in our fate being largely a matter of the *mores* and moods of the office-holders above us. Whether a social system is acceptable or awful, whether people are on the whole contented or miserable under it, depends very much on the variable personal traits of members of the bureaucracy. When the civil service is arrogant or corrupt or both, the managerial elite stony-hearted, the media mercenary and the 'technostructure' soullessly specialist, we have the 'unacceptable face of capitalism'. When those in charge genuinely want to serve the people and respect its 'legitimate aspirations', we get the Prague Spring and 'socialism with a human face'. It is not so much systems of rule, configurations of power which are conducive to a good or bad life, but rather the sort of people administering them. If the bureaucracy is not 'bureaucratic', the corporate executive is 'socially minded' and 'community-conscious' and the party apparatchik 'has not lost contact with the masses', private or state capitalism can be equally tolerable.

This is a tempting belief and easy to adopt. In turn, it gives rise to a live concern with how to make sure, or at least how to shorten the odds, that the *right sort of people* get to play the controlling, administering and managing roles. Each culture has its recipe for recruiting a good bureaucracy. Some place their faith in breeding and a stake in the land (England before the Second World War, as well as Prussia, spring to mind), others in the passing of examinations (France, Imperial China and lately perhaps the USA, are cases in point), while the socialist prescription recommends calloused hands or at least a credible claim to 'working-class origins'. (Mixed and contradictory criteria should not surprise us. An aristocrat with the common touch, a welder who went on to get an MBA or conversely the graduate who learnt all about life by doing a stint at manual labour, are particularly acceptable recruits into the 'power elite'. Among contradictory and mixed criteria, minor ones can in time become major. It is said that a contributory cause of Khrushchev's downfall was the embarrassment felt by the Soviet public, especially *vis à vis* the outside world, at his bumptiousness, clowning and lower-class Ukrainian accent.)

Hopeful ideas about the right way of recruiting the 'power elite' and the difference its personnel makes between 'savage' and 'responsible' capitalism, 'despotic' and 'democratic' socialism, condition civil society's approval of the composition of the bureaucracy. They also help explain the passionate interest of modern sociology in the statistical parameters of particular hierarchies, for if the behaviour of 'power elites' depends critically on where their members come from, it must matter a great deal whose father did what and went to which school. This preoccupation with 'socio-economic origins' is really the

complete negation of the belief that existence determines consciousness and hence the bureau determines that of the bureaucrat.[26] On
the latter view, whether it is principally made up of the sons of
toilers, schoolteachers or of other bureaucrats, the institutional
interest and hence the *conduct* of a bureaucracy will be esentially the
same, give and take minor cultural variations of style between the
moderately nice and the rather nasty. For the former view to hold,
the bureaucracy must be completely autonomous and obey no
master, in order to be able to follow its own personal tastes and
dispositions. For the latter, its master is its own existential, institutional interest, which may or may not happen to coincide with the
'maximand' of the ultimate beneficiary the bureaucratic institution is
supposed to serve – the state in state capitalism, shareholders in
private capitalism. On either view, the bureaucracy calls the tune,
though which tune it calls depends on the further particulars. Either
view is contingent on the thesis that the owner does not control, the
bureaucrat does. How good is this thesis?

In order for the separation of ownership and control to mean what
its disparate proponents, from Berle and Means through Trotsky,[27]
Burnham and C.W. Mills to Marris and Penrose intend it to mean, it
is trivial merely to show that the bureaucracy administers and the
managers manage with little apparent reference to their ostensible
masters. A more telling argument would be to establish that they
have non-trivial discretionary power. Evidence for such discretion
would be some measure (if a convenient one could be found) of a

26 A political philosopher of quiet distinction, whose 'socio-economic origin' was at least
consistent with some insight into these matters (for his father was the Premier of his country of
origin) has disposed of the question in the following 'holistic' terms: 'Why should we suppose
that ... [institutions], when they have to choose between their corporate interests and the
interests of the classes from which their leaders are mostly recruited, will ordinarily choose to
sacrifice their corporate interests?' (John Plamenatz, *Man and Society*, 1963, vol. II, p. 370).
27 The exiled Trotsky's social theory of the Soviet Union is that in it, capital belongs to the
workers' state (or, as he ended up by putting it, 'the counter-revolutionary workers' state'), but
the working class is prevented from exercising the owner's prerogatives by the bureaucracy,
which has won control of the state. The reason why the bureaucracy succeeds in usurping the
role of the ruling class is scarcity. Where people have to queue for what they need, there will be
a policeman regulating the queue; he ' "knows" who is to get something and who is to wait'
(*The Revolution Betrayed*, p. 112).

That abundance is not the *consequence* but the enabling *cause* of socialism has always
troubled socialist thought. It has led to much uneasy theorizing about the 'transition period',
classes in a classless state, the state withering away by getting stronger, etc.

Readers are no doubt aware that making explicit a doctrinal inconsistency or awkwardness,
as I have occasionally been moved to do, is severely condemned by Marxists as 'reductionism'.

divergence between the owner's presumable maximand and the maximand the managers seem in fact to be pursuing.[28]

This is not really feasible if the future consequences of the manager's present actions are uncertain, hence he can always be supposed to have aimed at consequence *A* (best for his employer) rather than *B* (best for him, less good for his employer), regardless of whether the actual result of his action turned out to be *A* or *B*. For instance, Montgomery's generalship in North Africa can be seen as self-serving, in that he would only really engage Rommel once his 'bureaucratic' insistence on a large sufficiency of resources gave him odds-on chances of spectacular victories. Yet it can always be argued (and it is hard 'objectively' to disprove) that though he earned fame at no risk by brazenly 'hogging' resources for the Eighth Army, he was in effect serving Britain's best long-term interest (e.g. because the resources he 'hogged' would not have done any greater good to the war effort in any other theatre). Likewise, the corporate manager who, in apparent pursuit of self-aggrandizement, goes for market share at the expense of current profit, can always pretend to be making future profit larger than it would otherwise have been – the sort of business school or management consultancy waffle one can dismiss with a shrug but not refute with science.

Nevertheless, it is at least possible deductively to assert that only security of tenure provides the *sufficient* condition for the state bureaucrat, the corporate manager or other hired power-elitist to exercise discretionary power regularly and in significant conflict with the owner's interest. The corollary of secure tenure is that in *delegating* control, the owner has somehow awarded it for keeps and has lost the faculty of recall, i.e. he has *lost* control. The standard argument to this effect is that once ownership has become fragmented and many owners have delegated managerial power to a single tenant (a bureaucracy, a management), each owner has only an infinitesimal influence on the tenant's tenure, and insufficient motivation to shoulder the cost of mobilizing fellow owners for joint

---

28 Gordon Tullock, in a paper of great clarity dealing with some of these issues ('The New Theory of Corporations', in Erich Streissler *et al.* (eds), *Roads to Freedom, Essays in Honour of F.A. von Hayek*, 1969), cites findings to the effect that apparent managerial deviation from profit-maximizing behaviour is greatest in regulated utilities and mutual savings-and-loan associations which have, so to speak, no owners or where regulatory barricades shield the sitting management from the owners.

action. In technical language, the bureaucratic tenant is protected by an 'externality'.

Precisely such an externality may protect a state from its unorganized subjects. The sheer money value of liberty to the subjects of a despotic state may be much larger than the money cost of suborning the praetorian guard, buying arms, copying machines or whatever it may take to topple such a regime. Yet no political entrepreneur would come forth and shoulder the cost if he considered it impracticable to recover it from the liberated subjects. He would lose his outlay if their liberty were an externality for which they could not be made to pay (except by enslaving them again).

The most casual reader of the financial pages of newspapers knows, however, that there is no such obstacle to organizing revolt against self-serving or just plain unsuccessful corporate managements. The take-over bidder, conglomerator, 'raider', 'asset stripper', proxy solicitor have (despite the regulatory hurdles well-meaning authorities put in their way) several ways of 'internalizing' some of the potential benefit accruing to the owners from the recall of the sitting management. These ways can be devious and unscrupulous, in keeping with the unscrupulous defences (such as 'scorched earth', self-denunciation on anti-trust grounds and 'saturation bombing' with frivolous lawsuits) put up by sitting managements to 'protect corporate property' from shareholders at the latter's expense. All in all, 'unfriendly' takeovers even in the face of desperate defences are often successful enough to shake the average hired management's confidence in its security of tenure.[30]

If the hold of the bureaucracy is precarious in the face of an unorganized multitude of dispersed owners, it is *a fortiori* precarious in the face of a single, concentrated owner. No externality protects the bureaucracy *from the state* it is supposed to serve. The discretionary power of a bureaucrat or a bureaucratic institution, no matter how important in the whole apparatus of the state, must not

---

30 Cf. Peter F. Drucker, 'Curbing Unfriendly Takeovers', *The Wall Street Journal*, 5 January, 1983. There is ample evidence of the tendency, noted with some alarm by Professor Drucker, that American corporate management is increasingly motivated by fear of the bidder. It is thus driven to instant profit maximizing behaviour, living from one quarterly earnings report to the next and having no time for the long view.

This is a far cry from the contention that 'owners want profit, managers growth', or 'peer approval', or some other, discretionally chosen 'managerial' maximand. In fact, the contrary contention is, if anything, closer the mark. Only owner-managers can afford to choose idiosyncratic ends. No *hired* chief executive could have ruled, as Henry Ford is supposed to have done, that 'customers can have any colour car as long as it is black.'

be confused with that of the state proper from which it is derived.

Nor is there much excuse for falling into traps of the 'good king, bad councillors' or conversely the 'wicked lord, kind-hearted bailiff' type. The bailiff may be kind-hearted, close to the villeins and especially to any relatives he may have among them, but his personal interest is seldom so far divorced from that of the lord as to make him let off the serfs all that lightly. He, too, wants the manor to function properly as a going concern. The reason the bureaucracy on the whole does serve the state's ends is not only that it has to, on pain of losing its precarious place, but also that, except in rare and easily identified historical situations where state power has just passed to an invader, a usurper or at least a culturally alien contender, there is a large and genuine harmony between their respective maximands. The greater the discretionary power of the state, the more scope the bureaucrat is likely to have for the fulfilment of *his* ends. He need not have the *same* ends the state is striving to realize. It is sufficient that his ends should be non-competing or subordinated. A loyal bureaucracy will find much of its happiness in a strong state. It would take disloyalty, safety from being found out, or perhaps a credible excuse in terms of the 'real', 'long-term' interest of the state, for it to side with civil society against its master. The chance of imposing its own will on *both* state *and* civil society by acting the role of ruling class looks, for all these reasons, doubly remote.

The true place and role of the bureaucracy in relation to the state were suggestively summed up by the historian Norbert Elias in what he called the Monopoly Mechanism. The state is the monopolist of 'the army, land and money' while the bureaucracy is the body of 'dependents upon whom the monopolist depends'. Of course the dependents are important, of course their qualities, their human types are interrelated with the type of state which depends on them; in Elias's example, while the free feudal nobility went with an earlier type, a later one produced the courtly nobility.[31] In a less neat sequence, we might add the clerics, the lay legists and commoner court servants, the landless administrative nobility, Chinese mandarins, Prussian Junkers, French 'enarques', American congressional staffers, dollar-a-year men and socialist party apparatchiks. Within each type, there is no doubt room for human variations leaving their

31 Norbert Elias, *The Civilizing Process*, vol. II, *State Formation and Civilization*, 1982, pp. 104–16.

stamp on the life of the society they help administer. Undeniably, they can lend socialism a human face, or an inhuman one. It is very much a matter of each subject's personal destiny what proves to be of greater import to him, the system or its face.

For any schema of social explanation which runs in terms of classes, however, putting the bureaucracy or some rough equivalent administrative, managerial, insider, expert and authority-carrying category in the place of the *ruling class* is liable to prove confusing. Doing so is to attribute to such a category a durable and well-defined identity ('the New Class'?), a degree of discretionary power and a liberty of action which it can in general hardly possess. It is to lose sight of the political significance of the pattern of capital ownership, reducing it to irrelevance in terms of power over others. Finally, it is by implication to allot to the human qualities of this category an overriding influence on the quality of social life, as if the *variable* disposition and character of office-holders could altogether swamp the systemic *constants* which are the source of the power delegated to such offices. Confusion of this sort yields such gems of incomprehension as that a certain despotism was, or has resulted from, 'bureaucratic distortion' or the 'personality cult'. If the system of state capitalism is to be thought of in traditional class terms, the role of the ruling class can only be ascribed to the state itself. This imposes no anthropomorphism and does not require the state to be personified by a monarch, a dictator or by the party elders. Nor need it be identified with a specific institution, assembly, central committee or cabinet. More non-committally and generally, it is sufficient for the state (to adapt a famous phrase of Marx) to be *armed force and capital endowed with consciousness and a will*.[32]

On the Plantation

Money, markets and the habit of choice are best weeded out by shaping the social system as a well-run plantation.

The universal employer, not content with pushing string, will have to end up owning his employees.

Completing mastery over civil society in maximizing discretionary power can be seen as a chain of corrective moves, each one being

32   K. Marx, *Capital*, 1959, vol. 1, p. 152.

aimed at making the social system both amenable to the state's purpose and internally consistent, although these two requirements are not necessarily or even probably compatible. Each corrective move is consequently capable of creating some new systemic inconsistency and of necessitating other corrective moves. This sequence drives on the political dynamics, such as it is, of state capitalism.

The first and perhaps most decisive of these moves, whereby civil society is purged of decentralized capitalist ownership and the state becomes the universal owner and employer, removes the *inconsistency between political and economic obedience* involved in serving two masters. As I argued at the beginning of this chapter, however, the fusion of political and economic power into state power is in turn inconsistent with electoral competition for its tenure. Having to run for office would involve the universal employer in soliciting his employees to keep voting themselves more money for less work. The next corrective move, therefore, must be one from competitive to monopolistic politics, to match the corresponding changeover in the pattern of ownership. Classical 'bourgeois' democracy needs to be transformed into socialist or people's democracy, or whatever else it may be called as long as it is a set of adequately enforced rules under which consent to the tenure of the essentials of power is *not subjected to electoral tests*.

Under the resulting system, then, the tenant of the state is not menaced by recall; it cannot be unseated by non-violent means; it owns all capital, though its subjects continue to own their labour. Inconsistency, however, manifests itself again, calling for new moves, new adaptations of the social system.

The state alone owning or hiring all factors of production, it must alone take (or delegate) all the who-does-what decisions, whereby inputs of capital and labour are allocated to produce various outputs. This is not only a responsibility but also a satisfaction; to direct resources to chosen uses, to cause certain goods rather than certain others to be produced, is a natural component of any plausible maximand, of any worthwhile employment of discretionary power. Its prosaic symptom is the state's (and its ideology's) treatment of 'planning' as a coveted *prerogative* rather than a *chore*.

Jointly with factor allocation, the state must make the matching distribution decisions. The two sets of decisions are mutually entailed. This is so if only because various people must be rewarded for performing various allotted tasks. (It is probable, though not certain, that the state as sole employer can get them to perform their tasks for less than private capitalists, competing against each other, would have ended up conceding. The relative wage under the two systems would depend, in part, on how much labour of what kind would be wanted under either arrangement. Our argument does not require that the particular 'subsistence wage' which a rational monopsonist would agree to pay, should always be less than the wage competing capitalists would have offered.)

The interdependence of the allocation and distribution decision means that the two *need* be consistent and not that they are *bound to be*. If under the set of distribution decisions, wage-earners get sums of money to be spent as they choose, nothing ensures that they will choose to spend them on the stream of goods the set of allocation decisions is causing to be produced. There is no built-in mechanism stopping them from (unwittingly) repudiating the plan.

Inconsistencies between the supply of goods and the demand it entails, manifest themselves differently under flexible and fixed prices. The symptoms under the latter – queues, quotas, black markets and (on the road to abundance) piles of leftover goods – seem to be less repugnant to socialist states than those under the former – waltzing prices. Regardless of its symptom, however, the inconsistency will subsist and react back on allocation and distribution, frustrating the state's plan. If it allocates workers to produce guns and butter, and they want more butter than they are producing, the sub-plan dealing with gun production will run into difficulties which may be only a little more (or is it a little less?) manageable if butter is rationed than if its price goes up.[33]

How, then, can consistency be ensured? 'Market socialism' is the most frequently recommended solution. It amounts to adjusting output to what people want, in return for the effort they agree to exert in producing it. This can be done, without further ado, by

---

33 If the inputs of all butter-making and gun-making efforts depended on the output of butter alone, there would be (at least) one ideal allocation of the labour force between the dairy and the armaments industries (which, incidentally, would have to start way back with the training of young people to be dairymaids and gunsmiths), ensuring the maximum output of guns. Putting too many people in the armaments industry would reduce the outputs of both butter and guns.

However, gun production is only one of the ends entering into the maximand of the totalitarian state; some of its other ends may conflict with giving people the amount of butter they want, particularly if eating butter makes them more rebellious, or raises their cholesterol level and hence the costs of health care. Beyond these pragmatic considerations, the state may feel that indulging people is bad, and *it is not for them to say* how much butter they should have.

banks of computers feeding on market research and production engineering, solving some very large number of simultaneous equations and using the results for enticing people into the activities which will produce the precise pattern of supply of goods which people engaged in those activities can usually be relied on to want. All that is required is that the equations should correctly express *enough* of the relevant relations between people's tastes, capacities and skills, the capital equipment and materials available and the known ways in which all possible inputs can be combined to produce given outputs.

If this suggestion is ruled out as facetious, recourse could be had to real, non-simulated markets and to letting their feedbacks reconcile allocation and distribution. This is done (to summarize the workings of delicate mechanisms rather radically) by the touch of the invisible hand acting on some out of a large number of separate, decentralized decisions, each of which had best be relatively small. Under state capitalism, the marginal touch of the invisible hand can only perform what is expected of it, if the managerial bureaucracy is made severally to maximize the separate profits of a large enough number of 'profit centres'. This, in turn, means that bureaucrats must be exposed to the incentives and penalties dealt out by the sellers of labour and the buyers of goods, rather than by the state. Asked to serve two masters, the success of the bureaucracy would then depend on how well it served *one* of them.[34]

Bureaucrats would increasingly find themselves in the anomalous position of quasi-owners, deriving a measure of autonomy and security from the market success of the enterprises or profit centres they managed. No totalitarian state in its right mind can risk condoning such an evolution, the less so as the resulting political threat is to *its* tenure while the advantages of greater economic efficiency accrue in part, if not wholly, to its subjects. The on-again–off-again history of experiments with decentralization, markets, self-regulating mechanisms in the economic management of socialist states, is strong circumstantial evidence that totalitarian regimes seldom lose sight for long of the 'primacy of politics'. They

---

34 It could be argued that managers of private capitalist enterprises are also serving two masters, the owner and the customer. However, those who are very successful at serving the latter do not, by their success, endanger the tenure of the former. Managers are not the owners' rivals.

do not, except in absent-minded moments, let their security of tenure be jeopardized for the sake of pleasing shoppers.[35]

Yielding to the temptations of market socialism would take care of the consistency of allocation with distribution through decentralized decision-making, inspired by money and markets. This, in turn, would generate a new inconsistency between the imperative need that people (including the managers) should be dependent on the state, and the economic mechanisms which would restore some independence to some of them.

Any mechanism, however (even if it could be politically neutral and innocuous, in the manner of networks of docile computers), under which resource allocation is subjected to what people want, is at bottom a surrender of some of the state's hard-won power. The rational state, finally possessing and intending to hold on to the extensive power afforded by the joint monopoly of arms and capital, should seek a method of adjustment involving no such surrender. Rather than letting junk food, porno-pop video, amphetamines, socially wasteful private motorcars and other deleterious trash be produced because people wanted them, it can produce 'merit goods' and cause people to want them instead.[36]

---

35   The case of Hungary which despite occasional backtracking has, since the late 1960s, gone quite a way towards decentralized profit maximization, meaningful prices and even the toleration of an undergrowth of private enterprise, is paradoxically enough a possible confirmation of this thesis. If the country is living proof that 'market socialism works', it is so by virtue of the trauma of the 1956 rising, suppressed by Russia, which has created a tacit understanding between the regime and its subjects. After its reinstatement by Soviet armour, the Hungarian state had the intelligence to grasp that its security of tenure is assured by geography and need not be doubly assured by the belt-and-braces of a social system where everybody's livelihood is precarious. Civil society, having learnt its lesson, is treating politics with a shrug. Thus, although more and more managers of enterprises and spurious cooperatives, professional people, small businessmen and peasants are building independent livelihoods, there is no parallel rise in demands for political participation and self-government.

In these rare and propitious circumstances, the Hungarian state can safely afford to concede as much economic freedom as it can get past its neighbours and especially, of course, Moscow. The one real constraint is Russian devotion to a number of socialist principles and the mounting irritation of Russian visitors at seeing their conquered colony wallowing in superior standards of life.

Moscow, which has no larger neighbour's friendly tanks to invite in and 'normalize' matters should the leading role of the party be challenged by self-confident technocrats, fat peasants, perpetual postgraduates and all the other independents who proliferate without control when the vestiges of decentralized economic power begin to reappear, would no doubt be rash to listen to all the expert advocacy of 'economic reforms'. It has more at stake than the greater efficiency of a self-regulating economy.

On the other hand, it is less clear why Czechoslovakia, whose peoples received in 1968 an albeit bloodless but no doubt nearly as effective lesson in political geography as did the Hungarians in 1956, refuses to let in the invisible hand to wake up the economy from its comatose sleep. It must be supposed that the national propensity to stay on the safe side, is attracted by the double security of dependent subjects *and* fraternal aid.

Adjustment to the resource allocation the state wants must then take place, if at all, through the bending of people's tastes, mode of life and character to what they are offered. It may be a slow process to make them actually like, say, wholemeal flour, national defence, Schönberg's music, sensible hard-wearing clothes, public transport (and no traffic-choking private cars), fine government buildings and fully standardized housing. While letting time and habit do such slow work as they will, the state can advance more rapidly towards these objectives through a short cut. It can directly attack the habit of choice itself, from which many of its troubles are derived, by no longer paying people with the universal voucher, money.

Having money provides wide scope for choice and trains people in its exercise. Specialized vouchers you can only spend on a much narrower class of goods, only on lunches, the education of children, transport, vacation accommodation, medical care and so on, restrict the scope of choice; they also help unlearn the habit. As a perhaps secondary convenience, they render consumer demands somewhat easier to predict for planning purposes. More fundamentally, they transfer part of the power over the disposal of incomes from the recipients to the state, which can within reasonable limits vary the 'mix' of vouchers and can, consequently, shape the kind of life people will live. Vouchers, therefore, provide direct satisfaction to the state which wishes to have its subjects live in a particular way, say healthily, for whatever reason, because it is good for them to be healthy, or because they work and fight better when healthy, or because it just values health.

Anything special vouchers do, the truck system will do better. A luncheon voucher or a food stamp at least leaves the choice of the actual food, and an education voucher the choice of school, to personal whim. It recognizes and to some extent even encourages a consumer sovereignty of sorts. Factory and office cafeterias, a range

---

36 'Merit goods' are considered by the state good for people. If *A* is a merit good, its supply is to be arranged in such a way that no one should be able to increase his consumption of any non-merit good *B* by reducing his consumption of *A*. It must not be possible, for instance, to swap school milk for lollipops, nor for beer for the child's father. This is achieved when school milk is on tap, with every child drinking as much as he wants.

When beef cattle are fed from self-filling feed bins, they are believed to eat just enough. Likewise, when merit goods are on tap, the presumtion is that people will consume just what they need. With some important merit goods, this leads to ambiguous outcomes. Free health care and free university education are notorious cases in point. Because of emulation, jealousy or other reasons, the consumption of these goods tends to get out of hand and seems almost impossible to stabilize, let alone to reduce.

of basic and nourishing foodstuffs at giveaway prices, an allotted dwelling, the sending of children to a designated school and the sick to a specific dispensary, remove some of the remaining occasions for choice and affirm the state's prerogative to decide. Life for the subject becomes simpler, its conundrums fewer and his communal (as distinct from individual and family) existence more all-embracing.

Beyond paying people less money and more selected goods, lies the limiting case where they are not paid at all, but just get their specific needs provided for by the state. *Exclusion,* with people's access to goods regulated by the money or vouchers they earn, is then replaced by *free access*: subway tickets are abolished, hospitals do not charge, there is free milk, free concerts and free housing (though not everybody gets all the houseroom he would like), and certain goods which people need but do not want, such as safety helmets or edifying printed matter, are given away to all comers pending the time when all have to come and get them. The frontier between public goods and private goods, ill-marked at the best of times, becomes unguarded, and state planning displays a steady bias in favour of public goods, which will be 'over-produced' (at least by the standard of a Pareto-optimum satisfying the taste of a 'representative man' – the useful fiction allowing us to pretend, without saying so, that everybody is like everybody else and all are unanimous).

Public goods by their intrinsic character and private goods by virtue of the progressive atrophy of money and markets, are supplied to people as a function of who they are and where they are situated (e.g. citizen, town dweller, mother, student, member of the hierarchy of a given 'collective' such as a place of work, school, or housing development, a police officer or bureaucrat of a given rank, etc.), their place in life largely determining their access to goods. Somewhat sweepingly, we can say that they all get what the state considers appropriate to their existential situation. Putting it more directly, *they get what they need.* It is in this way that the state's rational interest ultimately converges upon the matching ideological tenet – which is a prediction and a command as well – of giving 'to each according to his needs'.

As ever larger numbers of people get things primarily as a function of their nominal *life-situation* and *rank,* rather than as a function of how well they do what they do, however, one systemic inconsistency is resolved at the cost of provoking another. There are always those who positively enjoy certain kinds of effort, say teaching or driving in traffic, and have the good luck of being entrusted with a classroom or a taxi. But why should the rest do what the plan of resource allocation calls for them to do, and why should they do it well when they would rather shirk and bludge? The shape the evolving social system is taking at this point encourages, or at least fails to deter, shirking. Moreover, where people work in groups, the group imposes shirking, a slow rhythm of work or poor workmanship on its members on pain of ostracism, contempt or retaliation against the *Streber* ('striver' does not convey the ironic hostility of the German term). This phenomenon is an upside-down replica of the sanctions a group needing a *high* level of group effort will use against the free rider who will *not* exert himself.

If this inconsistency between the need for effort and the lack of any built-in reason for exerting oneself were not corrected, the state sitting on top of this social structure would be maximizing its potentially accessible ends no better than if it were pushing string.

The corrective move is to enforce the *quid pro quo* that goes with the provision of needs. If the state looks after people's subsistence, it is hardly justifiable for them to continue *owning* their labour, withholding it partly or wholly as the mood takes them, and devoting it, if at all, to jobs of their own choosing. In equity, they *owe* their capacity for effort to the state, so that it may fully be used for the common good.

With general obligations arising from people's *status* crowding out specific *ad hoc contracts,* the state ends up owning its subjects. Its task becomes more ambitious and more exacting. Its attention must now extend to matters that used to be non-political concerns settled within civil society (as well as to questions that cannot arise at all except in a totalitarian system), rather along the lines of the all-embracing concerns of the rational plantation-owner in the ante-bellum South:

> No aspect of slave management was too trivial to be omitted from consideration or debate. Details of housing, diet, medical care, marriage, child-rearing, holidays, incentives and punishments, alternative methods of organising field labour, the duties of managerial personnel, and even the manner and air assumed by a planter in his relationship with his slaves . . .[37]

37   Robert William Fogel and Stanley L. Engerman, *Time on the Cross: The Economics of American Negro Slavery,* 1974, vol. 1, p. 202.

Most of the implications of having to run the state as a large, complex and self-reliant plantation, are fairly evident. Some are depressingly topical. They need not be laboured, but only touched upon. There has to be a degree of direction of labour to where it is needed rather than where it wants to go. Educational opportunity has to be allocated to raise and train the people needed to fill the future roles and situations the state expects to create. Armed force, surveillance and repressive capacity have to be doubled and re-doubled, as they have to cope not only with political disobedience, but also with sloth, waste and free riding. The state cannot tolerate strikes. Nor can it tolerate 'exit', voting with one's feet; the frontier must be closed for keeping its property in, and perhaps secondarily also for keeping any alien, discordant influence spoiling the condition of its property out.

Is this social system at last well-rounded, efficient in operation, perfectly consistent? Is no part of it geared to rub against, let alone clash with the working of another, ultimately breaking up vital innards? Does it deliver the satisfactions of governing – tempting the state to sit back and contemplate its finished design, concerned only with the enjoyment and preservation of its place within it, *willing history to stop*?

If there is a plausible answer to the question, another and equally speculative book would be needed to argue it. At first glance, however, the prospects for any definitive settlement of outstanding affairs between state and civil society look doubtful – perhaps reassuringly so. In the event the state's striving for self-fulfilment were successfully to issue in a well-managed totalitarianism, the human types (the addict no less than the allergic) which such a system is apt to breed, would before long quite likely frustrate and disappoint the state's expectations. That may indeed be its inescapable predicament, just as it is probably the inescapable predicament of civil society to be disappointed in the state.

Index